Also by Gwenda Blair

The Trumps: Three Generations That Built an Empire

Almost Golden: Jessica Savitch and the Selling of Television News

Laura Ingalls Wilder

DONALD TRUMP
Master Apprentice

GWENDA BLAIR

Simon & Schuster

New York   London   Toronto   Sydney

SIMON & SCHUSTER
Rockefeller Center
1230 Avenue of the Americas
New York, NY 10020

For information regarding special discounts for bulk purchases,
please contact Simon & Schuster Special Sales at 1-800-456-6798
or business@simonandschuster.com

Designed by C. Linda Dingler

Manufactured in the United States of America

10   9   8   7   6   5   4   3   2   1

Library of Congress Cataloging-in-Publication Data

Blair, Gwenda.
    Donald Trump : master apprentice / Gwenda Blair.
        p.   cm.
    Includes bibliographical references and index.
        1. Trump, Donald, 1946–   2. Businesspeople—United States—Biography.
    3. Real estate developers—United States—Biography.   I. Blair, Gwenda. Trumps.
    II. Title.
    HC102.5.T78B52   2005
    333.33'092—dc22
        [B]   2005041267

ISBN 0-7432-7510-1

This book is comprised of selected chapters from *The Trumps*, which have been
revised, as well as additional new material.

To

Newell, Sasha, and Matt,

and to the memory of my father, Newell Blair (1907–2004)

Contents

Preface

On a warm fall afternoon, the world's most famous businessman sat in a large showroom next to a pile of 12-inch-tall male dolls. If this were somewhere other than New York City—the South American jungle, say, or ancient China—they might have been mud-and-twig fetishes designed to ward off evil, or ceramic objects destined to accompany the man into the afterlife. But it was Times Square in September 2004, and Donald Trump was launching a sales campaign at Toys R Us for a plastic action figure made in his likeness—more or less. Laser technology had provided the billionaire's pursed mouth and bushy eyebrows, but a shoe-polish-brown pompadour had replaced the famous orange comb-over and there were no genitals.

No matter; despite its single-breasted suit and wing-tip shoes, the Apprentice Talking Donald Trump Doll is not really a replica, or even a toy. Instead it's a pint-sized, personal mentor for viewers of the hit reality television series *The Apprentice*, on which fresh-faced young contestants compete for a job with the Trump Organization. Embedded in the doll's chest is a digital sound chip that allows it to declare, in Trump's own voice, "Have an ego," "Think big," and other pithy bits of advice similar to those Trump offers each week on the show.

What the doll doesn't reveal are the sources of Donald Trump's own extraordinary success. These include a number of lucky breaks, among them his father's real estate wealth and political connections, his surname (changed by a prescient German ancestor from Drumpf to Trump), and his ex-wife Ivana's gift of a catchy nickname, "The Donald," which became instant newspaper fodder.

Of equal importance are what we might call The Donald's Five Commandments: Do whatever it takes to win. Don't spare the chutzpah. Turn everything into an advertisement for yourself. No matter what happens, claim victory. And above all, *always* use the superlative. While he's heeded business basics like "Location, location, location," his own personal mantra is "Exaggerate, exaggerate, exaggerate."

Following these guidelines, Donald Trump has carved out a career in self-aggrandizement that has netted him fortune, fame, and enthusiastic fans. Hundreds plunked down $26.99 for a doll and waited in line for hours for the one-time-only opportunity to have The Donald scrawl his autograph in metallic gold across the face of the box. They knew him from *The Apprentice* as the archetypal boss: ready to pounce on mistakes, dismissive of excuses, and ever aware of the bottom line. What they didn't know was that behind this most recent claim to fame lay a life history with more twists and turns than any television producer could possibly imagine. Nor did they know that Donald himself had been a lifelong apprentice to a powerful man whom he had admired, rebelled against, studied, competed with, and eventually surpassed.

Fifteen years earlier, that mentor had watched with a bewildered look as Donald sat in another Manhattan toy store, FAO Schwarz, and autographed a Monopoly-like board game with his name and face on it. The man was Donald's father, Fred Trump. Like his son, he was in real estate. Also like his son, he was immensely wealthy. But the father had made his money building ordinary homes for ordinary people, not by constructing super-luxury apartments, running casinos, engaging in financial manipulations, and turning himself into one of the most celebrated figures of the century. Whereas the erstwhile apprentice lived in the center of photographers' lenses, his master existed outside the media's glare. The two men's lives were vastly different—as different as business in the middle of the twentieth century and at its end, as different as the America of the World War II era and what the country had become as the cold war drew to a close.

This apprentice did not always follow his master's advice. When Donald ignored his father's old-fashioned all-brick aesthetic in favor of modern glass-walled skyscrapers, he achieved great success; when he disobeyed his father's financial precepts and signed personal financial guarantees for nearly $1 billion, he created a disaster. Only a year after the FAO Schwarz event, Donald's empire lay in shambles. But unlike other magnates of the time, he emerged from financial turmoil to create a second, virtual empire. He would no longer own everything with his name on it; instead he would market himself as the embodiment of the American dream of wealth and fame. He would be the people's billionaire: the personality brand created by the dark suit, the improbable hairdo, and the over-the-top description of every undertaking as the world's most fantastic, amazing, and incredible.

Only a dozen years earlier, many had considered him finished, but his current life seemed to be, quite literally, gold-plated. To the contestants on his show as well as the world at large, he seemed the quintessential man in charge. But the reason Donald Trump had survived and flourished was that he had, once again, been an apprentice, resolutely adhering to his father's most fundamental rule: No matter what happens, never, ever give up.

January 2005

DONALD TRUMP:
Master Apprentice

CHAPTER ONE

Born to Compete

On June 14, 1946, the day Donald Trump was born, school bands and Boy Scouts marched up Fifth Avenue, and there were plenty of American flags waving—a festive touch, although in honor of Flag Day rather than Donald's birth.

He came into the world with thousands of other babies, as part of the first onrush of what is now called the baby boom.[1] Given that America's biggest war had just ended, and hundreds of thousands of GIs and sailors had only recently returned home after years away, demographers were hardly surprised by the upsurge in births. But they were astonished by its duration, which the precomputer Census Bureau recorded on punch cards riffling through dishwasher-size calculators.

In the 1950s, the UNIVAC, an early computer the size of a two-bedroom apartment, reported that the birthrate still had not slackened. When the level finally decreased, in 1964, statisticians found that there were almost 76 million new Americans—about 18 million more than had been expected.[2] For the first time, immigration played only a minor role, for almost all the new arrivals were born in the United States. As might be expected, being part of the largest demographic cohort in the nation's history would affect these baby boomers more deeply than anyone could have anticipated.

Although their strongest tie would be to their own families, they would also be members of the baby boom family. Together with their boomer sisters and brothers, they would grow up on television, rock and roll, and the cold war. But for those born, as Donald was, at the beginning of the boom, there may have been something more. Because World War II had interrupted normal patterns of marriage and childbearing, the first baby boomers, regardless of their actual birth order, tended to act like firstborns: assertive, ambitious, and, above all, successful.[3]

Donald was one of these faux firstborns. Although the fourth-born in his family, by all accounts he was self-assured, determined, and positive from the start. Obviously his own genes and family contributed mightily to the person who emerged. But it just may be that growing up in an unprecedented wave of firstborns had a shaping influence on the man who would come to define success to so many.

IT WAS A GOOD TIME to be born. America was on a roll. Wartime price controls would soon be lifted, and cars were once again pouring from Detroit's assembly lines. A small bank in Brooklyn was readying Charge-It, the nation's first third-party credit plan, which allowed customers to charge purchases within two blocks of the bank and eventually led to the modern consumer economy.[4] Ethel Merman was starring on Broadway in the new feel-good musical *Annie Get Your Gun*, Dr. Benjamin Spock published his first book on child care, and NBC gave the few thousand Americans with television sets one of their first live broadcasts, a welterweight bout at Madison Square Garden.[5]

At the time of Donald's birth, his parents, Fred and Mary, and the older children—Maryanne, nine, Fred Jr., seven, and Elizabeth, four—lived on Wareham Street in Jamaica Estates, the Queens neighborhood where Fred had constructed dozens of early American and English manor houses early in his real estate career. Their two-story mock Tudor, shoehorned into a tiny lot, was bursting at the seams, but the solution lay right outside the back door. On a double lot that backed onto the Wareham property and fronted on a wide, tree-lined boulevard called Midland Parkway, Fred built his dream house.

A redbrick colonial-style structure with white shutters at the windows and door, the Trumps' new home was far larger than the house on Wareham. But because it also covered almost the full width of the plot, it had the same sandwiched-in look. Outside, a winding brick walkway led up to an entrance flanked by two-story columns, and inside there were 23 rooms and nine bathrooms. By enlarging and repeating an ordinary floor plan, Fred created an enormous bungalow/ranch house/tract home—but with touches of 1950s-style luxury, including an intercom system and, in the library, which had more shelves than books, an early TV set, a huge console with a tiny screen. Finally, there was plenty of space for the family, which welcomed a fifth and last child, Robert, in 1948. There was also room for a maid (a middle-aged white woman named Emma) as well as a black chauffeur named George and two Cadillac limousines with license plates that read FT1 and FT2.[6]

Although he was already a wealthy man, Fred did not take much time off to enjoy his new home. Often he left for work before dawn, and he spent his day driving from one site to another and keeping on top of things with an early car phone. After he came home, long after dark, he sat in the library and returned phone calls. The only difference on the weekends was that he took the kids along and met with his brother-in-law to go over company books.[7]

"Dad was always checking on some building or construction site," Maryanne recollected years later. "What else would he do on a Saturday?" Robert, too, remembered weekends dedicated to inspecting Fred's buildings from roof to boiler room. "Dad would take the elevator to the top floor and then walk down," he said. "Supers had to be there, because weekends were when you rented."

Fred's success was due not only to his relentless effort, but to his instinct for how far to push the envelope. It was a legacy from his own father, who had once boldly asserted nonexistent mineral claims on a choice parcel of land in Monte Cristo, Washington, and built a hotel on it, even though someone else had a legal hold on the property.

During the Depression, Fred's construction business had gone belly-up and he was working as the manager of a supermarket. But writing on special stationery that displayed a trim model bungalow, he presented himself as a highly successful real estate executive to a federal bankruptcy court charged with doling out the remnants of the Lehrenkrauss Corporation, a once-dominant investment bank in Brooklyn. The court decided to award a mortgage-servicing contract to Fred that would eventually make him one of the biggest real estate developers in the borough. Later this gutsy approach brought him large subsidies from the Federal Housing Administration, a New Deal institution designed to rescue the construction industry, and allowed him to exploit loopholes in FHA regulations.

Yet worldly success notwithstanding, Fred was so shy and uncomfortable in person that he once took a social-relations course designed by Dale Carnegie, author of the popular book *How to Win Friends and Influence People*. What Fred lacked in public speaking and conversational skills, however, he made up for with his steadfast belief in optimism's transformative power. Long before Norman Vincent Peale's best-selling book, *The Power of Positive Thinking*, made this notion a national cliché, Fred was living by it and drilling it into his children.

" 'You can do it if you try,' that was his motto," Maryanne remembered. His attitude never varied, even when, after the birth of their last child, his wife Mary had to be rushed to the hospital for a series of operations that included an emergency hysterectomy. "There were four [operations] in something like two weeks," recalled Maryanne, who was an adolescent at the time. "My father came home and told me she wasn't expected to live, but I should go to school and he'd call me if anything changed. That's right—go to school as usual!"

By contrast, Mary, an immigrant from Scotland, loved the spotlight. Even when she was ill, she rallied for family events and relished having everyone's eyes on her. "When the lights went up," Maryanne said, "she was the star." She was also a role model for Donald, who picked up pointers as he watched her command the attention of everyone present. Later on, he would credit her as a source for his own sense of showmanship. "She always had a flair for the dramatic and the grand," he wrote in his autobiography, *The Art of the Deal*. "My mother loves splendor and magnificence."[8]

Rounding out the family circle was the Trump children's paternal grandmother, Elizabeth Christ Trump. She had grown up next door to the family of her husband-to-be, Friedrich Trump, in Kallstadt, a small winemaking village near Mannheim, Germany. Friedrich had emigrated to the U.S. at 16, and despite having trained as a barber, ended up supplying food, liquor, and women to miners during the Klondike era. On a visit back home, he married Elizabeth and they set up housekeeping in the Bronx. Although they lived in a heavily German area, she was desperately homesick, and after the birth of their first child, a daughter, they returned to Kallstadt. But because Friedrich had not served in the army, German authorities refused his request to repatriate and instead expelled him and his wife, then pregnant with Fred. For better or worse, Friedrich, Elizabeth, and the generations to come were to be Americans after all.

Friedrich, who became a small-scale developer, died during the influenza epidemic of 1918. Elizabeth hoped to carry on in the same field with their three children, but ultimately it would be Fred who kept the Trumps in real estate. Because he was underage when he started, Elizabeth signed the incorporation papers, and well into her seventies she still collected the coins from Laundromats in Trump buildings in Queens and Brooklyn. After Fred's marriage she left the house they had shared, but she lived nearby and eventually moved to an apartment building that her son built across Midland Parkway from his own house. Impeccably dressed and hardworking, the family matriarch seemed a stern figure to neighborhood children. "She wasn't a grandmother you'd leap on for kisses," recalled Heather MacIntosh Hayes, who grew up in the house next door.

Fred inherited his mother's formal demeanor. Even on weekends, he disdained wearing a bathrobe and slippers, and when he came home from work, he would shower and then don a jacket and tie for dinner. He corrected anyone who called and asked for "Lizzie" instead of Elizabeth, and he looked down on the use of terms he considered indelicate for female conditions. Years later, he scolded Maryanne for talking about her own pregnancy. "My father said, 'Your mother had five children and never used that word,' " she said afterward.

Inside the big house on Midland Parkway, there were curfews and lots of rules. "You didn't utter a curse word in that house, or you'd get your neck broken," recalled Louis Droesch, a friend of Fred Jr., known as Freddy. Cookies or other snacks between meals were forbidden. When Fred came home at night, Mary gave him a report on who had done what to whom during the day, and he would mete out the consequences. Depending on the seriousness of what had occurred, malefactors might be grounded for a few days; according to the children's friends, occasionally wrongdoers were also paddled with a wooden spoon.

Fred and Mary made sure their children had a good grounding in life. Sundays meant the First Presbyterian Church at Jamaica, and all week long both parents preached the value of a dollar. Sometimes it seemed that life's highest priorities were to turn out the lights, eat every bite, and remember all the poor children around the world. At their father's building sites, the kids collected empty bottles to turn in for the deposits. They all had summer jobs, and the boys had paper routes; when it rained or snowed, Fred made the single concession of allowing them to make deliveries in a limousine.

Perhaps the highest value was belonging to a family so close that it shared not only the same surname but the same first names (except for Robert). Thus the children were named after their mother (Maryanne), father (Fred Jr.), grandmother (Elizabeth), and maternal and paternal uncles (Donald John). When Maryanne was expecting a child of her own, she later recalled, she asked her father for suggestions for names. "He said, 'Oh, a proper name like Elizabeth or Maryanne,' " she said. "That was it, that was the entire list." It is hardly surprising that family would remain the highest loyalty for this generation. For at least one member, Donald, it would be a source of warmth and security that nothing else in life could ever quite match.

———◆———

IN THE LATE TWENTIES, when Fred began building in Jamaica Estates, the area was a remote, genteel enclave, almost a square mile in size, without stoplights or streetlights.[9] Much of the area was undeveloped forest dotted with springs and streams. But by 1946, when Donald was born, the woodlands were gone, there was a parochial school on Midland Parkway, and there were red lights at intersections. The once-bucolic refuge had become a magnet for successful professionals, with so many doctors that the local public school's PTA stamped its envelopes "Dr. or Mr." But the community was still a relatively homogeneous white area, with one or two black families, no Asians, and little truly conspicuous consumption. Neighbors knew one another, and each winter the kids sledded together down Midland Parkway.

Nobody bothered to lock doors or minded when children wandered over to a neighbor's house in search of adventure. Almost every day Elizabeth, Donald, and Robert, all blond and fair-skinned, visited the lady next door, Bernice Able MacIntosh, and her daughter, Heather. Bernice's father, a retired jeweler and land developer who had sold Fred the lots on Wareham and Midland Parkway, was a surrogate grandfather to these towheaded neighbors. He made them toy boats, and he hung a swing from a high tree branch in the backyard. In the summer, the squeak from early morning rides by the Trumps would wake up his daughter.

"It seemed like every morning I would have two or three Trumps at the breakfast table with Heather," Bernice remembered later. "There were three cookie jars, and they were always open. So was the refrigerator. The Trumps didn't have that [freedom] at their house, so they came over to mine." The Trumps also had no pets, so they came over to play with the MacIntosh kittens and rabbits. Donald's special passion, Bernice recalled, was toy vehicles, and for Christmas and birthdays she would give him the strongest one she could find. "He'd always take it apart immediately," she said. "By the time my daughter got home from his birthday party, he'd have dismantled it. 'Oh, Mom, he's got it all in pieces,' she'd say."

When Donald was three he went to the Carousel Pre-School, a new nursery program in Jamaica Estates. "Donald was a beautiful little boy, very blond and buttery," recalled the founder and director, Shirley Greene, who had trained at Columbia University's Teachers College and Bank Street College of Education, both noted for their progressive early childhood education program. "He wasn't fat, but he was sturdy and really quite jolly." Considered avant-garde at the time, Carousel emphasized individual development and hands-on learning experiences like gardening and collecting snowflakes. Regardless of the season, Donald's favorite activity was building with blocks.[10]

Among his closest playmates was his younger brother, Robert. When they weren't next door with Heather or her grandfather, they were down in the family playroom with model trains and toy construction equipment. His hair slightly darker, his build more slight, and his manner more quiet and easygoing, Robert usually ended up doing things Donald's way. In later years, one of Donald's favorite childhood stories was about using all his own blocks on a particularly ambitious structure and then borrowing Robert's to complete it. When Donald finished he was so pleased with the results that he glued everything together. "And that was the end of Robert's blocks," he later remembered.[11] It was also the model for how things would continue to go between the brothers, who would play and work together for years to come—always under Donald's direction.

At age five Donald went to Kew Forest, the private school in nearby Forest Hills attended by his older siblings. Unlike Carousel, it was a traditional, structured environment where students sang hymns at morning assembly and wore uniforms. Although the Trumps did not seem to realize it, their father's success, reflected by the limousines, the chauffeur, and the many billboards around Queens and Brooklyn advertising Trump buildings, had already distanced them from other children in Jamaica Estates. But these things were not a problem for another Kew Forest pupil, Peter Brant. His father was also wealthy, and Peter would be Donald's best friend for many years.[12]

With his short, chunky build and dark coloring, Peter was the physical opposite of Donald, a tall youngster with a fair-haired, choir-boy look. But in every other respect they seemed a perfect match. Both were in the bottom half of their class, and both excelled as athletes, playing on every team and bringing home medals and trophies. "Sports was our whole life then," Brant said afterward. "We were in our own world, [which] revolved around watching the Brooklyn Dodgers play."[13]

Despite family wealth and winter vacations at luxury hotels in Miami, everyday life for the two boys was modest by contemporary standards. Like Donald, Peter earned money by delivering papers and returning empty bottles. One of their favorite games was Land, which consisted simply of drawing a line in the dirt, then throwing a pocketknife at it and seeing who could get closest. Once they both wanted a particular baseball glove that cost $28, a hefty sum in the 1950s, and each got an emphatic no from his father. Peter asked relatives and raised enough money to buy it on his own; Donald received a cheaper model.

"They were extremely competitive and had to be on top whichever way they could," said another classmate, Fina Farhi Geiger. "They really pushed the limits in terms of authority and what they could get away with." Cracking loud jokes and launching spitball offensives, they worked nonstop to get attention from classmates and a rise out of teachers. "Everyone [else] basically went by the rules," Geiger said. "They did their own thing. Donald was very sharp and knew just what he could get away with."

In seventh grade the two boys had crew cuts and pegged pants, and Donald wore Thom McAn black flapjack shoes, so named because a piece of metal running up the tongue made the shoes snap shut when a wearer put them on. That year kids started having coed parties, where they would stack up Elvis Presley and Chuck Berry 45s on little RCA record players and stand around wondering whether to dance. "You'd be looking at girls," Brant said, "but not really admitting you were interested."

One of the things they liked to do most was go into Manhattan and buy stink bombs and plastic vomit at a magic store. Another favorite item was hot peppered gum, which they gave to unsuspecting schoolmates. After they saw *West Side Story*, they purchased a series of increasingly larger switchblades. "There was nothing bad in it," Brant said. "We just wanted to play Land and listen to the noise of flicking the blade."

One day their parents found the knives. Fred, an active member of the school's board of trustees, was already disturbed by reports about Donald's behavior in the classroom and at church, where he had managed to annoy Sunday school teachers and youth group leaders. Discovering the switchblades and learning that the boys had been going into New York was the last straw. "That was the incident that turned Donald's father into thinking he should go away to school," Brant said.

———————

OCCASIONALLY THE FAMILY piled into the limousine and drove to the Concord, a sprawling Catskills institution about 90 miles northwest of New York City.[14] Among the largest of many hotels in what was called the Borscht Belt, the Concord was a vast hodgepodge of tennis courts, swimming pools, putting greens, and dozens of brick buildings connected by covered walkways. Catering to a mostly Jewish clientele, it offered city dwellers a chance to take a drive, breathe in the pine-scented air, then disappear inside familiar-looking structures and re-create a scaled-down version of the urban scene they had just left. Fred saw men he knew from business and politics, and his kids hung out with their kids. Then families ate dinner together at tables piled with platters of kosher food and watched entertainers like comedian Buddy Hackett and crooner Vic Damone.

But for the Trump children, summer really meant two other Catskill establishments: Camp Hilltop, which offered eight weeks of outdoor activities to boys, and, next door, Camp Hill Manor, with the same for girls.[15] The camps were exceptionally carefully supervised, a priority for Mary Trump. "I hated to see the children go away," she said later, "but we knew they would be taken care of."[16]

Every morning boys and girls, who were strictly segregated despite sharing facilities and being within hailing distance all day, put on the official camp shorts and shirts. Then they made their beds, stood for cabin inspection, and trotted off to a busy day of sports and crafts. In the evening counselors in each cabin filled out "poop reports," in which they noted what children did and ate, when they had brushed their teeth, and whether they had a bowel movement.

Even in such a well-regulated environment, certain kids found ways to assert themselves. Fred Jr. toed the line himself but induced others to misbehave. "He would come up with some mischief he'd like to see," said Richard Hillman, a son of the owners and a camp counselor, "then plant the idea in another kid's mind and watch what happened." Once Freddy and his cabin mates hitchhiked into a nearby town in the middle of the night and on the way back had the misfortune to be picked up by the wife of the camp owner. As punishment they had to strip down to their underpants, lean over a sawhorse, and receive a paddling.

Donald found camp life boring, but he learned from his brother's experience. Instead of creeping into town and risking a spanking, he concentrated on doing only what he wanted to do around camp. "He was an ornery kid, the kind that tried to get out of activities whenever he could," recalled Stanley Hillman, another of the owner's sons. "He figured out all the angles." One safe outlet was to paint "Don Trump 59" inside the door of his cabin. Whenever camp got to him, he could lie down on his bunk and look over at the sight of his own name. It was a reassuring sight for a boy about to be swept into the uniformed impersonality of military school.

———◦———

IN 1959, when he was 13, Donald Trump went off to New York Military Academy (NYMA).[17] Located on the outskirts of Cornwall-on-Hudson, a tiny hamlet about 55 miles north of New York City and next door to West Point, it had first opened its doors in 1889. Founded by a Civil War veteran as a place to curb unruly young spirits, it looked like a life-size version of a child's toy soldier set. Crenellated, fortress-style buildings surrounded a central courtyard, and nearby were parade grounds where cadet squads marched and the school band steamed through one military march after another.

As soon as they arrived, cadets underwent a crash course in everything from how to give a proper salute to how to face right and face left. Taped to the door of their rooms were typewritten instructions and a diagram that showed how to fold and stow linens and clothing, a task made easier by a complete ban on civilian attire. Weekday mornings they rose before dawn to the sound of a bugle, put on gray shirt and pants and maroon tie, and marched to meals, chapel, classes, and military drills. On Saturdays they cleaned their rooms, scrubbed their gloves, and polished their belt buckles and shoes.

"It's not an easy task for a boy away from home, having people barking at you, do this, do that," said Colonel Ted Dobias. A World War II veteran, he had graduated from NYMA and then stayed on as a tactical training officer and athletic coach. "Kids would burst into tears and beg to go home."

But somehow, what might have been utterly Dickensian was not. After a few dazed weeks the cadets rallied and began to compete for cleanest room and most impeccable uniform. By Thanksgiving most boys had gotten more or less used to the routine. "It builds character," said Dobias. "It teaches them to be organized, to know exactly what they're doing all the time."

For the first time, Donald was in a place that encouraged and channeled competitiveness and aggression instead of tamping it down. In the barracks, he could compete for shiniest shoes; in the classroom, a flair for spatial relations, which would serve him well when he became a real estate developer, would help him earn the highest grade in geometry; and on the athletic field, he could be a star. At last Donald was in a place where winning really mattered, and he poured himself into doing better than everyone else at everything.

———— ◆ ————

LIKE TEENAGE BOYS EVERYWHERE, the cadets had contests for who would be first to have a wet dream, swore that the school put saltpeter in food to keep testosterone under control, and took pride when condoms left a small round mark of distinction on leather wallets.[18]

Donald did his best to fit in, at one point refusing to let his parents visit unless they left the chauffeur at home, and went on a chaperoned trip to Bermuda in his senior year.[19] That year classmates voted him "Ladies' Man," although like the other cadets, he saw girls only at mixers and occasional school dances.

Nonetheless he never had truly close friends. "I think it was because he was too competitive, and with a friend you don't always compete," said Ted Levine, Donald's roommate their first year at NYMA. "It was like he had this defensive wall around him, and he wouldn't let anyone get close."

The warmest relationship Donald had was with Dobias. Accustomed to students who routinely ignored his advice, the coach was pleasantly surprised to find someone who actually wanted to learn. "He caught my eye right away because he was so aggressive but so coachable," Dobias said. "If you told him he wasn't throwing the baseball correctly, he'd do it right the next time. He was very sure of himself, but he also listened." Because he considered Donald promising, Dobias pushed him constantly to keep up his grades and made him unofficial assistant baseball coach his senior year.

As Donald remembered it, he "finessed" Dobias by showing that he was respectful but not scared. But perhaps the coach finessed him as well. By protecting and promoting him, Dobias elicited a performance and level of self-discipline well beyond what the young man from Jamaica Estates had seemed capable of. When Fred and Mary came up to see their son, as they did nearly every weekend, they found him transformed. "The academy did a wonderful job," Mary said afterward. "I would never have sent Robert there, he was too sensitive. But Donald was different. He was never homesick, or at least if he was, he never let on. He loved it."[20]

When Donald and his senior-year roommate, David Smith, hung out in their room, Donald liked to "hit the beach" by lying down on his bunk under a UV bulb and pretending that he was basking in the Florida sunshine. Smith had only the vaguest notion of his own plans, but Donald seemed to know exactly where he was headed. Dropping the family's usual reticence about its wealth, he pegged his father's worth at $30 million and bragged that the number doubled every year. "He was already focused on the future," Smith said. "He used to talk about his dad's business, how he would use him as a role model but go one step further."

In effect, Donald had long since apprenticed himself to his father. During childhood visits to construction sites, he saw how Fred's constant vigilance kept everyone on their toes. When he was a teenager and worked in the machine shop at Gregory Apartments, a foreclosed FHA project his father had bought in Seat Pleasant, Maryland, he took in the emphasis on regular maintenance. "I loved it, working with my hands," he said years later. "I saw a different world, the world of the guys who clean and fix things."[21] At Fred's largest project, Trump Village, in Brooklyn, Donald ran errands and saw how to coordinate hundreds of workers. When he chauffered his father, he noticed that even on coffee breaks, Fred was busy scribbling in a notebook and doing paperwork. Day in and day out, Donald watched, worked, and learned. "You could already see the motor running in his head," said one Trump Village tenant.[22]

FOR HIS FIRST TWO YEARS of college Donald attended classes in business administration at Fordham University, a Roman Catholic institution in the Bronx, and commuted to his parents' home on Midland Parkway.[23] According to Donald, he chose Fordham because he wanted to be near his parents, but when Maryanne was asked why her brother went to Fordham, she offered another explanation: "That's where he got in."

It was not an obvious fit. His military bearing stuck out in this civilian setting, and with his little red sports car and well-tailored clothes, he was obviously wealthier than most of his classmates. In an era when cigarette smoking was a symbol of sophistication and independence, he did not smoke; more unusual, in a school culture where alcohol played a big role, he was a teetotaler. And on the squash team, where players were often tardy and had tantrums when they lost, Donald was never late and never had a meltdown. "He was more of a gentleman than we were," said Rich Marrin, a teammate. "More refined, as if brought up in a stricter family, with more emphasis on manners. We weren't that rowdy, but we didn't always know the right forks."

Squash was new for Donald and he worked hard at it, every afternoon doggedly squeezing into a station wagon with his teammates to ride to practice. Eventually he won a spot on the first-string team, and when it traveled to matches, he seemed like just one more curfew-breaking student. Along with his teammates, he stayed out late and went to parties to meet girls; the only difference was that he handled himself better than his teammates, most of whom came from parochial schools. "We sometimes acted like jerks or were shy or just got drunk," Marrin said. "He could talk easily and get girls' attention. He had a certain savoir faire."

Occasionally that savoir faire showed through in other ways. Whenever a *Wall Street Journal* or *New York Times* was lying on a bench at practice, he'd grab it and start scanning the pages. When the team went to Washington, he tried out the new set of golf clubs in his car trunk and hit half a dozen new balls into the Potomac River without a second thought—a gesture so extravagant that his teammates remembered it decades later.

But perhaps the most important event occurred shortly after Donald's arrival at Fordham. One rainy, cold day in November 1964 he accompanied his father to opening ceremonies for the Verrazano-Narrows Bridge, which joined Staten Island and Brooklyn and was the longest and highest suspension bridge in the world. It was the last hurrah for Robert Moses, who had reshaped the city through massive construction projects, and an obvious occasion for politicians to deliver remarks and receive applause. But what Donald noticed was that Othmar Hermann Ammann, the 85-year-old Swiss-born immigrant who designed the bridge, was alone and ignored. "I realized then and there something I would never forget," the young developer-to-be told a reporter many years later. "I don't want to be made anybody's sucker."[24]

By the end of his sophomore year Donald was ready to move on. He was interested in business development, which he called "the what-if kind of stuff," and he could learn more about it at Wharton, the University of Pennsylvania's business school.

At the time, Wharton was on the margins of the campus both geographically and culturally.[25] Opposition to the Vietnam War was beginning to heat up on campuses around the country and within Penn's own liberal arts division, but the business school remained resolutely unaffected. Wharton students still wore coats and ties to classes, and those enrolled in ROTC wore their military uniforms to class without incident.

But Donald wasn't there to participate in the counterculture. He wasn't concerned that Wharton students were the most straight-arrow on the entire campus. Nor did he mind that as a transfer student he was ineligible to play on varsity sports teams and that he seemed to have even fewer friends at Wharton than at previous schools. What he cared about was that Wharton had one of the few real estate departments in American academia. His older brother had identified the school as the top choice for Fred's successor but had been unable to gain admission. Heeding Freddy's example, Donald had not applied to Wharton right off. Instead he earned two years' worth of respectable grades at Fordham, had an interview with a friendly Wharton admissions officer who was one of Freddy's old high school classmates, and then transferred into the real estate department.

"My father wanted me to finish and get a degree," Donald said later. "It was the only thing I could see studying." For the next two years Donald and the other students, most of whom were there because their families were in the industry, studied mortgages, accounting, and banking. Working on a team with classmates, he learned how to analyze neighborhoods and make appraisals by going into bars to see what ethnic groups were present. For the first time in his life, what he was studying seemed relevant.

"It didn't take me long to realize that there was nothing particularly awesome or exceptional about my classmates," he later wrote in *The Art of the Deal*.[26] "I could compete with them just fine." Sometimes the department's lone professor and Donald would have asides about what was really going on in the business. "I remember the professor talking to Donald like one insider to another," said Peter Gelb, another real estate major. "We were the students, and they were the pros."

ALTHOUGH HE WAS BARELY old enough to vote, Donald Trump had already won what might have been the toughest competition of his career.[27] On his dresser at NYMA was a photograph of his older brother standing next to an airplane. Lying on his back and discussing the future, Donald told his roommate that Fred Jr., his elder by nearly six years, had opted out of the family business to become a pilot. This choice, which Donald hastened to say he would never have made, left Donald in line to take over. Before he had finished high school, what could have been the most difficult conflict of his entire career was over, and he had come out on top.

It wasn't supposed to turn out that way. In a family where an older sister was not considered a candidate, Fred Trump Jr. was the heir apparent.[28] The problem was that he did not act like one. Blond, skinny, and nervous, he was always in motion. Even when sitting down, he would invariably be tapping his toe or jiggling his chair, behavior which made him what was known then as a live wire but would today be seen as possible symptoms of attention deficit disorder.

Freddy was closer to Maryanne, who was a year and a half older, than he was to his other siblings. He played with her and, more often than not, lost to her—the usual outcome between older and younger siblings, but with Freddy it seemed to happen way too often. Like his father and his younger brother, he was fiercely competitive; unlike them, he did not have the skills or the strategic sense to get what he wanted.

"He wasn't as intelligent as Maryanne, and I think the other kids outshone him," said Ginny Droesch Trumpbour, a counselor at the Hillman camps. "He wasn't quick enough to grasp what their father was telling him, which must have been hard given that he was the oldest boy."

What Freddy did have was a sense of humor. He was a wise guy who specialized in raised eyebrows and double entendres and was always ready to poke fun at anyone and everyone, including himself. It was the behavior of a younger child, fitting in where he could; the difficulty was that he was expected to act like a firstborn, to be a leader and a winner. "Be a killer," Fred Trump told his sons—not the class clown. Unlike Maryanne, Freddy did not stay at Kew Forest for high school but instead enrolled at St. Paul's, an Episcopalian boys' prep school on Long Island. Neither a jock nor an academic type, he nonetheless ended up gravitating toward a handful of fledgling intellectuals. They rode the same train to and from school each day and over the years formed a tight group that shared everything—pizzas and Cokes at first; then as they became older, cigarettes and beer. Often they hung out in the recreation room at Freddy's house, where they played at putting together a band. On nice days they went for rides in Freddy's little red motorboat, *Dixie Cup*.

To his friends, Freddy spoke admiringly of his father as a shrewd, corner-cutting businessman and boasted that he intended to step into his old man's shoes. But even to them, Freddy seemed far too anxious for attention and approval to take on the top job. "He [wanted to] show his dad he could be a tough little street fighter," one classmate said. "But he was a real pussycat, not mean and aggressive, kind of pathetic, really."

Freddy's obvious vulnerability made his friends feel protective, but it brought a harsh response from his father. "He wanted tough people," said the same classmate. "That was his bottom line, and he put a lot of pressure on Freddy." When one of Freddy's crowd mentioned that he was going to study liberal arts at an Ivy League school, Fred bristled with rage and spoke contemptuously of how little money his own brother made as a full professor at MIT. "I think Freddy's father feared that he was having the aggressive instincts schooled out of him," said the classmate. "He [thought that Freddy] was being turned into an Ivy League wimp."

In fact, the Ivy League, in the form of Wharton, rejected Freddy, and he ended up at Lehigh University, a second-tier school in central Pennsylvania. There he enrolled in Air Force ROTC and began to daydream about being a pilot, but when he graduated in 1958 he went to work as his father's general assistant. Finally he was face-to-face with the business he had been slated to take over, and for the next several years he gave it his best.

It was not close to good enough. When Freddy made what his father considered a mistake, such as installing new windows when old ones were still marginally serviceable, his father didn't hesitate to chew him out in public for wasting money. At the same time, when Freddy did something well, as when he finished off the roof and the final touches on a six-story Brooklyn building called the Falcon, his father never mentioned it. "When I asked him why not," Maryanne recalled, "he said, 'Why? He's supposed to do a good job.' It never occurred to him to actually praise Freddy." Under the stress of state hearings into alleged profiteering by Fred on Trump Village, a state-subsidized project, tensions flared between father and son. They rose further when Freddy couldn't push forward a Coney Island housing development that had ground to a halt after his father's political allies failed to deliver necessary zoning variances.

Freddy married a beautiful blonde airline stewardess from the Midwest named Linda Clapp, had two children, and continued trying to fit into the heir-apparent role. But the strain was becoming unbearable. The occasional cigarettes of high school had turned into chain smoking; the occasional beers, into serious drinking. Everyone could see that he would never be able to fill his father's shoes. They could also see that another candidate—a substitute firstborn, as it were—had emerged. "Donald was a lot younger, not close enough in age for heavy competition," Maryanne said. "I don't think Freddy thought Donald was a cold wind at his back, and he wouldn't have cared if he was."

Whether Freddy minded or not, Donald was blowing at his brother's back as hard as he could. "Our family environment, the competitiveness, was a negative for Fred," he later told one reporter. "He was the first Trump boy out there, and I subconsciously watched his moves." [29] Donald saw that cowering when Fred was mad caused further anger; that hanging around pointy-headed types brought on a rage; that showing any vulnerability was a mistake; and that smoking and drinking, both of which Freddy did a lot, were considered near-fatal flaws. The more Donald watched his sweet, generous, funny older brother, the more it looked as if Freddy would probably be spending his life behind the eight ball. If Donald didn't want to be there with him, he would have to show that he was the killer his father had wanted.

CHAPTER TWO

Manhattan Bound

One morning in January 1964, when Donald was still a cadet at New York Military Academy, his father had gotten on a plane, flown to Cincinnati for the monthly sheriff's auction, shelled out $5.6 million for a 1,200-unit garden apartment complex called Swifton Village, and flown back home in time for a dinner given by a powerful local political organization, the Madison Democratic Club. "Other men like playing golf," Fred told the man sitting next to him that night. "I like buying apartments." [1]

Fred had little connection to Cincinnati, but he had made his fortune building housing backed by the same FHA mortgage guarantees used for the construction of Swifton. Built in the early 1950s for about $10 million, it was the largest apartment complex in town. [2] It was also one of the most dilapidated and was then more than half-empty. Even though the FHA had cut the unpaid mortgage by one-third, Fred was the sole bidder. To everyone else, including his own mother, Swifton looked like a disaster. "That's the worst news I've had all day," she said when she heard about the purchase.[3] But to Fred, it seemed a compelling opportunity. "I don't see how you people can resist a steal like this," he told a local developer standing next to him at the auction.

From Chase Manhattan Bank, where he was a member of an advisory board and reportedly the largest depositor in Queens, Fred obtained a $5.75 million first mortgage, enough to cover the purchase and part of the renovation necessary to turn Swifton around. Every Tuesday he would fly to Cincinnati to make on-site inspections and take local real estate figures out to lunch. Back in New York, he would phone them and ask how much they paid for a gallon of paint or a yard of carpeting, then check their numbers against what his staff reported to him. At Christmas a huge neon sign wishing Cincinnati a happy holiday from Fred Trump went up in front of the project. "This was his baby," Roy Knight, who worked at Swifton as a carpenter, told a local reporter.

When Donald was at Fordham, his father occasionally took him along on his Tuesday flights. While Fred spent what was known at Swifton as "T-Day" charging in and out of buildings and firing questions at employees, his son did yard work and cleaning with the maintenance crew. As the months went by, he saw how his father's insistent, demanding approach brought the ailing complex back to life. New paint and appliances, neatly landscaped grounds, and beefed-up security increased occupancy rates, and Swifton gradually returned to a more even keel—for a while.

In June 1969, Haywood Cash, a black stock clerk at a nearby General Electric plant, inquired about an apartment at Swifton. After the rental agent told him he did not meet income requirements and there were no vacancies, Cash and his wife contacted a local civil rights organization called HOME, which then rented an apartment within the Cash family's income eligibility. When HOME attempted to turn over the apartment to the Cashes, the Swifton general manager called a HOME representative a "nigger lover" and threw her and Haywood

Cash off the premises. The Cashes filed a discrimination suit under the Civil Rights Act of 1968, and a lawyer for Swifton, acting on Fred's orders, offered them an apartment. They moved in and dropped the suit but asked for damages, eventually settling for the maximum allowable award of $1,000. Outwardly that was the end of the matter, although Donald would continue to insist that his father had done nothing wrong. Donald saw what had happened as a loss, and he did not take losing well.[4]

In the meantime, urban problems were closing in on Cincinnati. An interstate highway had sliced the city in half, and waves of unskilled immigrants from Appalachia had permanently disrupted many formerly stable neighborhoods. Once again, Swifton began to slide downhill. Tenant turnover accelerated, and this time the absentee landlord from Brooklyn could not stem it. By the fall of 1972, it was time to sell.

In *The Art of the Deal*, Donald takes considerable liberty in his depiction of his role at Swifton, including giving himself personal credit for its purchase and upgrade. But there's no doubt he showed a certain savvy in its sale. Rather than rely on his own sketchy knowledge of the area when showing around a potential buyer, Prudent Real Estate Investment, he called Franklyn Harkavy, the owner of a nearby apartment complex, and asked to stop by. Although they'd never met, Donald gambled that it would be in Harkavy's interest to give the visiting Prudent executives a positive picture of the neighborhood. The gamble paid off: Harkavy spoke in glowing terms, and in December 1972 Prudent announced it had bought Swifton for more than $6.75 million in cash.[5]

At the age of 26, Donald Trump had sealed his first multimillion-dollar deal. It was a sweet thing for a young man who had been his father's full-time apprentice ever since graduation from Wharton. Every morning they drove from Jamaica Estates to Fred's modest office, located in Beach Haven, the second of the two large FHA-backed housing developments he had built in Brooklyn in the early 1950s. Inside a nondescript three-story brick building on Avenue Z, the headquarters of the Trump empire still looked like the dentist's office it had once been, with a linoleum floor and chest-high partitions between cubicles.

There Donald learned where to stand when knocking at the door of a nonpaying and possibly violent tenant and how to handle purchases and repairs. When he raised neighborhood hackles with a clumsy attempt to lease tenant parking spaces to McDonald's, his father showed him how to use political ties to make things go his way. When Fred walked into a closing and told the buyers, who'd already syndicated the deal and could not afford further costly delays, that it was just too embarrassing to get such a low interest rate on promissory notes, Donald saw how to pull off a last-minute renegotiation.[6] When his father put a plant and a mirror in vacant apartments and got a more favorable response from prospective tenants, Donald saw how an extra touch can make a difference. When, in order to save on boiler-cleaning bills, Fred donned old overalls, climbed inside a boiler with an experienced cleaner, and emerged covered with soot but ready to instruct his supers himself, Donald saw how to pinch pennies. When his father wore a jacket and tie to building sites even on weekends, he saw the importance of looking professional at all times.

The son taught the father a few things, too. Gradually Donald overcame his father's reluctance to refinance his holdings, then about 80 buildings with an equity value on the order of $200 million, and they raised cash for new investments. But the younger man could not convince his father to operate in Manhattan, where both costs and potential benefits were far higher. Indeed, his father seemed willing to consider getting involved in projects almost anywhere except right across the river. "Manhattan just didn't make sense to him," Donald said later. "Why pay thousands of dollars for a square foot of land in Manhattan when out there [in Brooklyn] he paid thirty cents?"[7]

In the early 1970s, Donald received a promotion. His father had kicked himself upstairs to be chairman of the board, and Donald became president of the family business. One of his first acts was to bypass all the pedestrian corporate names used by his father in favor of a single, classy-sounding label: the Trump Organization.[8]

As befit his new station, he moved into a mid-building studio apartment on Manhattan's Upper East Side and blithely referred to it as a penthouse. "Moving into that apartment was probably more exciting for me than moving, fifteen years later, into the top three floors of

Trump Tower," he later wrote.[9] Every morning he drove a new company-owned white Cadillac convertible in a reverse commute to the far end of Brooklyn, but in the evenings he could savor his new identity as a Manhattanite. A first step was to join Le Club, a East Side members-only restaurant and nightclub. There he became acquainted with various powerful players in real estate and banking, including the lawyer Roy Cohn.[10]

Permanently tanned and famously pugnacious, Roy Cohn had been a celebrated bad boy ever since he first burst on the national scene in the 1950s as Senator Joseph McCarthy's assistant in the relentless hunt for communist subversives in the U.S. government. A master fixer who lived a conspicuously lavish life, he insisted on cash payment, scorned income taxes, and stonewalled his way through numerous IRS audits. Over the years he had faced charges for bribery, conspiracy, and bank fraud, gone to trial three times, and won acquittals on every occasion. Now in his mid-forties, Cohn radiated power in a way that repelled many but drew in Donald, who seemed intrigued to find someone else who would do anything to win. "I think Donald was attracted by the fact that Roy had actually been indicted," said Eugene Morris, Cohn's first cousin and a prominent real estate lawyer.[11]

Morris had met the Trumps in the late 1960s, when Fred retained him to handle his donation for a new wing at a Queens hospital. When the attorney asked Donald how he planned to handle his father's mini-empire, the young man said he didn't want anything to do with it. "I want to be in mid-Manhattan, where all the top stuff is going on," he told Morris. "I'll never be involved with the old man's property except when he needs me."

Perhaps in part because of this independent streak, Fred seemed to listen to his middle son in a way he listened to few others. At a later point Morris did a total overhaul of Fred's city tax assessments and obtained what he thought was an impressive rollback. His client peremptorily rejected it as grossly inadequate, and Morris complained to his cousin. Cohn passed on the complaint to Donald, who managed to convince his father to accept the deal he had just turned down. To Morris's amazement, the man who would still spend an entire afternoon meticulously explaining to a maintenance man how to mix liquid cockroach spray so as to avoid calling an exterminator promptly signed the paperwork. Afterward he put an arm around the lawyer and said, "Oh, Gene, it's only money, after all."

Once in a while, though, it wasn't just money. On October 15, 1973, the U.S. Justice Department slapped the Trump Organization with a suit charging that blacks seeking apartments in Trump-owned buildings were turned away or quoted inflated rents. The Trumps had faced similar charges in Cincinnati, but the new president of the Trump Organization no longer followed his father's policy of quiet diplomacy. Instead he held a press conference at the New York Hilton and announced that he had hired Cohn to fire back at the government with a damage suit for $100 million, a jaw-dropping amount at the time. Denying any discrimination, Donald said that the government was trying to push major landlords into accepting welfare tenants despite their precarious finances.

The presiding judge dismissed Trump's countersuit as "wasting time and paper," but Cohn's stalling tactics delayed the federal investigation for another year and a half. Donald testified repeatedly that he had nothing to do with renting apartments, although in an application for a broker's license filed at the same time he said that he was in charge of all rentals. In June 1975 he signed a settlement described by the Justice Department as "one of the most far-reaching ever negotiated." It required him to advertise vacancies in a black newspaper, to give first notice to the Urban League for a certain percentage of vacancies, and to include welfare payments when determining an applicant's income.[12]

This time around, he simply declared victory and went on as before. He had seen that such a boast was unlikely to be challenged. He had also seen that being charged with discrimination did not seem to deter anyone in the public or private realm from doing business with him. Practically speaking, the entire matter appeared to add up to little more than "a spit in the ocean," as Roy Cohn said dismissively. But perhaps more to the point, Donald Trump now had something far bigger and juicier on his plate.

ON JANUARY 26, 1968, a chunky, balding man with dark-rimmed glasses and a bulldog set to his jaw stared out from the cover of *Time*.[13] His name was Stuart Saunders, and he had just pulled off a stunning corporate coup: the merger of the Pennsylvania and New York Central railroads. The staggering cost of labor, government regulations, and cutthroat competition from trucks and planes had pushed these rail giants to the edge of bankruptcy. But now, with Pennsy chairman Saunders at the helm and Central president Alfred Edward Perlman as second in command, the two behemoths would morph into a slimmer, more robust entity called the Penn Central.

Headline writers dubbed the Penn Central "the Railroad of the Future," and *Saturday Review* named Saunders "Businessman of the Year." Strategic planners and transportation experts applauded, and business schools like Wharton, where Donald was finishing his senior year, looked upon Saunders with awe. Preaching the gospel of postmodern railroading—that the industry would survive only if lines got bigger in size and fewer in number—Saunders had taken over at the Pennsy in 1964 and revived long-stalled plans for consolidation with the New York Central. Four years later the new era began.

It lasted exactly 872 days. Late on the afternoon of June 21, 1970, the Penn Central, listing badly since the moment it came into being, went belly-up.

One of the biggest problems was that the merger never went beyond a paper transaction into a truly functional arrangement. Indeed, the two chief executives never had more than chilly relations and long before the end had ceased speaking to each other.[14] In turn, their huge joint workforce of 94,000 employees had lacked a common sense of purpose or even a common computer language. Supposedly headed for peak efficiency and profitability, the railroad of the future had instead produced a record-breaking deficit of $4 billion.

The Penn Central collapse would help spawn a profitable new bankruptcy industry peopled by turnaround specialists, assessors, and even publishers of newsletters devoted exclusively to this rapidly expanding field. More than that, though, the Penn Central story would produce important lessons about the modern corporate world, the nature of capitalism, and how to profit from seeming disaster. As events in coming years would show, Donald, then only 24 years old, would be an apt pupil.

Public admission of insolvency did not solve the Penn Central's problems. Because railroads were considered vital national interests, federal law required them to file for reorganization. Doing so suspended the Penn Central's debts, but it also meant that the railroad had to maintain the passenger and freight operations that had been losing $1 million a day.[15] Ultimately, court-appointed trustees came up with a proposal to transfer rail services to government ownership, pay the Penn Central's debts by selling everything not needed for rail operations, and reorganize the holding company in charge of the few subsidiaries that actually made money.[16]

The remaining problem was getting the many creditors to sign on—not easy, given that most were busy maneuvering to push everyone else further back in the line for the railroad's assets. "It was trench warfare, right out of World War I," said one Penn Central trustee.[17] But the railroad had "debtor's leverage": Its potential loss was so large that it could cow the banks, institutional investors, stockholders, and government authorities that were its creditors into accepting crumbs out of fear that if they held out for what they were owed, they would end up with nothing at all.

The next task was to come up with the crumbs. The solution: liquidating the vast real estate holdings that the Pennsylvania Railroad and the New York Central had spent the last century accumulating.[18] The New York Times reported on July 6, 1973, that the bankrupt railroad planned to hire a Los Angeles businessman to handle the deal. His name was Victor Palmieri, and he would be marketing properties worth more than $1 billion.

Only six months earlier, Fred and Donald had announced that the Trump Organization was finally entering the Manhattan market and would be turning a site on the East Side into rental apartments. At the time Donald had been thrilled, but the deal paled in significance when he picked up the *Times* that July morning. He knew that the list of sites on the block would include the one property he wanted more than anything in the world: the Penn Central rail yards, consisting of two huge parcels of land stretching along the eastern shore of the Hudson River. The total size of the yards was 120 acres, one-seventh the size of Central Park.[19] Remarkably, they were the same sort of undeveloped tracts on which his father had built so successfully in Brooklyn. The same, that is, in all but one respect: They were in Manhattan, a location that would have ruled them out for Fred Trump but made them a magnet for his son.[20]

As soon as Donald read the article, he wrote Palmieri a letter, but he received no response for six months. The reason for the delay was that Victor Palmieri, known for cutting through complex tasks with singular efficiency, was stumped.[21] The Stanford-trained lawyer, then 42, had already had his share of high-intensity careers. Stylish and sophisticated, he had been a high-profile corporate attorney, developed vast Southern California orange groves, and served as deputy chair of the Kerner Commission, established by President Lyndon B. Johnson in 1968 to investigate urban riots. Along the way he had also been the host of a public TV show and had salvaged one of Penn Central's numerous subsidiaries by paring it down to a string of amusement parks in southwestern states called Six Flags.[22] But even he was not prepared for what confronted him when he accepted Penn Central's offer.

Reduced to basics, what most people thought of as a huge railroad with a lot of property turned out to be a huge railroad plus a huge real estate company. Penn Central appeared to be one of the largest private landlords in the nation, but its real estate portfolio was so disorganized that no one could be sure what property it owned or where it was. To find out, Palmieri tapped his former assistant on the Kerner Commission, an efficient young graduate of Yale Law School named John Koskinen. A blond, cherubic-looking information machine, Koskinen hunkered down over old railroad maps and got to work. Because existing records were inadequate, obtaining exact coordinates of sites often involved going to them and walking the boundaries. Ultimately Koskinen pegged the Penn Central's holdings, initially thought to include about 450 items, at over 8,500 parcels of land, including everything from large sites in midtown Manhattan to thousands of rights-of-way obtained from the federal government during the original construction of the railroads.

Of those properties, nearly one-third were in New York City and were among the most valuable real estate in the world.[23] Ordinarily this enormous asset would be all the rescue package needed by any corporation, no matter how dire its straits. But in December 1973, New York City was in such poor shape that it seemed impossible to cash in these holdings for anything close to their real value. The manufacturing sector that had made the city a magnet to Friedrich Trump and millions of other immigrants was shrinking, major corporations were jumping ship, and public employees were on strike. Construction, a vital economic sector, was at a standstill, in part because the federal government, staggering under the tab for the Vietnam War, was making drastic cuts everywhere, including the subsidies from which Fred and other developers had made fortunes.

New York State was also on the ropes, due in part to former governor Nelson Rockefeller's exuberant expansiveness. In his zeal to subsidize middle-income housing, Rocky had tapped bond lawyer John Mitchell to finesse the debt limitations in the state constitution. Mitchell, an ingenious sort later famous as Richard Nixon's campaign manager and attorney general, had come up with a deceptively simple solution: replacing the usual "full faith and credit" phrase in state revenue bonds by the term "moral obligation." To protect its credit rating the state would have to make good on such bonds, but technically they would not count against the debt ceiling. Soon other states adopted this handy model, making Mitchell, later excoriated as a friend to wealthy elites, indirectly responsible for providing decent housing to millions of middle-income families all over America. But by the early 1970s, even moral obligation bonds were in trouble in New York. The housing program that had financed Trump Village had ground to a halt, and the Urban Development Corporation, which had used Mitchell's clever device for hundreds of projects, actually went into default.

Still worse, New York City, famed for its generosity to schools, hospitals, and the poor, was relying increasingly on costly short-term bonds just to finance daily operations. To attract buyers, the terms for the city became ever more onerous, and underwriting firms issued ever louder alarms over the city's financial condition. Seeing the city spiraling toward disaster, John Lindsay, the elegant East Sider who had ushered in the era of deficit financing, prudently declined to run for a third term as mayor. By the time his successor, Abraham Beame, moved into Gracie Mansion, the pressures of the fiscal crisis were so severe that Beame was barely able to exercise his mayoral powers.[24]

In sum, it was not the best market to sell large real estate parcels in New York City. But Ned Eichler, the former business school professor charged with the initial selection of buyers, had both a long-term perspective and a certain commonality with Donald Trump. The son of a successful developer who built what were known as "Eichler homes" near San Francisco at the same time Fred was doing FHA housing in Brooklyn, Ned had gone to work for his father and expected to take over the prosperous family business. But in the 1960s his father had ignored his advice, abandoned the well-designed single-family houses, and plunged into high-rise apartments. The two had an enormous row, the younger Eichler left the company, and his father went bust.

Hired by Palmieri to help divest Penn Central of surplus real estate, Ned Eichler had farmed out much of the task but reserved for himself the plum: the New York properties, which were the most valuable and the most challenging. Because the West Side rail yards looked like a particularly hard sell, he figured that the best shot was not to think of it as a conventional sale. "I knew that nobody would buy the yards for cash," he said afterward. "Effectively we would be going into a joint venture where we'd be putting up the land and the developer would be putting up the skill."

It seemed to Eichler that he needed a seemingly impossible package: a developer who knew how to do the job and could handle big-city politics but didn't already have other Manhattan projects competing for attention. "I knew we would be riding a horse here," Eichler said. "The only question was which horse—which developer—would be the right one."

One December day he opened a file of correspondence on the yards and found Donald's letter. After ascertaining that no one in Palmieri's office recognized the name, Eichler called the Trump Organization. "Donald just came right through the telephone from the start," Eichler said. "He was selling from the beginning of the conversation. He told me about his father, all these buildings they'd built, when was I coming to Brooklyn, he'd show me around, he'd send a car to pick me up, don't worry."

Taken by the sheer energy on the other end of the line, Eichler made the trip in mid-January and took the Donald Trump tour. He was impressed by the real estate he saw, and he was fascinated by the young man spouting off grandiose plans to build an enormous residential development on the site now occupied by the rail yards. "He seemed like an epic character, straight out of Stendhal," Eichler said. "An ambitious boy from the provinces, full of his own ego, wanting to make his way in the city."

But Eichler was unsure that this unknown developer-in-training could take care of the heavy-duty politics, financing, and rezoning such a massive undertaking would require. When Eichler asked for proof that he could handle these issues, Donald suggested that he speak to the new mayor, Abe Beame, in office only a few weeks. Playing along with what he assumed was a joke, Eichler said off the top of his head, "Okay, how about tomorrow at one-thirty in the afternoon?" Without an instant's hesitation, his host said he would send his car to pick Eichler up. What Eichler didn't know was that the new mayor had started his political career as a precinct worker in the Madison Democratic Club and counted both Fred Trump and Trump's longtime attorney, the legendary Brooklyn political insider Bunny Lindenbaum, among his closest friends.

The next day Eichler found himself walking into the mayor's office at exactly 1:30 P.M. for a meeting with Abe Beame, Fred and Donald Trump, and John Zuccotti, the newly appointed chair of the City Planning Commission.[25] After a few pleasantries Eichler told the mayor why he was there. To Eichler's astonishment, the tiny chief executive of New York City managed to reach an arm around each of the Trumps, both six-footers, then looked out directly at Eichler and said, "Whatever my friends Fred and Donald want in this town, they get."

The normally voluble Eichler was dumbfounded at what seemed a mayoral blank check. "What else could I ask after that?" he said. "Beame had answered all the questions in one sentence." Afterward Eichler stood chatting with the Trumps on the plaza in front of City Hall. Many successful fathers, including Eichler's, were ambivalent about having their sons step into their shoes, but Eichler was struck by how easily Fred ceded the spotlight to Donald. "It seemed clear to me that this was a very unusual relationship," Eichler said. "His father seemed totally supportive that this was Donald's project."[26]

What Eichler could not have realized was that for Fred, this was an opportunity to live out his own fantasies and longings and to provide the paternal tutelage he had not gotten from his own father, who had died when he was only 12. In a way, Fred was acting as father both to his son and to himself. This dual identity gave great intensity to their relationship, and it had a powerful effect on a number of observers, including Eichler. In the end, what may have sealed his choice of Donald to develop the rail yards was the close tie he saw between father and son.

Palmieri was less taken with the untried neophyte from Brooklyn. For several months he and Eichler argued about whether to back Donald's bid for the option on the yards. But there were no other credible candidates, and Palmieri's national Democratic credentials were worthless in New York, where what counted was local ties. With pressure from all sides to act quickly, Palmieri had to find someone who already had the necessary connections and was what he called a "hard charger"—a risk taker with a nose for the market and enough energy to keep pushing throughout the five to ten years a major development could take. Reluctantly, Palmieri gave his okay to a deal that would allow Donald to pursue financing and rezoning on the yards in exchange for cutting the Penn Central in on future development proceeds.

If Donald hadn't existed, Palmieri would have had to invent him—and vice versa. Although Fred's political connections and real estate portfolio gave Donald legitimacy, they did not provide financing per se. Even if Fred had put his entire fortune into the deal, he could not foot the bill for what his son had in mind. The money would have to come from government programs, then being cut back, or from banks and other institutions that were loath to lend even to experienced builders because of the city's chancy financial state. What Donald needed was someone who believed that his intense drive would somehow make up for his lack of both experience and cash—someone, that is, like Ned Eichler and, albeit grudgingly, Victor Palmieri. "We were backing him for effort," Palmieri said later. "With us, Donald could operate without money, just energy, and that was key for him at that point."

Over the months that followed, Donald tried again and again to come up with a way to strike a deal on railroad property. Every day or two he would show up at Eichler's office, in an old Penn Central building, and go over everything that was potentially for sale. Most of the time, though, he talked about the rail yards, which were bundled together for sale purposes. The smaller parcel (also the one with more rail traffic), known as the 34th Street yards, was 44 acres and extended from 30th to 39th streets along the Hudson River; the second, known as the 60th Street yards, was about 75 acres (18.5 of them underwater), went from 59th to 72nd Streets, and was partially covered by an elevated section of the West Side Highway.[27] Urban planners had long been eyeing the yards, which were used for freight traffic and were the last large undeveloped stretch left in Manhattan. But it was not until the 1970s, when rail freight carried down the West Side had dwindled to little more than the newsprint for the *New York Times*, that the property became available for other uses.[28]

The use Donald was envisioning was a gigantic middle-income housing complex, which would require a zoning change from industrial to residential as well as enormous government subsidies. "Donald made all sorts of outrageous demands and had no tolerance when I would say something was impossible," Eichler said. "But that's true of all successful real estate developers—they don't want to hear the negatives. If they just keep pushing and pushing and don't listen, they'll get there."

The developer-to-be tried every which way to get what he wanted. At times his conversation included heavy innuendos—but never concrete offers—that he was willing to pay for favors. "Once we passed a headline about a mayor in New Jersey being arrested for an enormous bribe," Eichler recalled. "Donald looks at the headline and says, 'There is no fucking mayor in America worth that much money—I could buy a U.S. senator for less than that.' He had that way of talking—was he kidding, was he serious, was he sending me a message?" After Eichler sent back a Christmas present of a chauffeur-delivered television set, Donald threw up his arms in exasperation. "I don't know how to deal with you," he told Eichler. "Anybody else in your position would have $10 million in a cigar box tucked away."

Like his father, Donald labored morning, noon, and night. Sometimes he would call Eichler up at one or two in the morning to argue over details. One fall day they drove out to Winged Foot, the classy Westchester County golf club that Donald had joined the year after he graduated from college, and Eichler interrupted his business spiel to comment about the gorgeous trees alongside the highway. "I suppose so, if you like that sort of thing," Donald said, then plunged back in. For him there was no downtime; once at the golf course he was still going full throttle, playing not to relax or even just to win, but to vanquish.

On another occasion Donald asked Eichler to join him and Roy Cohn for lunch at the fashionable Four Seasons restaurant. Eichler was offended by Trump's many tales of hiring Cohn to keep tenants he considered undesirable out of his properties, but he was also curious to meet the famous fixer. Donald came late and announced, with such loud enthusiasm that Eichler was sure diners on all sides could hear, that he'd just met with Democratic gubernatorial candidate Hugh Carey, then a member of the U.S. House of Representatives from Brooklyn. "He's perfect," Donald declared gleefully. "He'll do anything for money."

Mostly, though, Donald worked harder and was more focused than anyone Eichler had ever met. "I saw it again and again," Eichler said. "He'd be in a meeting, performing and carrying on, and then some guy would ask him a technical question and he'd be on it like a tiger." No matter what the time of day, the only topic of conversation was business. "You didn't talk about any of the ordinary things, like movies or books," Eichler said. "With Donald, there was no small talk."

Eichler often wondered why someone who already had family money would be so driven. Once when they lunched at another elegant Manhattan restaurant, the '21' Club, Donald supplied a clue in an uncharacteristically reflective moment. He told Eichler that he assumed he would not marry and would be dead before he was 40, but in the time he had left he intended to be bigger than Harry Helmsley, then the largest real estate magnate in New York. "I knew that whole world of builders," Eichler said, "and the guys who really cared about making money were very private. Donald was different. For him, the purpose wasn't the money. It was to be famous."

Such behavior didn't make him likable, but Eichler wasn't looking for likable. He was looking for someone unlike all the other developers in town, someone who wouldn't just sit on the property until he had all his other development ducks in a row. "I wanted somebody who got up every day thinking this was his main thing in life, what he wanted to make work," he said. And to Eichler, that meant Donald.

———◈———

LATE ON THE AFTERNOON of Monday, November 11, 1974, Donald Trump, then 28, sat at a table in a Philadelphia courtroom and watched as a hearing on the disposition of the Penn Central rail yards opened. Next to him were Fred Trump and Bunny Lindenbaum. Nearby were Ned Eichler, John Koskinen, and nearly a dozen attorneys for various creditors and interested parties. They were there because the Penn Central trustees wanted to grant the Trump Organization an option to buy the rail yards and needed permission from Judge John Fullam, the federal magistrate assigned to the reorganization.

A former Pennsylvania farm boy, Fullam was a World War II vet and Harvard Law School graduate who ended up in judicial robes after he lost two races for Congress. "In chambers he was this really little guy who wouldn't stomp a fly," said one Penn Central lawyer. "But he was a terror up there on the bench. He controlled all of the creditors and all of us, kept us all in place."[29] With one of the most valuable sites in the entire Penn Central inventory at issue, observers expected the proceeding to be long and contentious. Instead it unfolded with unaccustomed smoothness, for unbeknownst to almost everyone present, the important deal-making occurred before Fullam ever lifted his gavel.

Most of those sitting in the courtroom had expected strident opposition to the trustees' request to give Donald the option. They assumed the source would be David Berger, the lawyer for the Penn Central's stockholders, then at the bottom of the creditor heap. A stout man with a penetratingly loud voice, he had built a successful practice in Philadelphia representing clients in class-action suits. "His job was to yell and scream," recalled one Penn Central lawyer, "and he was very good at it."[30] Protesting, complaining, and stringing everything out, Berger was doing precisely what he was hired to do: make himself so annoying that other creditors might cut his clients in on a settlement just to get rid of him.

When Eichler said that Berger could be a problem, Donald said nothing. But a few days before the hearing, Eichler received middle-of-the-night calls from both men informing him that they had met and summoning him to Berger's office. There the lawyer announced that because the developer and he had completely overhauled the terms of the sale, he now favored it. As Berger later explained in court, the price would remain $62 million, but because payment would not occur for some time, it would come with interest, plus a larger portion of any future increase in the yards' value and an option to acquire a larger percent of the equity. The total "improvement," as Berger termed it, could amount to as much as $20.5 million.

There was also an "improvement" for Donald. As before, he would pay no deposit and receive $750,000 in start-up money from the Penn Central, but now he would not have to pay back a dime if the project went nowhere. Somehow he had convinced Berger that a nebulous future promise in return for the cancellation of any refund was an excellent deal for Berger's clients. "It was a very clever accomplishment," Eichler said. "If someone's in your way, deal with him yourself—kill him, buy him, deal with him however. This wasn't the only problem, but it was a big one. Then all of a sudden it disappeared."

Berger's sudden switch from adamant foe to ardent supporter was puzzling. A possible explanation would emerge some years later. In 1979 federal prosecutors investigated allegations that Berger's abrupt turn-around was related to Donald's decision to join several other New York landlords as plaintiffs in a $100 million lawsuit Berger was preparing at the same time. The suit charged major oil companies with fixing the price of heating oil. As was standard in such cases, Berger's fee would be one-third of any settlement, and the settlement's size would depend on the number of apartments represented by the suit. This number was also the basis for the advance that plaintiffs paid Berger up front. The partic-ipation of the Trump Organization, which had more apartments than any other party to the suit, was clearly to Berger's advantage, but the federal probe did not find sufficient evidence of wrongdoing to yield criminal indictments.[31]

Whatever quid pro quo may have taken place, the deeper expla-nation for why things went Donald's way had at least as much to do with the two men sitting next to him in the courtroom. It was because of his ability to handle such problems that Bunny Lindenbaum had become a Brooklyn real estate fixture, and Fred himself had nearly always been able to see his way around obstacles. Forty years earlier, he had encoun-tered an oddly similar situation. Like Donald, he had been 28 years old, he had been trying to gain control of one of the most valuable parts of a bankrupt empire, and he had encountered opposition. Another devel-oper had topped his offer for the mortgage-servicing department of the Lehrenkrauss Corporation, and a group of disgruntled creditors had threatened to block the sale of any assets. Fred promptly joined forces with his rival, won over creditors by adding an attractive but meaning-less new provision, and nailed the mortgage-servicing contract. In this Philadelphia courtroom, Donald was simply following in the footsteps of his father and his lawyer, doing whatever it took to make things end up where he needed them to be.

With Berger in the Trump camp, the only opposition to the trustees' proposal came from an elderly New York real estate broker and his associate. But because their ostensible client did not appear at the hearing or send an attorney, Fullam gave this competing bid scant at-tention, and his decision to postpone a final ruling seemed little more than a formality. Still, Donald left nothing to chance. During one break he went over to the broker's associate and attempted to neutralize him. "Bring me deals," Donald said. "Represent me. I'm interested in expanding, and you seem very knowledgeable about real estate."[32] Afterward the Trumps and Lindenbaum walked out into the night, climbed into the black limousine waiting at the curb, and headed north.

Four months later Judge Fullan awarded the Trump Organization the option to buy the rail yards. Finally, Donald could pursue his own middle-income apartment complex. He had diverged from his father's model by focusing on Manhattan; now he would make his second departure. Instead of looking only for maximum profits, he would set out to build the largest such project in the world.

"The biggest project, the one with the most apartments, that's what was exciting to him," Eichler said later. "He thrived on conflict, the bigger the better. He loved it. People like him always do."

CHAPTER THREE

From Brick Box to Glass Fantasy

S ix days before the Penn Central hearing in Philadelphia, the people of New York State elected a new governor.[1] A Democrat, an Irish Catholic, and the father of a dozen children, Hugh Carey had been a lawyer for his family's fuel oil business when he entered electoral politics in 1960 and won a seat in the House of Representatives from what had long been a solidly Republican district. In six terms he had nailed down choice committee assignments and consolidated his position on Capitol Hill. By his seventh term, in 1972, he had become so powerful that he had tacit support from Republican governor Nelson Rockefeller.[2]

Two years later Carey, then 55, launched his gubernatorial campaign against Rocky's handpicked heir apparent. Polls showed that Carey was unknown to nine out of ten Empire State voters, and only a few weeks into the race his wife died from cancer. Channeling his grief into his quest for higher office, he hired a media consultant and got to work. By election night he had lost his spare tire, his graying hair was again brown, and he was jubilantly hosting a crowded victory party at the Commodore Hotel in Manhattan. It was the first time in 16 years that a Democrat would occupy the governor's mansion in Albany. Moreover, the winner was a Democrat from Brooklyn, with strong ties to New York City mayor Abe Beame, former mayor Robert Wagner, and Bunny Lindenbaum. In short, a Trump kind of Democrat.

Earlier that year Donald had hedged his bets by offering support to both Carey and his opponent in the Democratic primary, Howard Samuels, the progressive millionaire who had invented Baggies.[3] "My antenna went up," said Ken Auletta, campaign manager for Samuels and later a prominent journalist. "He was a big developer with big plans, and if he was going to come off as a major contributor, I was worried. What was the money for?" Auletta turned the developer down, but Carey's campaign evidently had no hesitation. Accordingly, the Trumps gave early—they funded the Carey campaign's first phone lines—and often. Carey rolled over Samuels in the primary, and the Trumps and Trump-owned companies would go on to become Carey's second-largest source of donations, topped only by his own brother.[4]

Like any good politician, Hugh Carey knew how to say thank you. In the first round of appointments after the election, the governor-elect named Donald to a blue-ribbon task force on housing even though he had not yet constructed a building.[5] With Hugh Carey in Albany and Abe Beame in City Hall, that would change.

——————⋅◉⋅——————

AMONG THE HUNDREDS of supporters gathered to cheer the governor-elect was a tall woman with a round face and an assertive manner. She was expensively dressed and heavily made up, her reddish blond hair well coiffed and heavily sprayed. Her name was Louise Mintz

Sunshine, and she would arguably have more influence on Donald than any other woman except his own mother. On this victory night she was the executive director of Carey's finance committee, but until the Democratic primary she had been a key fund-raiser for Howard Samuels. Gracious and warm to her wide range of friends and acquaintances, Sunshine could be tough when she deemed it necessary. "She made people pay their dues," recalled one campaign insider. "Fund-raising is full of bullshit artists who want to be at the party but don't want to pay. She wouldn't put up with that."[6]

A Brandeis graduate from a prosperous New Jersey real estate family, Sunshine had married a successful doctor and had three children. Only a few years earlier, her work as a parent volunteer at Dalton, a prestigious Manhattan private school, had seemed an adequate outlet for her considerable skills. But when she lost a bid to join the school's board of directors, she redirected her formidable talents toward politics and developed connections in Manhattan and the Bronx. After seizing the reins in Carey's campaign, she overhauled his precarious finances. Early in 1975 she became treasurer of the Democratic State Committee and a national committeewoman from New York. On the side, she continued to do volunteer work. By now, though, she was not donating her services to education or politics. Instead her cause was helping Donald, whom she had gotten to know as a Carey contributor, to develop the Penn Central properties.

Because Sunshine was still Carey's chief fund-raiser, her work for the Trump Organization had to be on an unpaid basis—a "truly ridiculous" situation, she later commented to the New York Times. But like Ned Eichler and Victor Palmieri, she found Donald's mix of high energy and high-level political connections irresistible. The brash go-getter from Queens, she said, was "the most incredible person I ever met in my life."[7]

For Donald, Sunshine, a powerful political player who could deliver the favorable government treatment he needed, seemed the answer to his prayers. Her access to Carey and other state officials would prove invaluable as the all-but-bankrupt city came more and more under the control of the state. But working with her also gave Donald his first opportunity to join forces with someone whose drive, aggressiveness, and stamina matched his own. Someone who already had the approval of his quasi-mentor, Roy Cohn, a patient of Sunshine's husband. Someone whose advice he could take without offense, because she was an older, married woman. Yet at the same time, someone not that much older, not Fred's associate but his own, someone he had found and selected himself. In short, a colleague.

Even with Louise Sunshine's aid, Donald's proposal was far from realization. He had managed to obtain an option on the Penn Central rail yards, but before he could dig a spadeful of dirt he would have to convince the city to rezone the site and banks to finance construction. And before he could do either of these formidable tasks, he would need a design.

The logical choice for that task was the firm led by Jordan Gruzen and Peter Samton, two MIT-trained architects who a decade earlier had designed a 5,000-unit apartment complex on an enormous platform over the tracks.[8] As soon as Donald fired off his initial Penn Central yards letter, he summoned Gruzen and Samton to Brooklyn to discuss a small apartment project. It was never built, but the designers evidently passed muster. One year later Donald hired them to produce the first plan for housing on the yards that would not have a railroad running underneath.

What he wanted, he told them, was big. In initial press stories he suggested 20,000 units for the 60th Street yards and 10,000 for the 34th Street yards.[9] Taken together, this two-part, 30,000-apartment complex would surpass the Trump Organization's entire real estate portfolio, variously estimated at between 15,000 and 20,000 units. Fred's first structure had been a garage for a neighbor; his son's initial venture would be the largest apartment complex in the world. It was a breathtaking proposal, and it was also impossible. The once-plentiful subsidies Fred used to build large-scale middle-income housing had disappeared, but a market ready to pay the staggering cost of basic infrastructure—that is, to pony up market-rate prices—had not yet emerged.

Donald's vision was almost comically out of sync with what almost everyone else in the city had in mind. City Planning Commission chairman John Zuccotti said flatly that the 34th Street yards should remain dedicated to industry and that the 60th Street yards should be "residential but not monster high-rise."[10] Former city construction coordinator Robert Moses, never known for advocating small-scale anything, declared that there should be no more than 1,300 apartments, built solely on the northern yards.[11] Richard Dicker, general counsel for Penn Central's largest creditor and subsequently the head of the reorganized railroad, thought building anything at all was out of the question and that Trump's option to do so was like "paying me $1,000 for the option of delivering me to Mars."[12] Even Ned Eichler, for whom more apartments meant a higher sale price and a bigger commission for his employer, the Palmieri Company, believed less density would be easier, faster, and better for the neighborhood.

Donald paid no attention. Instead of scaling the project down, Gruzen and his partners found themselves drawing continuously, turning out sketches, studies, elevations, renderings, and site plans for a client who literally could not wait to see their work. When the architects got to their office in the morning, they would find him already there, looking over drafting tables and leafing through papers.

"He talked a mile a minute, and he knew everything," recalled Paul Willen, one of the architects working on the rail yards. "Of course he didn't know everything, didn't in fact know very much, but he had that air of confidence."

Although Donald's impatience could be irritating, his overwhelming eagerness was engaging. "He was hot to trot," said Jordan Gruzen. "He was excited and anxious, wanting to see what was going on, how far we'd gotten." Often these encounters would lead to spontaneous discussions between the architects and the developer about alternative possibilities. "He would play dumb a lot, ask a lot of questions, what do you think of this or that," Gruzen said. "After a while I realized he wasn't as uncertain as it seemed, that he was playing a game."

Of all the obstacles Donald faced, the most intractable may have been neither financing nor design but the community, whose backing would be necessary to obtain a zoning change from industrial to residential. By the 1970s, the area around the 60th Street yards was on its way up and attracting savvy, well-connected residents unwilling to let a developer decide what would happen to their neighborhood. "We felt this land belonged to us," said Sally Goodgold, member and later co-chair of the local community board. "We would look into it and see what was best. We were not going to have a developer-driven process."[13]

As soon as Goodgold and other board members heard about Donald's ideas, they obtained planning chairman Zuccotti's commitment not to accept any proposal that lacked their approval. Then they began a seemingly endless series of meetings with Donald, his architects, his lawyers, and his consultants. Board committees and subcommittees made countless phone calls and produced a flood of letters, questions, recommendations, thank-yous, and you're-welcomes. Gradually the project shrank. From 14,500 units, which the board summarily rejected, the project contracted to about 5,000. But this was still too big for the board, and meetings with the developer grew increasingly contentious.[14]

It was Donald's first construction project and his first large-scale dilemma. Needing somehow to produce a project large enough to pay for itself but small enough to be approved by the community, he bobbed and weaved. Again and again he would unveil a new plan and insist that it was ideal for the community and financially feasible, but he declined to provide any specific hows and whys.

"Trump was very young, and he would throw numbers around in ways that seemed to me to make no sense," recalled the community board consultant, an architect named Jonathan Barnett. "The whole thing seemed like a variation on the old joke where a vendor says he's selling potato peelers and he's losing four cents on each one, but he expects to make up the loss in volume."[15] To Barnett, the only strategy that could work, and what Donald may well have been doing, was to say whatever was necessary in order to get the zoning change. Then, with the new zoning in hand, he would be able to obtain financing from a large institutional investor with deep pockets and use the investor's clout to push the city into paying for the infrastructure.

Occasionally Fred attended community meetings. No doubt his

son's situation reminded him of his own experience a decade earlier, when he had tried to build apartments at Coney Island. He, too, had presented one scheme after another, bobbed and weaved, and ultimately failed to win community backing for a necessary zoning change. Now, though, he sat in the back row of the auditorium as his son delivered an upbeat pitch and showed slides with leafy trees, beautiful parks, and, in the background, shadowy clusters of buildings.[16]

At Donald's side was an all-star team with what architect Barnett called "a very general 'Don't worry about it, we know how to do it' approach—plus 'Don't get in our way or we'll run over you.' "[17] In addition to Sunshine, the group included Fred's publicist, Howard Rubenstein. Raised in Brooklyn, he was now a Manhattan-based public relations czar, and his list of business, political, and real estate clients was so large that he occasionally represented both sides in disputes.[18] Another member was Sandy Lindenbaum, the son of Fred's longtime attorney, Brooklyn power broker Bunny Lindenbaum. One of the few real estate lawyers who had mastered the city's arcane zoning restrictions, Sandy was known for his aggressive style and boasted that he was "the last of the gunslingers."

Nonetheless, Donald's plans for the 60th Street yards remained stalled. Ultimately it was a Manhattan project, and his Brooklyn and Albany ties could not make it happen. But at the 34th Street yards, a different story was unfolding.[19] It had begun back in the Lindsay administration, when major hotel and business interests wanted to replace the multilevel New York Coliseum, located just north of midtown Manhattan at Columbus Circle. By the time of Beame's inauguration, advocates of a new hall were pushing for a huge single-level structure that would allow giant displays on the same floor. The leading plan, designed by the prestigious architectural firm Skidmore, Owings & Merrill, spread out horizontally on a spaceport platform that extended out hundreds of feet over the Hudson River at West 44th Street. Despite its Jetsonian design, nearly everyone in the city, including Mayor Beame, had signed on to the scheme.[20]

When Ned Eichler and, later, Jordan Gruzen pointed out that the nonresidential neighborhood around the 34th Street yards made more sense for a convention center than housing, Donald insisted that it was out of the question.[21] He wanted to build housing, he said, and 44th Street looked like a done deal. Gruzen persevered. Warming to the prospect of a huge project with tens of thousands of jobs and a vast payroll, Donald told him to work up a sketch of a convention center and leave it unsigned. Together they showed the drawing to John Zuccotti, whose eyes lit up immediately. "If you have a viable, less costly alternative, here's your chance to prove it," he said. "But do so quietly."

This time the group that had been stymied at 60th Street moved ahead like a precision drill squad. Louise Sunshine worked the phones to build support, a more conciliatory Donald addressed small community groups, and the Gruzen firm turned out a design for a two-level structure made of bronze-colored glass.[22] Unlike its 44th Street rival, this building rested squarely on terra firma, was accessible from all four sides, and boasted a solar collector on the roof, per instructions from Donald, who said he wanted the public relations value.[23] Estimated to cost between $100 million and $140 million, this structure would be vastly cheaper than the $231 million budgeted for 44th Street.

As Zuccotti had predicted, Beame eventually shelved the 44th Street center for lack of funds. But just as Donald's campaign was picking up speed, the mayor abruptly endorsed a different alternative: Battery Park City, an enormous and, at the time, faltering state-sponsored development project planned for a landfill area at the southern tip of Manhattan. Beame may have been concerned that promoting a site controlled by the son of his old friend Fred Trump would look like cronyism. Probably more important, the mayor was under siege from the governor, who was facing pressure from business and financial leaders to rescue Battery Park City and jump-start the publicly owned World Trade Center, opening across the street and desperate for tenants.

Undaunted, Donald began drafting press releases headlined RIP-OFF AT BPC. By the next week the selection of the convention center had become a major story.[24] Then he unveiled at a press conference what he called, with a nod to the popular film of the same name, the Miracle on 34th Street. Before him were midtown business leaders and city officials, reporters from every major paper, and TV crews. Calling the Battery Park City proposal "a tragic mistake," he claimed that his Miracle Center would be the largest such facility in the country, would be done in one-fourth the time scheduled for 44th Street, and would cost only one-fourth as much. In fact, other facilities were larger, Trump's cost and time estimates were low, and his projections of potential revenues were high, but most press coverage omitted these details.[25]

For Howard Rubenstein, the actual press conference was an anticlimax. He already knew it would be a success. He'd spent hours the previous day going over possible questions and answers with Donald, whom Rubenstein considered a public relations natural. Better yet, that morning the *New York Times* had run a pro–34th Street story. The product of a Rubenstein-arranged briefing, the article quoted Ted Kheel, born in Brooklyn and now a well-known labor negotiator, saying that a convention center in Battery Park City would be "like putting a nightclub in a graveyard."[26]

By most accounts Donald began to rise to power only when he moved to Manhattan. And such was the case, but not because of leaving Brooklyn behind. Rather, his ascent was due to his ability to turn Manhattan projects into Brooklyn projects. The real "Miracle on 34th Street" was not the convention center design unveiled at the press conference. It was how Donald himself managed to combine his father's political connections, his advisers' collective wisdom, and his own budding development acumen to outmaneuver his competitors. The borough he had fled would be among his most important sources of strength.[27]

———◦◉◦———

ALTHOUGH DONALD'S INITIATIVES on the two West Side rail yards were impressive, they were not what would establish him in the New York real estate pantheon. Instead he would secure his reputation with the redevelopment of another Penn Central property: the 65-year-old Commodore Hotel, which was named after nineteenth-century tycoon Commodore Cornelius Vanderbilt.[28]

Located next to Grand Central Terminal, the Commodore, one of five hotels in Manhattan owned by the Penn Central, had 2,000 guest rooms and had offered modest but reliable lodging to several generations of railroad travelers. Now, though, it was falling apart. Hotel management had roped off whole floors as unusable. The occupancy rate had slipped well below 50 percent,[29] a massage parlor had set up shop, and prostitutes occasionally propositioned guests in the lobby. Although it was losing close to $1 million a year, a strong union contract required the hotel to continue paying its workers even if it shut down altogether. After years of nonpayment, the overdue real estate taxes on the building stood at $6.6 million. Given that the building's market value was estimated at no more than $10 million, it was hardly surprising that Ned Eichler viewed the Commodore as a losing proposition. "I felt as though we should pay someone to take it off our hands," he said afterward.

When Donald had first inspected the Commodore, he, too, was repelled by the sleaziness and squalor of both the hotel and the neighborhood. But at the same time he noticed prosperous commuters flooding in and out of Grand Central Terminal. "The problem was the hotel, not the neighborhood," he later wrote. "If I could transform the Commodore, I was sure it would be a hit."[30]

His plan for this transformation was relatively simple. He would buy the hotel for $10 million, obtain a tax abatement, and gut-renovate the building into a new hotel. The only problem was that to everyone else, each of these steps, not to mention all of them combined, seemed beyond the realm of possibility.

He started with the design. Because he had admired a striking skyscraper at 44th and Broadway with a huge diadem projecting from the top, he arranged to meet the architect, Der Scutt, for dinner. When Donald arrived at Maxwell's Plum, a popular singles bar on the East Side, he found a tall, square-faced man with an intense and sometimes abrupt manner. Surrounded by faux Tiffany lamps and baroque mirrors, the developer-to-be told the architect, who was about ten years his senior, what he had in mind. As the younger man laid out a plan to encase the Commodore's traditional brick-and-masonry facade in glass, the older man covered one of the restaurant's oversize menus with preliminary sketches of a tall, glass-enclosed building rising next to Grand Central.

They proceeded to Donald's current apartment, a bona fide penthouse a few blocks away on East 65th Street. Perched on the thirty-second floor, it had one bedroom, one and a half bathrooms, and a sweeping view that included the George Washington Bridge to the north and Brooklyn and Long Island to the east. At the moment it also boasted a prodigious amount of large modern furniture, most of it in brown or beige and so new that it still had brown wrapping paper around the chrome legs. "Donald said, 'What d'ya think, what d'ya think,' his favorite line throughout his whole life—he usually says it twice, not once," Scutt said later. "He was very proud." After telling Donald that he had enough couches and chairs for two apartments, Scutt pushed the bulkier items into the hallway and rearranged the rest to make the apartment look more spacious.

The two men hit it off immediately, for they spoke the same earthy language and relished confrontation. Perhaps more important, they shared a passion for mirrored surfaces and shiny metal as well as an understanding of how to market to the public. "Donald had a way of not exactly exaggerating, but issuing public relations statements that were exciting," Scutt said. "If they were slightly exaggerated, okay, that was how he could sell." Soon Donald asked Scutt to come up with a few ideas for remodeling the old New York Central office building. "Nothing old-fashioned or colonial," the developer scrawled in the margin of Scutt's drawings. "No cornices, no brick, no round columns."

Donald would retain Scutt to work with Gruzen and Samton on both the Commodore and the convention center.[31] But to move forward, he also needed an experienced hotel operator. By 1974, he had his sights on Hyatt, which was owned by the wealthy Pritzker family of Chicago and was the one major national hotel management chain without a New York base.

Hyatt had first come to the Pritzkers' attention in 1957, when Jay Pritzker had stopped at an airport coffee shop in Los Angeles called Fat Eddie's. To his surprise, it was packed with other travelers between flights. Then he noticed that the attached motel, named after its builder, Hyatt von Dehn, had no vacancies. A lightbulb went off. Pritzker scribbled on a napkin an offer to buy the motel and Fat Eddie's, and the Hyatt Hotel chain was born.

Ten years later another lightbulb went off. After every other hotel operator in America had passed on the idea, Hyatt bought its first atrium hotel: a 22-story facility in Atlanta with a vertical atrium that went all the way to the roof and housed brightly lighted, glass-enclosed elevators. Architect John Portman's eye-catching design was perfect for the dawning era of business travel and conventions. The elegant lobby and lavish suites drew executives on the road and on expense accounts, and the huge meeting rooms and banquet facilities attracted convention planners. Soon Hyatt had similar atrium-style hotels in every major city except the one city that counted most, New York.

Donald's first contact with Hyatt was not promising. On the phone he sounded like "a kook" to Hyatt executive vice-president Joseph Amoroso, and things did not go much better when Amoroso met him and saw a pre–Der Scutt rendering. "Trump showed me this awful-looking drawing in an awful part of town," Amoroso said. "I wasn't too interested." But after Donald intimated that he had a tax abatement deal with the city, Amoroso did a one-eighty. The young developer, Amoroso reported back to Jay Pritzker, was "very intelligent, very glib, and very persuasive." He was also very optimistic, for at the time a tax abatement was little more than a gleam in his eye.

Donald's next step was to call up another member of the East Side's prestigious Le Club, a sophisticated mortgage banker named Ben Lambert.[32] The son of a wealthy jeweler, Lambert had an upper-class Park Avenue childhood and majored in art history at Brown. But instead of becoming a museum curator, he went into real estate finance and changed the basic nature of high-end urban real estate marketing. Until he came on the scene, most sales had been relatively simple exchanges between buyers and sellers; under his influence they became elaborate, complex processes in which real estate became "product," deals were "transactions," and getting the best price involved "strategies for raising the selling price floor." Along the way, prices went up and the business became a field in which everyone made a whole lot more money.

What mattered to Donald was that Lambert knew Jay Pritzker. Lambert didn't remember the developer from Le Club, but he accepted his invitation for lunch at the '21' Club. "Donald came to my office, and we acted like we'd met before," Lambert said. When they went downstairs and got into the back of Fred Trump's stretch limousine, Lambert discovered that his host had lined up renderings of the Commodore all along the back seat. "He's taking me to lunch by way of his office, which is also his car, which is actually his father's car, and he's really giving me this marketing pitch on the way to this lunch he's supposedly taking me to," Lambert said. When they got to the '21' Club the owner didn't recognize Donald but greeted Lambert warmly and showed them to a prime table.

In turn, what mattered to Lambert was not Donald's gaffes but his intuitive understanding that the essence of marketing is setting the stage for a deal to go forward. "Donald is very good at that," Lambert said. "That's what he did when he invited me to lunch." When Donald asked for help with Hyatt, Lambert made some introductions and received a payment he described as nominal. Donald then asked him to write a letter saying that the renovated Commodore would be the greatest hotel in New York, and Lambert balked. "I thought it was a great location, that it had potential, but I couldn't write that letter," he said. Donald exploded, and the two men did not speak again for a year.

But the initial groundwork had been laid, and more Hyatt officials headed east. Soon Donald was hammering out a deal with them.[33] When they reached a preliminary agreement, the *New York Times* announced it with a full-page article. Such coverage was remarkable given that Donald had never built anything, had obtained neither the tax abatement necessary for the financing nor the financing itself, and did not even have a final design for the hotel, but he told friends he was disappointed because the article was not on page one.[34] Almost before the ink was dry on the deal, he was exploring using a cheaper facade, saving on escalators, and reusing old Commodore guest rooms and baths as ways to save money on the project. "Fuck Hyatt," he said when asked whether this would affect the quality image that he and Hyatt had just endorsed. "I have them signed, now I can do what I want."[35]

AS DONALD KNEW, Hyatt would not sign a final agreement until he had the tax abatement. Making this already difficult goal even harder, there was growing alarm in Albany over the city's deteriorating finances. In 1965 the city's short-term, high-interest debt accounted for $526 million, or 10 percent of the city's total debt; by the summer of 1975 it was $5 billion, more than one-third the total. New York City could not raise another cent, and even the normally unflappable mayor was distressed. On a visit to Israel, Beame stuck a note in a crevice in the Wailing Wall with a one-word plea: "Help."[36]

First aid was already under way. Under the leadership of real estate magnate Lew Rudin, the city's largest taxpayers agreed to prepay their quarterly real estate taxes. The state set rescue efforts in motion, and the city actually fired some civil servants, a huge step in such a heavily unionized town.[37] Nonetheless, the Beame administration had lost all credibility. Panicked business and financial leaders demanded that Governor Carey take effective control of the city.

Some went further, pushing for the removal of the mayor, but in the end the man who walked the plank was his top aide, James Cavanagh, who was a close friend and old Brooklyn hand.[38] To replace him Beame tapped city planning chair John Zuccotti, a Yale-educated real estate lawyer. It was a good move for New York City, for the mayor's two harshest critics, the unions and the banks, both favored Zuccotti, who had a reputation for calling the shots as he saw them.

But what was good for the city was not necessarily in the best interest of Donald Trump. Zuccotti, who had no Brooklyn ties, had no reason to stick his neck out for an untried developer. It was time for Donald to try yet another route, which is why, one day in the fall of 1975, he headed downtown to the tiny office of Mike Bailkin, an obscure attorney in the mayor's Lower Manhattan Development Corporation. Bailkin, a dark-haired, thickset man in his mid-thirties, was not expecting him. When they had first met a few weeks earlier, Donald had made his usual get-acquainted gesture of inviting Bailkin to lunch at the '21' Club. But Bailkin said that he couldn't afford it and didn't want Donald to pay. Instead they had sandwiches at a restaurant with

Formica-topped tables, and Bailkin turned down the developer's request for help on a side project, a small property at the tip of Manhattan.[39]

It had been the worst sandwich of his life, Donald later told Bailkin. But he said that he was impressed by the lawyer's spunk, so he had come back. It seems likely that he was also impressed with Bailkin's ready access to John Zuccotti, the man who now controlled the fate of the Commodore. Flourishing a drawing by Der Scutt of the renovated hotel, Donald immediately started rattling off a long list of reasons it was a great idea: a revived Commodore would be the first new hotel in almost 15 years;[40] it would give 42nd Street a shot in the arm; it would revitalize the whole city; it would show the nation that New York was still in business. To cover the $70 million price tag, he could get a bank loan—but only with a tax abatement.

Then Donald outlined his argument. At the anticipated interest rate of 10 percent, the debt service on a $70 million loan would be $7 million a year. If, as was the general expectation, the hotel made about $9 million a year and had to pay $2 million in real estate taxes (these would be levied before any other obligations) plus about $2 million in operating expenses, there would be only $5 million to pay the mortgage. This would leave a potential shortfall of $2 million, something that no lender would take on because a municipal bankruptcy would inexorably lead to higher real estate taxes and an even larger shortfall. Accordingly, the only way to swing the deal was to abate the taxes until the hotel had the ability to pay them. Indeed, as far as Donald was concerned, the only question left was how to obtain the abatement, so logical was the scenario he had created.

Bailkin came up with the answer: Have the developer buy the hotel, sell it to the New York State Urban Development Corporation (UDC) for the token sum of $1, then lease it back. The UDC, a Rockefeller-era agency that had issued more than $1 billion in tax-exempt moral obligation bonds, was now facing the reckoning that John Mitchell, the creator of these financial instruments, had said would never come. The market for UDC bonds had dried up, the state legislature and big banks had scorned its rescue pleas, and in February 1975 the UDC had gone into default.[41] But having been a deputy counsel at UDC, Bailkin was aware that any property it owned would still be tax-exempt, and that the bureaucrats left minding the empty store were desperate for new projects.[42] The agency's shell ownership of the Commodore would remove the hotel from tax rolls, allowing it instead to pay rent until its income could cover all real estate levies. Trump Village and other housing programs had employed similar tax abatements to pay for residential construction, but this would be the first use for a commercial project.

Bailkin knew that to gain approval, the abatement would have to be available to other developers, but he thought he could push it through the inevitable obstacles. And in contrast to Donald's first proposal to him, Bailkin wanted to do this one. He had realized at once that the Commodore would not be just one more deal. It would be the only major development in town, and putting it together would put Bailkin in direct contact with key city officials, including the mayor.[43] Because the Beame administration felt itself to be under intense scrutiny, the Commodore abatement would receive more review than Bailkin had ever seen. From all directions, he received the same message: Take it through cleanly, touch base with everyone, and don't make any mistakes.

As the months went by, Bailkin gradually developed a grudging respect for Donald. "Something about the guy intrigued me," he said later. "He was always the salesman, selling all the time, and he never doubted he was right. Even when he'd lost a point, he'd say time would tell that he was really right." Because such qualities seemed the mark of a great businessman, Bailkin was taken aback to see the developer's impatience with details and his reliance on the high-powered experts on his payroll to take care of everything. "In his mind," Bailkin said, "once he had bought the land rights, put up a little money, and gotten a bank to come in, things should have been over and done with."

Bailkin was also annoyed by Donald's incessant competitiveness, particularly with regard to women. He seemed to date only occasionally, and the women were often models chosen to make him look good. According to a knowledgeable source, one particularly exasperating experience occurred when Donald and Bailkin were dining. Reportedly, Donald spotted Jay Pritzker with a striking blonde who nodded at

Bailkin. Donald demanded to meet her, and Bailkin managed to arrange a small get-together. Incredibly, Donald arrived late, brought another, younger blonde, and left shortly afterward. The next day he cheerfully explained that although he had originally intended to show Pritzker up by stealing the woman he had assumed was Pritzker's date, he had subsequently learned that she was merely a friend and had lost all interest in her.

NO MATTER HOW GORGEOUS the Commodore's design, how generous the tax abatement, or how capable the hotel operator, nothing was going to happen unless Donald arranged the financing. There was only one possible way: hire the most established and respectable broker in the city.

His name was Henry Pearce, and he was a real estate industry fixture.[44] Afterward Donald described him as "this white-haired guy with whom [bankers] had been dealing forever."[45] Then in his late sixties, Pearce had gotten into real estate back before the Depression, when he'd worked as a rental agent to pay for night classes at law school. He had intended to open a law office after graduation, but instead, nearly 40 years later, he was running mortgage brokerages in half a dozen cities and directing a staff of more than 100 employees.

"Donald was young, bright, and a pain in the ass," Pearce said later. But in the mid-1970s Pearce was hungry for business, and he immediately got to work on his new client's project. "Forty-second Street was not very attractive then, and the Commodore was a drab hotel," Pearce recalled. "There weren't many institutional lenders for that sort of thing." But he had heard that the Equitable Life Assurance Society, which probably had deeper pockets than any other such lender in New York City, was interested in hotels. So he cold-called Bill Frentz, the point man at Equitable for such proposals.

After Donald laid out his game plan, Frentz said that Equitable would be interested, but only if Donald could deliver all the necessary permits and waivers from the city and state. "This wasn't just a new investment that easily fell into place," Frentz said later. "Lots of folks within Equitable were saying, 'Why should we invest in Manhattan when other insurance companies aren't?' " At that point the odds were running strongly against Donald's proposal making it to the next level of review.[46] But every time Frentz met with him, Donald had taken care of two or three more steps. "There was little question he was heading in the right direction, that he could pull it off and put all these pieces together," Frentz said.

Eventually Frentz and Donald brought the proposal to a well-appointed conference room on the thirty-second floor of Equitable headquarters. It was the floor where all the real estate deals were done, and only one out of every 20 proposals that made it to this point went any further. By the time the hour-and-a-half presentation was over, it seemed this could well be the one. "Donald was sort of green then, the newest kid on the block," recalled Ben Holloway, a senior real estate investment manager and second in command of Equitable's vast real estate department. A quarter century earlier, Ben Holloway had worked at FHA headquarters in Washington and had processed Fred's plans for the Beach Haven apartment complex in Brooklyn. Although Donald was hardly a flower child, his longish hair and flashy clothes seemed jarring to the courtly, patrician Holloway, a member of the North Carolina tobacco family. But when Donald started talking about his elaborate and extensive plans to revamp the Commodore, Holloway forgot all about his appearance. "The fact that he'd really done his homework sold everybody," Holloway said.

But not long after Donald's winning presentation, the Chrysler Building, a signature New York skyscraper located directly across the street from the Commodore, went into foreclosure. The consensus that had existed in the conference room gave way to second thoughts and backpedaling. "That's just the way those things work," said Bill Frentz. "A senior executive wakes up one morning and feels comfortable, and then the next day another company threatens to pull out of the city and that causes concern, so you step back another foot or two." At the end of months of discussion, Equitable was still interested—and still uncommitted.

ALL THE WHILE, the Commodore itself continued to lose money.[47] A recent refurbishment failed to boost the occupancy rate, and another would cost at least $2 million—one-fifth of the appraised worth of the hotel. Taking it down to the ground and selling the land was not a realistic option, given the cost of demolition and the vast network of subway and railroad tracks under the building. Even purchase by Donald Trump did not seem a surefire solution, for there was no guarantee that he would obtain financing for the desperately needed renovation.

In December 1975 the Palmieri Company upped the ante in Donald's favor by announcing that unless its cash flow improved immediately, the Commodore would close before the expiration of the current union contract the following June 1. This meant that when delegates to the Democratic National Convention arrived, one of the city's largest and most centrally located hotels would have a padlock on the door. In February, workers at the Commodore went on a brief strike. Then, as the tax abatement program that Donald needed for financing took shape down at City Hall, other hoteliers began to complain of unfair treatment and favoritism.

There were other rumblings of discontent. Richard Ravitch, newly appointed chair of the Urban Development Corporation, objected to the whole idea of a tax abatement on a potentially profit-making project. Third-generation scion of a wealthy real estate family, board member of half a dozen nonprofit institutions, and developer of two major Manhattan projects, Ravitch had toyed briefly with buying the Penn Central rail yards himself.[48] Instead, he decided to dip his toes into the public sector prior to a possible run for political office. When Donald and Louise Sunshine showed up at his office, Ravitch declared that it was completely unethical for the governor's chief fund-raiser to lobby a state agency for a commercial project. Sunshine burst into tears and promised she would stay out of the way. When Donald threatened to call Carey and have Ravitch fired, he ordered them both to leave.

Ravitch remained troubled and urged two City Council members to make a fuss. They teamed up with a state assemblyman, and the three legislators held a press conference outside the Commodore to ask for better terms. To their surprise, Donald bounded up to the podium and declared that no investor would put in ten cents if the legislators' points were included. "He provided some confrontation and drama," said then–council member Henry Stern, one of Ravitch's recruits. "Donald helped make our event."

Perhaps, but he also helped defuse it, and there was no serious follow-up effort within the council or elsewhere in city government. After the Penn Central board voted to close the Commodore, the city's top decision-making body, the Board of Estimate, approved the deal. Four months later, the UDC met for a formal vote on the transaction whereby it would end up owning the Commodore Hotel and leasing it back to the Trump Organization for the next 99 years. Richard Ravitch still disliked the deal, but he was under intense pressure from both Albany and City Hall to vote yes. He did. Donald would have 41 years tax-free, a savings of more than $111 million,[49] and a slowly escalating rent that would never come close to the total sum abated.

Because the city was acting, in effect, as a joint venture partner with the developer, Bailkin had included a net profit-sharing mechanism in the terms of the abatement. Or so he had thought. Some years later, at Donald's request, he gave a lecture before a real estate industry group and noted that because of this arrangement the city was sharing in the project's eventual success. Afterward Donald gleefully piped up, "No, I'm able to write depreciation off as an expense!" That was when Bailkin learned that after he left city government and other attorneys drew up the final version of the abatement, the developer had managed to insert a depreciation clause that would drastically reduce the city's portion of any profits.

Because Bailkin had believed that keeping the Commodore open had been critical for the city, he had not minded that the agreement he had done so much to produce had been a great deal for Donald. But the budding young developer, who had learned from his father never, ever, to let up, had made a great deal better.

CHAPTER FOUR

The 28-Sided Building

In the late fall of 1976, Donald was a 30-year-old licensed real estate broker whose first development project was less than half done. Despite the headlines, the tax abatement, and the UDC agreement, he did not have a valid option on the Commodore Hotel. He had returned the necessary legal papers to Penn Central with only his signature on them and had never produced the required $250,000 deposit. He still lacked a formal commitment from Hyatt and comprehensive financing, and he faced negotiating with nine different governmental bodies, including the relevant local community board, the City Planning Commission, two city bureaus and three departments, the Board of Estimate, and the UDC. Neither he nor any other party had made any binding commitments. Everyone could still walk.

But that December, at a major New York real estate industry event, a benefit dinner dance for a medical research center, Donald received the annual Honor Award. Real estate leaders, an entrepreneurial breed that tends to shun publicity, did not welcome his flamboyant style and penchant for the limelight. Nor, had they known about it, would they have liked his inquiring whether the award was sufficiently prestigious to bother accepting it.[1] But they respected his ability to pull off a whopping commercial tax abatement and to use the UDC as a vehicle, something none of them had apparently ever thought of trying.

Doing so without putting in any of his own money or having the rest of the deal together impressed the real estate *machers* even more. Keeping up in the air some half a dozen elements, each of which requires all the others to be finished before it can be completed, having the timing to pull separate irons in and out of the fire in the nick of time yet keep everything going until the whole thing is a done deal—they knew that is what real estate development is all about. And they knew that Donald was doing it.

———————

IN SEPTEMBER 1977, Abe Beame, politically tainted by the city's fiscal crisis, suffered a crushing defeat in the Democratic mayoral primary. Two months later, Ed Koch, the five-term Democratic congressman from Manhattan who had beaten him, won election as New York City's 105th mayor.[2] As the year drew to a close, outgoing officials scurried around City Hall wrapping up loose ends before the change of administrations. High on the list of outstanding items was finalizing the tax abatement for the Commodore.

"Everyone in the Beame administration was determined to get it done," said Richard Rosan, then head of the city's Office of Economic Development. "Donald knew he had the momentum, and he and Louise played every angle they could." Once again Donald provided the exuberance and the self-confidence, and Sunshine the access to state officials. "If something didn't happen at the city level," Rosan said, "or I had trouble with the city corporation counsel's office, which always found fifty or sixty things wrong with everything, there would be a call [to the party causing the delay] from the governor's office."[3]

Shortly before Christmas, First Deputy Mayor Stanley Friedman convened the parties. The tough-talking son of a taxi driver, Friedman had worked his way through Brooklyn Law School and the Bronx Democratic organization. Along the way, the cigar-chomping, goateed politico had earned a reputation as someone with singular street smarts, contacts, and bravado, and he had replaced John Zuccotti as Beame's top deputy. But at this particular moment, he was struggling. As soon as the Beame administration closed down, he was supposed to assume a lucrative position with Roy Cohn's law firm. Friedman's prospects at the firm would improve if he could deliver for Donald, one of Cohn's most highly publicized clients; however, if Friedman failed, those same prospects could vanish. Worse, leaving any details to be resolved in the new administration could be a disaster, for incoming mayor Koch had campaigned as a reformer, blasting both sweetheart deals and the city's political establishment. He might well scuttle the Commodore abatement as a handout that New York could not afford and should not provide.

In the six weeks since the election, Friedman had been scrambling to make the abatement happen. Like all such complicated arrangements, it was full of time-consuming details, but there was one seemingly unresolvable problem: Donald's package still did not have financing. Determined not to let the deal unravel, Friedman went after an unusually open-ended version of what was called "an escrow closing." What this meant, underneath the fine print, was a selective closing—that is, one that bound the city and UDC, but not Donald. Regardless of whether he came through, the government entities would be committed to the deal.

The closing took place at the offices of Dreyer & Traub, where Jerry Schrager, Donald's chief real estate lawyer, was a partner. Unlike Cohn and Friedman, Schrager, a graduate of New York University Law School, had a soft voice and a shy manner. But he used them to such good effect that after seeing him defend the other side in another real estate transaction, Donald retained him for the Commodore deal. From the morning of December 20 until the middle of the next day, lawyers, city and state officials, and representatives of Penn Central roamed around Dreyer & Traub's large conference room and the surrounding hallway, conferring and amending papers. Periodically food from a local delicatessen appeared, and the tables filled with empty soda cans. Schrager pored over thick piles of legal documents, Friedman buzzed from one group to another, and Louise Sunshine, alternately smiling and scowling, monitored everything.

Unlike Fred, who would never have thought of missing a closing, Donald was spending this evening at a Lincoln Center concert, showing he was boss by being absent. But Sunshine insisted he remain on call. At one point she dispatched his chauffeur with instructions to get into the concert hall, find Donald, and drag him to the phone to answer an urgent question. "You belong here," she said. "Get the hell over here now."

But the developer still had to nail down the financing, a task so daunting that even he felt discouraged. Equitable had seemed all but on board, but then it delivered what Henry Pearce called "a real karate chop" by cutting a tentative $70 million to a more firm $25 million. Another bad moment came when an institution Donald was absolutely sure would say yes instead said no. "Let's just take this deal and shove it," he told Pearce. The broker, who would not be paid unless he got someone to sign on a bottom line, walked across the street from the Commodore to the Bowery Savings Bank and pointed out to its chairman just how devastating it would be to look at an empty, shuttered building. The chairman agreed and helped Pearce cobble together a consortium of banks to make up the $50 million shortfall.[4]

As was common real estate practice, Donald planned to cover his $70 million costs with a short-term bank loan that he would repay, after construction was done, with a permanent loan from Equitable and the Bowery group. There was a hitch: So far he did not have a short-term loan. But there was also a solution: Jay Pritzker.[5]

Getting Pritzker on board would require that the hotel bear the name Hyatt—an important asset, given Hyatt's prominence in the field, although Donald complained bitterly about the prospect of "ten-foot-

high Hyatt letters across the face of my building" and insisted on naming a restaurant inside the hotel "Trumpets."[6] In addition, Manufacturers Hanover required that Fred Trump and Jay Pritzker co-guarantee the
entire construction loan, and in the end each side put up about $2 mil-
lion.[7] At Donald's prodding, the bank also required Hyatt to sign a noncompete clause, promising that it would not open another hotel within
New York City.

This request apparently seemed innocuous to Hyatt executives,
for the chain had noncompete clauses in other cities and evidently assumed that future modifications would be possible if necessary. "Hyatt
approached this as, 'Look, this is an upstart young man,' " Schrager recalled. "They were still skeptical about his putting the pieces of the puzzle together." But Pritzker himself never had a chance to argue the
point. Although each partner supposedly had 10 days to respond to any
suggestion from the other, Donald shrewdly bypassed Pritzker by waiting to bring up the issue when the hotelier was on his way to Nepal and
unreachable. Pritzker would keenly regret that he ended up locked out,
for New York City was reviving and would soon enter an extraordinary
boom period, particularly in the hospitality industry.[8]

The Beame administration wanted to save the Commodore;
Donald's aim was to knock the Waldorf-Astoria off its perch as the city's
premier luxury hotel, a goal that would cause the renovation to go
wildly over budget. The first step toward this lavish vision would be to
reconfigure the old structure's 2,000 tiny cubicles, which felt more like
closets than rooms, into 1,400 larger and more comfortable units. Because the banquet and meeting rooms were directly over the lobby, installing a vertical atrium was impossible. Instead the present lobby,
basically a large, ugly box, would become a multileveled space filled
with plantings and fountains and connected to a glass-enclosed garden
restaurant cantilevered out over 42nd Street.

Behind the scenes, Fred continued to advise his son. "The two of
them together in the same room was very strange," said Mike Scadron, a
New York Military Academy classmate who worked for Donald in the
mid-1970s. "I was sure neither of them heard what the other was saying.
They talked right past each other." Or perhaps, in their own fashion, to

each other, for in many ways Fred was the 70-year-old version of his son: a high energy force field, always in motion, with bright blue eyes and bushy Salvador Dali eyebrows. "He came through like a rocket ship," recalled Jeff Walker, another former NYMA classmate who was Donald's second-in-command. "It was all I could do to keep up with him."

Somehow it worked. Fred kept tabs on the job site and dispensed builder lore, including his practice of adding a bucket of water to every bucket of paint in order to stretch it. But this time, Fred's penny-pinching practices were counterproductive. To comply with the short-term construction loan that had been obtained, Donald and Fred had shaved to the bone the budget they negotiated with HRH Corporation, the firm contracted to do the actual construction.[9] However, unlike his own projects, where Fred could stick to a spartan budget because he was familiar with the type of building, the Grand Hyatt was more elaborate than anything either Fred or HRH had ever seen.[10] Attaching a glass skin to the 60-year-old brick shell was much harder than they had anticipated, and reusing existing plumbing systems meant that pipes were constantly popping up in unexpected and sometimes disastrous places.[11]

Meanwhile, Donald acted like someone at a combination revival meeting and barn raising. He ignored Pritzker's objections to the construction budget as unrealistic and stuck to the numbers he needed to get the project up and running. He dashed around town from dawn to midnight, returning calls from his car phone and other people's offices and having anything that needed his signature brought to his restaurant table, often at the '21' Club. He heaped praise on his staffers, huddled on the old hotel's half-demolished top floor in space that was unheated and under a roof that leaked during rainstorms. They were the best, he told them over and over, because only the best worked for Donald Trump; inspired, they redoubled their efforts.

Whenever a nettlesome detail appeared, he simply rolled over it. Required by his agreement with UDC to turn over a portion of his tax savings for improvements to Grand Central Terminal, he hung a huge TRUMP banner over the station and said that he was donating triple his actual contribution. It was a gross exaggeration, but the press dutifully repeated it. Similarly, when the head of the prestigious, preservation-minded Municipal Art Society called to chew him out about the offending streamer, he spoke of his delight that his mirrored hotel would reflect Grand Central's architectural splendor and cheerfully removed the hanging—for a day or two.[12]

———◆———

TWO YEARS EARLIER, in June 1976, shortly after the Board of Estimate had approved the tax abatement for the Commodore, Donald turned 30. He'd moved from the bachelor pad that Der Scutt had rearranged to Olympic Tower, a new high-rise across from St. Patrick's Cathedral. With a two-bedroom luxury apartment to come home to and the top spot at work, he had arrived at that station in life where thoughts of marriage tend to make an appearance. But the ambition and tenacity that led to one of the biggest real estate deals in recent city history translated into a kind of gauche flashiness that did not endear him to women. Apparently, an evening that consisted of a ride in a limo, a visible table at a chic restaurant, and an expansive monologue about his plans to remake the Manhattan skyline seemed less like a date than a sales pitch.

On one double date with Jeff Walker, the developer pulled out a massive wad of bills to pay the tab. "He didn't have a wallet like a normal person," Walker said. "He was still really pretty awful with the clothes, too."[13] Donald seemed drawn to a look that was overdone even by flamboyant mid-1970s standards, choosing for his first lengthy interview with the *New York Times* a burgundy suit, a white shirt with his initials stitched in burgundy on the cuffs, and burgundy patent-leather shoes.

One evening he and another Le Club man-about-town, a private investment banker named Jerry Goldsmith, stopped off at Maxwell's Plum. Among the usual assortment of bright-eyed singles, several slim, long-legged models from Montreal stood out. The slimmest and most long-legged was a 27-year-old blonde with hazel eyes named Ivana Zelnicekova Winklmayr. A Czech émigré to Canada, she was in New York to model at a fur show and to publicize the 1976 Olympic Games, to be held that fall in Montreal. "There were lots of pretty girls around," Goldsmith said, "but right away Donald latched on to Ivana."

That night Donald arranged for a table for Ivana and her friends and picked up their tab. The next day he sent a dozen roses to her room at the Americana Hotel. A few weeks later he showed up at a fashion show in Montreal where she was working, said hello, and left.[14] Soon she was riding around Manhattan in a silver Cadillac limousine with DJT license plates, dining at Le Club, and trotting out to Jamaica Estates to meet Donald's parents. Wherever he went with his "Ivaska," as he called her, he marveled aloud at her appearance. "Isn't she gorgeous?" he asked everyone within earshot. "Have you ever seen anybody more beautiful?"

At the time, Ivana was living with George Syrovatka, her longtime Czech boyfriend. A champion skier back in Prague, Syrovatka now sold sports equipment in Montreal and was a serious contender in European ski races. Ivana was also an excellent skier, although not on the same level, much less an Olympic alternate as later claimed by Donald in *The Art of the Deal*. In the early 1970s the couple had decided to leave communist Czechoslovakia. On a skiing trip to Austria, Syrovatka defected, which meant that he would not be able to return to his homeland. Ivana chose instead to make a cold war–style marriage of convenience to one of Syrovatka's skiing friends, an Austrian named Alfred Winklmayr. With an Austrian passport, she would be able to return to Czechoslovakia to see her parents.

Divorced from Winklmayr by the time she joined Syrovatka in Canada, Ivana changed her dark brown hair to a brassy blonde and looked for modeling jobs. Although Donald touts her in his autobiography as "one of the top fashion models in Canada," in reality she lacked the requisite height and cheekbones to advance beyond showroom work. But her athletic training, which included a master's degree in physical education, had given her an eye-catching self-assurance, and her smile, which tended to look harsh in photographs, was magnetic in person.[15]

Such a commanding presence would have seemed unlikely for a premature baby who spent month after month in a hospital crib. But pushed by her demanding father, the young Ivana had become a daredevil skier who charged downhill with such abandon that she broke both legs repeatedly. Her striking physical self-confidence was one of so many similarities between Donald and Ivana that he sometimes referred to her as his twin. Perhaps the most important of these parallels was having strong fathers who had nipped youthful rebellion in the bud. Donald's father had placed him in military school, where he had flourished; Ivana's had yanked her out of school and put her on the assembly line in the shoe factory where he worked as an electrical engineer, a move that sent her back to her books within weeks.

Like the man she would marry, Ivana was wildly ambitious and fiercely competitive, in part because of her early sports training. "Going down a ski slope at a hundred miles an hour, you have only yourself to count on," she told one reporter. "It takes incredible discipline." But it was also because once she had left Czechoslovakia, where it had been acceptable to excel at sports but prudent to remain an anonymous mediocrity, she reveled in the opportunity to stand out. She was intelligent, not brilliant, but she had something that was perhaps better suited to life in the new world: She was shrewd. She did not question why things were the way they were; she sized them up and made them work for her.

Above all, she radiated the same raw energy that distinguished Donald and would be the tie that bound them together. "I think what attracts us so much together is not only the love and all that stuff," Ivana once said. "It's the energy. We are very much alike in that way. I can't sit still."

On April 9, 1977, the day after a bachelor's party at Maxwell's Plum, Donald and Ivana recited marriage vows at Marble Collegiate Church in Manhattan. It was the Saturday before Easter, and fragrant white lilies filled the landmark Dutch Reformed sanctuary. Among those present at the ceremony and at the reception at the '21' Club was Roy Cohn. When Donald told him he planned to marry, Cohn had insisted on drawing up a prenuptial contract. An early draft stipulated that the bride return all gifts in the event of a divorce, and Ivana countered by demanding a "rainy day fund" of $150,000 in cash. After stormy arguments and lengthy negotiations, the couple finally found common ground and the ceremony went ahead on schedule.

It was a Trump affair in every way. Because Ivana could not afford airfare for both parents and was evidently too embarrassed to ask her husband-to-be for the money, only her father was there. But the Trumps were present in full force, with the groom's brothers serving as best man and usher and his sisters as bridesmaids. Even the church was Trump territory; Fred and Mary Trump had joined it only recently, but they were regular attendants and had long felt an affinity for the head minister, Dr. Norman Vincent Peale, who conducted the ceremony. Starting out in upstate New York at the same time Fred began building in Brooklyn, Peale put worldliness and godliness together into a practical-minded theology that encouraged self-promotion and valued success. Critics called him crass and commercial, but supporters saw an up-to-date Protestant ethic that promised rewards for hard work in this life as well as in the next. Known as "God's salesman," he acquired a huge audience through his radio show and newspaper columns, and his legendary bestseller, *The Power of Positive Thinking*, sold an estimated 20 million copies.[16]

Although the Trump children rarely attended services at Marble Collegiate, they had joined, and Mary was convinced that they shared her deep faith. After one service, she gave Peale's assistant a ride to the airport in her Rolls-Royce and told him that she had taught her children about faith when they were young. "I tried to get it into their heads that they had to believe," she said. "Whether it shows or not, it's in there because I put it in there."

——◦——

DONALD MARRIED AT 30, the same age at which his own father had wed; he chose a woman who, like his mother, was not an American citizen; and he told everyone that he, too, wanted five children. Unlike his father, he took time off and went to Acapulco for a honeymoon, but on his way out of town he put in a conference call to tell the architects back at the Commodore exactly what to do in his absence.

He seemed to expect a marriage more or less like that of his parents, but what evolved could hardly have been more different. After producing a son and namesake, Donald John Trump Jr., Ivana had launched herself into the New York social scene via the usual route of volunteer work for select charities. She'd busied herself with exercise classes and hairdressing appointments and exchanged Donald's flashy outer-borough wardrobe for expensive dark suits from exclusive Manhattan stores. In the family's new eight-room apartment in an old mansion at 800 Fifth Avenue, she'd installed beige velvet sectional sofas and mirrors framed with twinkling lights.[17] She'd revised her résumé, telling the *New York Times* that she'd gone to Montreal to visit an aunt and uncle, and she'd developed a promotional manner that complemented that of her husband. "The Donald is fantastic in the golf and very good in the tennis," she told the *Times*, inadvertently giving her husband his most lasting nickname.

But the woman who had been winning athletic competitions since she was six was not satisfied being the stay-at-home wife of a rising developer. She began showing up at the construction site in designer outfits, donning a hard hat, and conducting her own inspection tours. Less than two years after the ceremony at Marble Collegiate, Ivana Trump had become involved in the family business.[18]

Like her husband, she was inexperienced and aggressive; unlike him, she was not inclined to listen to others or even to learn their names. To many observers she seemed unnecessarily imperious; she declared that she had to act extra tough to get the job done. In any event, by being there, clipboard in hand, without any clear authority and yet demanding attention, she was a distraction and often a headache for the supervisors and construction managers. For her husband, however, Ivana was a crucial part of the operation. Because he was a hands-on soul who liked to know every detail, it was vital to have someone acting as his eyes and ears, looking over shoulders and taking notes. With Ivana on the case, he could devote himself to any entrepreneur's number one task—scouting out future deals—and still know exactly what was going on at the current job site.

Ivana was one management tool. Another was a Machiavellian tactic that Wharton students would have called "creative conflict": hiring someone to do a job, then bringing in someone else to do the same job, thereby pitting them against each other and forcing them to rely on

Donald to adjudicate their status.[19] Whether consciously or not, the developer set even Ivana and Fred against each other by soliciting from them whatever on-site intelligence they could provide. Off the job, father and daughter-in-law were dutiful relatives who shared family events, meals at the house on Midland Parkway, and visits to what was still Fred's favorite out-of-town spot, the Concord.[20] But at the work site they complained constantly about each other's presence. Ivana did not hesitate to take her grievances to her husband, which sometimes led to pitched battles between them—and, for Donald, another opportunity to reaffirm his authority.

In similar fashion, he "supplemented" the interiors team by adding Ivana and declaring her taste to be "tremendous" and "impeccable"— that is, just like his. Although the Grand Hyatt was on the edge of the classically tasteful Upper East Side, neither Donald nor Ivana bought into the notion that old and restrained is good, that less is more, or that quiet elegance is superior to sticking out. Instead they sought what architecture critic Paul Goldberger called "an out-of-towner's vision of city life."[21] To them, newer was better, more was more, and being noticed was always better than being one of the crowd. They shared the same flashy aesthetic and boundless appetite for more marble and mirrors, more shiny brass, and more dramatic lighting.

Creating an environment of extravagance was not simply a matter of taste; it was also a critical business decision. Forced to work around the old structure, Donald was determined to make the Grand Hyatt look different in every possible way from its dowdy predecessor.[22] Stuck with the same building height and footprint, he bypassed historic mementos or a traditional limestone facade, à la Grand Central Terminal next door, choosing instead to sheathe the old structure in a shimmering new skin; to create the illusion of additional height by changing the floor numbers, thereby transforming a 26-floor building into a 34-floor structure; and to assert that he had the largest ballroom in the city, even though a junior designer at the Gruzen firm had found that other facilities were larger. "He listened to us about plumbing and code issues," said architect Paul Willen, "but on anything that had to do with marketing or image, he got his way."

It was a way that worked. The Grand Hyatt, Donald's first opportunity to display his own glittering vision, was a grand slam. Construction crews were still in the lobby at the November 1980 opening and *New York* magazine scorned the gold Mylar tablecloths and blonde waitresses "lined up like Vegas chorines." But the public drank up all the spectacular, unquiet luxury. The same people who had been unwilling to pay $20 a night at the old brick hotel next to Grand Central eagerly forked over several times that amount now that the building was sheathed in glass, polished to a high gloss, and touted as new.[23] They took the Grand Hyatt's elevators to what they supposed to be the thirty-fourth floor, and they danced in what they believed to be the biggest ballroom in New York City. And if all that wasn't quite so, they didn't really care. Donald was right: It sounded so much better that way.

The gleaming, almost new structure did not come cheap. Design alterations and change orders had mushroomed during the renovation, and because they occurred after the signing of the construction contract, they were on the developer's side of the ledger.[24] The final tab was $130 million,[25] almost twice the contract and the construction loan. Going over budget was never good; doubling it would seem guaranteed to create a disaster, plunging the new hotel into an impossible financial hole.

Instead the Hyatt was a resounding success. In the short term, Fred rescued his son. When the huge bills came due, Donald met his half of the extra cost with help from his father's old bank, Chase, in the form of a $35 million unsecured line of credit and a $30 million second mortgage, plus another loan from one of his father's corporations. But the principal reason for the Hyatt triumph was that the city itself was gradually recovering. From 1970 to 1975, 30 of New York's largest corporations had left the city; between 1975 and 1978, 12 of them returned.[26] Similarly, hotel occupancy, down to 64 percent in 1975, rebounded to 78 percent by 1980. Midtown Manhattan stood at the center of this renaissance, and at the center of midtown was the Grand Hyatt, a shiny and prosperous symbol of urban recovery.

DEVELOPMENT OF THE OTHER Penn Central property, the West Side rail yards, continued to elude Donald. As it turned out, the 34th Street yards would eventually house a new convention center, although he would not build it—but not for lack of trying. Early in 1978, while the new Koch administration was still unpacking, the developer was down at City Hall pushing his project. "He sort of burst into the office," recalled Ron Marino, then deputy to newly elected Manhattan borough president Andrew Stein. "He was this big tall blond guy with this great physical presence, saying he had a great idea, that he would be doing us a favor." Rather than bothering with the time-consuming process of requesting proposals from any other developers, Donald suggested, the city could just turn over the land to him and he'd do the job.[27]

Ultimately the commission to design the convention center went to I. M. Pei, and the joint developers were UDC and another public agency, the Triborough Bridge and Tunnel Authority.[28] However, as stipulated by the agreement Donald had made with Palmieri and Penn Central, he stood to collect a broker's fee. At one point he suggested that he might forgo the money. He would be doing so only to help out the city, he told a reporter, because "from an economic standpoint for me, [waiving the fee] is a foolish thing."[29]

To Peter Solomon, then serving as Koch's deputy mayor for economic development, the offer seemed worth investigating. Most city officials enjoyed having the public come downtown, but Solomon, the multimillionaire heir to an old department store fortune as well as a Wall Street wunderkind, had long since found going to others' offices more effective. When he went uptown to meet with Donald, he found an aspiring multimillionaire intent on one-upsmanship. According to Solomon, Donald said that he would not collect his $4 million fee if the city put his father's name on the center. For further details, the developer said airily, Solomon could consult court records. "It wasn't, 'Put my name on it,' it was, 'Put my father's name on it,' " Solomon recalled. "Of course, that was his name, too, but he was clever the way he put it." After Solomon looked the matter up and found the fee was closer to $600,000, the mayor dismissed the whole idea as ridiculous.[30]

Meanwhile, Donald continued to express a strong desire to de-

velop the northern section of the yards, at 60th Street, and was scheduled to make a $100,000 payment on the option for the site at the end of
1979. At the appointed hour he walked into Palmieri's office, pulled out
what he said was a check for that amount, and then backed out of the
deal, citing problems with the title.

The project faced community opposition, zoning problems, and financing difficulties, and Donald had his hands full with the Commodore. Nonetheless, he insisted that he was not paying because the
map of the site showed a 1½-inch strip between the street and the yards
that nobody owned. As he well knew, such "gores"—minuscule strips
where adjacent plots do not match up exactly—are commonplace technical defects for which title companies routinely provide insurance in
the unlikely event that anyone tries to exploit them. "The so-called
title problem was a joke," said one close observer. "The guy just used it
as an excuse because he could not admit that he was defeated."[31] But although giving up the option seemed the end of a dream, it would prove
to be only an interruption.

———— ◦◦◦ ————

BY THE TIME the ground was actually broken for the Grand Hyatt,
Donald was already involved in another project that would identify him
at home and, eventually, around the world. In the process he would
hone the skills and tactics that would define his way of doing business
for the rest of his career. During his long apprenticeship, he had learned
what he needed from his father, including the need for that extra element that caught people's eye. For his father, it had been the garage
under a front stoop and the extra closet in a modest apartment; for Donald, it was the marble on marble and the gilt on gilt. From his father he
had also learned about paying for such visible flourishes by cutting what
was invisible—lopping an inch off the width of bathroom doors, say, or
reducing the number of cabinet hinges from three to two.

But now Donald's apprenticeship was over. From now on he was
the master. Instead of relying on his father's network of aging Brooklyn
politicians, he would be operating in a world where wealth, power, and

possessions would reach new orders of magnitude and the klieg lights would be permanently on. He already had bravado to spare, and with his newly cemented ties in the banking world, he would have access to financing. After training in the Brooklyn old-boy league, he was ready to play with the Manhattan big boys.

Donald had been learning what he could do; now he would be learning what he could get away with, knowledge that was both intoxicating and dangerous. It would make him one of the most famous people in the world, able to sell not only real estate per se, but also magazines, pizzas, cars, books, sunglasses, and even the notion that losing money is fun. And although it would take him to dazzling heights, it would also help set the stage for a calamitous fall.

Initially, the idea for the next project was a simple one: Construct a big building, name it after himself, and make a lot of money. The model was Olympic Tower, the 52-story luxury building that had been Donald's home when he met Ivana. Essentially a huge box covered in bronze-tinted glass, it was the first of what would be known as "mixed use" projects in Manhattan, with retail stores, offices, and condo apartments all under the same roof.

What most New Yorkers noticed about Olympic Tower was a large indoor public space that contained an arcade, a café, and a three-story waterfall. What other developers noticed was that real estate lawyers Jerry Schrager and Sandy Lindenbaum had used zoning loopholes to make more money for its owner, Greek billionaire Aristotle Onassis, than anyone had thought possible.[32]

One of the largest loopholes had to do with air rights, which refers to the right to build the largest possible building under existing zoning regulations. Just as the scarcity of water makes the right to its use a negotiable commodity in the American West, in Manhattan the lack of land makes air rights a valuable asset. Owners of buildings that are not "built out"—in other words, already at the maximum square footage allowable—can sell off unused air rights, which developers can use to make projects on adjacent sites larger than would otherwise be allowed. Quietly buying up air rights, Onassis had put together the first large-scale development in this exclusive section of Fifth Avenue. Then, by including public space, he earned further zoning bonuses. In the end he increased his building's size and income-producing floor area by more than one-third, giving Olympic Tower the highest density in the city at the time.[33]

Because it was a high-end building, the extra space meant record profits. Making the deal even juicier, Onassis also obtained a new 10-year real estate tax abatement available for sites that were underutilized or functionally obsolescent. In spirit, the relevant law, known by its section number, 421a, was meant to help distressed neighborhoods, not East Side elites. But by the letter of the law, Onassis's property qualified. Its previous occupant, the old-line department store Best & Company, was housed in a 12-story building far smaller than the site's zoning permitted, and Best & Company had long since lost out to other, more modern retailers. "It was the first time 421a was used on such a huge project," said former New York City Corporation Counsel lawyer Rochelle Corson. "Everybody watched Olympic Tower as the test for how far they could push the envelope on this."[34]

Not one to tamper with success, Donald scrupulously followed the example set by Olympic Tower. He hired the same lawyers, negotiated with the same bankers, and proposed a project with the same retail/office/residential mix. To capture the same high-end market, he selected a nearby Fifth Avenue location, and to get the same zoning bonuses, he chose a spot currently housing the ailing flagship of another celebrated department store chain, Bonwit Teller.

But there the similarities ended.[35] The most immediate difference was that Bonwit's had almost three decades left on its lease, and its owner, a Nashville shoe and apparel conglomerate named Genesco, showed no interest in making a deal. But in the spring of 1978, Genesco appointed a new chief executive who was eager to unload any assets not contributing to the company's bottom line, and Donald promptly bought two plane tickets to Nashville. Uncharacteristically for Donald, the project was hush-hush at first. He gave it the code name "Project T"—supposedly for the next-door neighbor, Tiffany & Co.—and refused to tell his traveling companion, Phil Wolf, where they were going. "It wasn't until we got on the plane that he showed me the letter he'd prepared," said Wolf, a contractor at the Grand Hyatt site who was in his late forties. "He was renting my gray hair for the day."

Donald was also renting Wolf's social graces. Upon arrival, Genesco brass whisked the visitors off to lunch at a private club, and Wolf exchanged pleasantries and shoe industry shop talk as the developer fidgeted in his chair. "Afterward, Donald said that if I hadn't been there, he would have jumped out the window," Wolf said. "He absolutely cannot do small talk—he wanted to steer the conversation his way all the time."

In November, Genesco gave Donald a six-month option to purchase the Bonwit leasehold for $25 million, even though he had put no money down. The signing took place at Genesco's Manhattan offices, located across the street from Bonwit's. When the developer and Jerry Schrager walked outside afterward, a light snow was falling. "We looked across Fifth Avenue at Tiffany, and there was a line of limousines around the block," recalled Schrager. "Without paying out a cent, we controlled the most fabulous location in all of New York City."

To build condominiums, however, the developer had to own not only the tenant rights but the property itself. In theory, current property owner Equitable Life Assurance Society should have been eager to sell because it was earning only about 4 percent a year at a time when interest rates were 8 to 10 percent and still climbing. Yet Equitable managers had refused every offer because they believed that when the lease finally expired, they could negotiate a new one so profitable it would make the long wait worthwhile.

Undaunted, Donald went to talk to Equitable, which had financed Olympic Tower. Just as he had told city officials that he considered taking over the 34th Street Convention Center to be doing New York a favor, he now told real estate executive George Peacock that he wanted to help out Equitable, one of the nation's largest institutional investors, by taking this low-yield site off its hands. When he finished speaking, Peacock burst into laughter. "If you just looked at the income, and not what we'd get when the lease was up, it was pretty miserable pay," Peacock said later. "But Equitable was paying me not to miss these things."

Unlike other developers George Peacock had brushed off, Donald

came back. When he said that he had obtained an option on the leasehold, Peacock's interest was piqued. With the New York real estate market at last picking up, Equitable had begun to think of owning not just
the land but what stood on it as well. Soon the owner of the property
and the holder of an option on the leasehold were drawing up plans for
a joint venture.[36] To Peacock, the developer's insistence that the project
bear his name seemed little more than a personal whim that could be
used to Equitable's advantage.[37] But later, this would prove a crucial step
in what would come to be known as branding—and in making Donald
one of the most famous people in the world.

With the Grand Hyatt under way, financing the construction of
what would be called Trump Tower was not a problem.[38] Donald simply
went to the first person he had approached for hotel financing: Conrad
Stephenson, regional vice-president in charge of commercial real estate
loans at Chase Manhattan Bank. A hearty, athletic man in his early
fifties, with only a hint of gray in his red hair, Stephenson had gone
through Fordham on the GI Bill and had headed for law school. But
after sitting in a tiny cubicle writing briefs, he opted for a "people" business and ended up in banking, where he was known for establishing special relationships with blue-chip clients.

When Fred Trump, the bank's real estate customer of longest
standing, brought in his son to inquire about short-term financing for
the Grand Hyatt, Stephenson had quickly arranged terms and gone off
on a European vacation. In his absence a colleague stepped in, the deal
collapsed, and Stephenson returned to an empty plate. "Putting it
mildly, I was very upset," he said. "Another loan officer went for that
extra ounce." When Donald returned to talk about a $130 million con-
struction package for his second project, Stephenson handled the negotiations himself.[39]

What the developer had in mind was essentially a variation on
Olympic Tower: a big vertical box sitting on top of a big horizontal box.
Too boring, Der Scutt said. He began to sketch out alternatives, including an ugly, chunky box that showed the biggest possible structure that
could be put up under existing zoning, called "as of right." The developer flaunted the sketch at a meeting with Tiffany's patrician chairman,

Walter Hoving, a famously haughty octogenarian who banned from his store such plebeian touches as men's diamond rings, silver plate, or the use of knots in the white ribbon used to tie Tiffany's blue gift boxes.[40] Aghast at Scutt's eyesore, Hoving eagerly agreed to sell his company's air rights, which the developer claimed would give him the space necessary to construct a more graceful tower.

Then Sandy Lindenbaum realized that the building could go still higher if the design included "public parks" in the form of tiny, nearly inaccessible fifth-floor balconies. Combining purchased air rights, Lindenbaum's micro-miniparks, and the same zoning bonuses for public space that had been used at Olympic Tower, Scutt produced a building that was neither chunky nor boxy. Instead it was a soaring 28-sided structure with an arresting sawtooth profile. Although it ignored city guidelines about how buildings were supposed to arrange themselves on sites and fit into neighborhoods, it would provide drop-dead views in two directions, one of which was Central Park.

Such a design meant that Donald would have to undergo a cumbersome review process and obtain multiple zoning variances at the same time that two other huge projects were under construction next door and the City Planning Commission had ordered a crackdown on large buildings. Apparently unfazed, he instructed Scutt to produce another hideous as-of-right version, this one a 77-story monolith cantilevered over Tiffany. Brandishing it in front of the commissioners, Donald promised to lease space in his preferred design to Bonwit's, a prime retail tenant the city was eager to retain. Crying uncle, the commissioners approved the obviously superior building with 28 sides and passed it on for quick ratification at the Board of Estimate.

Razing of the old building began in December 1979.[41] Although Donald did not have a demolition permit, he hired John Kaszycki to handle the operation. A hard-bitten former window washer, the white-haired Polish immigrant had never done such a job. But because he could pay undocumented Polish laborers less than half the union rate and make money selling whatever scrap he salvaged, he accepted a rock-bottom fee. His crews began sneaking into the building and pulling apart upper floors, even though the electricity was still on and they had to cut into live wires. Over the next six months nearly 200 illegal laborers worked with dozens of members of Housewreckers Local 95. Readily distinguished by their lack of hard hats, the Polish Brigades, as they came to be called, put in 12- to 18-hour shifts seven days a week and slept crowded together in slum housing, cheap motels, or, in some cases, on the floors of buildings they were tearing down. Despite dreadful working conditions and erratic pay, the Poles did exactly what the developer wanted—which proved calamitous.*

ON BONWIT TELLER'S FACADE were two notable art deco features. One was a pair of 15-foot-tall bas-relief panels, carved in limestone, that portrayed highly stylized, partially draped female nudes; the

---

* Kaszycki grossly underestimated the cost of this and other contracts. At least once he paid the Polish Brigades in vodka, and eventually he stopping paying them at all. In March 1980 they held a work stoppage, and Kaszycki gave them checks that bounced. Remarkably, given their vulnerability to deportation, half a dozen of the men went to John Szabo, a Queens storefront lawyer. His first case, it would turn into a pitched battle over who was to blame for this exploitation and subject Donald to his third FBI probe (the first was for racial discrimination in Trump-owned housing in Brooklyn and Queens, and the second explored how Donald had obtained the option on the West Side rail yards).

In 1983 the developer, Equitable, and Kaszycki were sued for unpaid union pension benefits, due on all workers regardless of immigration status. When the case went to trial, Szabo testified that he had been threatened with a $100 million lawsuit by a Trump Organization spokesman named "John Barron." Although the identity of the caller was never established, Donald and his construction supervisor admitted using the name on other occasions. Indeed, using a pseudonym was an old Trump family practice, according to Maryanne Trump Barry, who remembered her father's using "Mr. Green" to obtain information over the phone. "It was like 'John Barron' is for Donald," she said, "a name for an imaginary spokesman who is really Donald. My husband [a lawyer named John Barry] says when he's joking that he's going to call and say John Barron's been given a subpoena, and then we'll see how quickly John Barron falls ill and dies."

Sixteen years later, in March 1999, the case was settled out of court. The Trump Organization and Equitable would pay an undisclosed sum, presumably approximately the $4 million that had already been levied against them plus interest, to the pension and welfare fund of Housewreckers Local 95. The Polish Brigades had long since scattered, the lead plaintiff was dead, and few among the public remembered that the gleaming tower at Fifth Avenue and 56th Street had such an unseemly chapter in its early history.

other was an ornamental grille, 15 by 25 feet and made of solid nickel that consisted of intricate geometric designs. Three months after the demolition began, the *New York Times* ran an article at the front of the Sunday real estate section describing in detail Donald's plans to donate the artworks to the Metropolitan Museum of Art, a gift for which he would receive a tax deduction. Although removing the grillwork in one piece would be a simple matter, taking down the sculptures, which an independent appraiser suggested might be worth about $200,000, would be more complex and would cost perhaps $2,500.

Three months later the *Times* ran a second story on the Bonwit Teller artwork. This one, on the front page, said the sculptures had been jackhammered into smithereens and the grille had disappeared and perhaps been sold as scrap. Although museum officials expressed dismay at the loss of promised artwork, one John Barron, who identified himself in phone interviews with the press as a Trump Organization vice president, claimed the reliefs were worth only $9,000 and were "without artistic merit." Removing them, he said, would cost the developer $32,000 plus another $500,000 for project delays. Later Donald said that $32,000 was "nothing" because he contributed that much monthly to artists (although he provided no names). He said that he'd had the reliefs destroyed to protect pedestrians from falling debris and that there had been no damage to his project because the whole episode was attracting buyers rather than repelling them.

He was unable to admit that removing the badly weathered sculptures was harder and more expensive than he had first thought, or that, if consulted, the officials to whom he had promised the work might have agreed that he could not keep his promise at a reasonable cost. Instead he tried to blame everyone and everything else. He claimed that there had been no reneging on a promise to the Metropolitan Museum of Art because the museum had actually declined the art, and there had been no destruction of valuable art because the art was not valuable.[42]

Some years later, in his autobiography, he would make a measured apology, saying that he was sorry for his actions but his opponents were still phonies and hypocrites. But he did not see what he had said earlier as lying. In his mind, there was no more reason for saving souvenirs of

Bonwit's, an outmoded department store, than there had been for saving mementos of the Commodore, an outmoded hotel. Both were old, useless, and broke; his projects would be new, glamorous, and enormously profitable. "He couldn't stand anything from before," Der Scutt said. "He wants his own clean image, from A to Z, from inside to outside."

But there were additional reasons for his peremptory behavior. He did not want attention drawn to the undocumented workers who had torn down the artwork and was eager to end press scrutiny of the episode. Worse, a handful of well-connected East Siders had already formed an organization specifically opposed to the project, which they saw as an ugly successor to a beautiful old structure, and there was talk of a possible landmark designation.[43] "Bomb the shit out of that building!" Donald told his staff, urging them to get word out that it was structurally unsound, that windows were falling out, and that previous renovations had already drastically altered the building's original design.[44]

Even more problematic, the delays needed for careful removal of the artwork could end up costing him the 421a tax abatement he was counting on. With the city's financial crisis receding, the abatement, once deemed necessary to encourage housing, now seemed a giveaway to fancy apartment buildings, and civic leaders and city officials were pushing hard to eliminate it. Donald needed to file his application as soon as possible, but he could not do so until the old building was torn down and construction on the new one had actually begun—a situation that made even a modest delay intolerable. What was at issue for the developer was not $32,000, or even $500,000, but at least $25 million in additional taxes.

By 1981 Donald was finally able to submit his abatement application. Soon after, word leaked out that it was receiving special scrutiny. In the past he would instantly have started yanking strings in Albany and Gracie Mansion. But there was no state involvement in this project, and the current mayor was not a self-effacing accountant and Brooklyn political crony of Fred Trump. Indeed, Ed Koch enjoyed confrontation at least as much as Donald did. Koch had welcomed the developer and his wife to his victory party and had snipped ceremonial ribbons at the Grand Hyatt, but this mayor's relationship with the Trump Organization was not a happy one.[45]

Koch was bitter about a long-stalled pedestrian passageway under the Grand Hyatt that was meant to relieve subway congestion. After making a verbal promise to a mayoral deputy that he would provide a free easement, Donald procrastinated until he extracted a large condemnation award. To him, as to many others in real estate, a deal was not a deal until he signed on the dotted line, and the long delay was no more than his prerogative. To the Koch administration, though, an oral promise to a deputy mayor was a done deal, and the developer's refusal to go forward was infuriating.

The developer made a fence-mending contribution to the mayor's upcoming reelection campaign. But he also turned to pro-development Manhattan borough president Andrew Stein.[46] In the early 1970s, Roy Cohn had introduced the two men, who were both attractive, highly ambitious sons of successful, wealthy, and encouraging fathers. Over dinner at Trader Vic's, a trendy Polynesian-themed restaurant, the pro–rent control politician, then a state assembly member, and the anti–rent control developer had spent the evening arguing about whether rent regulation should be abolished. Hardly surprisingly, neither budged. Nonetheless, the two young men hit it off and remained on good terms.[47]

At the moment, Stein was wrestling with a dire threat from Manhattan's biggest real estate owner, Harry Helmsley. Unless the city handed over a playground of little apparent value, Helmsley said, he planned to build on two small, much-loved private parks in the middle of Tudor City, an apartment complex he owned on the East Side. City officials, wary of setting a possibly dangerous precedent by giving in to such blackmail, were reluctantly gearing up to approve the trade-off. But on the eve of the final vote, Donald provided the ammunition needed to kill the swap. He asserted—correctly, as it turned out—that Helmsley's parks were on nearly unbuildable sites, which meant that his threat to put apartments on them was a bluff. Donald also said that because the city playground fronted the East River, the site was worth far more than its appraised value, and thus Helmsley's proposed trade was not even close to fair. To back up his claims, Donald publicly offered, at a meeting in Stein's office, to buy the playground for more than Helmsley's assessment.

"This is good," Donald said, pulling out his own checkbook. "You can call the bank to find out."[48]

The proposal never came to a vote, Helmsley never built on the park land, and Donald's friendship with Stein grew warmer. A few days after Donald torpedoed the park swap, the borough president hosted a breakfast meeting at his Park Avenue apartment for the developer, Sunshine, and Tony Gliedman, the city commissioner charged with deciding on the 421a issue. Less than two weeks later, Donald made an early contribution to Stein's reelection campaign. Within three days, Stein provided a notarized letter stating that he had encouraged Donald to make his building residential based on the understanding that it would receive 421a tax benefits.

According to later affidavits from the developer and Sunshine, Gliedman seemed to agree with them that, legally speaking, the new building qualified for tax benefits. But the mayor remained unpersuaded and told Gliedman so in a meeting on March 20. Late that afternoon, the commissioner telephoned Donald and left word that the 421a application had been rejected. To Gliedman's surprise, the developer called back and denounced the decision as "dishonest." Then he added, "I want you to know that I am a very rich and powerful person in this town, and there is a reason I got that way. I will never forget what you did."

Three days later, Donald and Equitable sued the city and Gliedman. To avoid any glitches, Donald sent his brother Robert to serve the papers. The Trump-Equitable attorneys made a letter-of-the-law argument that Trump Tower, which replaced a department store that was 65 stories shorter than the maximum allowable height and drowning in red ink, couldn't have been more qualified for a 421a tax break. The city's attorneys countered with a spirit-of-the-law position that granting such a benefit to one of the most expensive buildings in New York was flagrantly contrary to the law's intent.

The case dragged on for three years, twice going up to the state's highest court. At one point Donald's attorney, Roy Cohn, asked for a meeting with the city's lawyer, a dignified, highly respected septuagenarian named Edith Spivack, to discuss a settlement. It was one of the few times that Donald ever publicly considered such a step, and it was certainly the only time anyone ever showed up in Spivack's office dressed like Cohn, who wore a white T-shirt, a purple suit, and loafers with no socks. But no deal was struck.[49] Finally, in July 1984, the court of appeals ruled in Donald's favor. Koch denounced the decision as utterly outrageous and unfair; Donald called it "a very positive thing for the city." Later, in what Koch could not fail to perceive as a pointed rebuke, the developer hired Tony Gliedman for his own staff.[50]

TO A FAMILY that had already known success, Donald Trump brought more. His first Manhattan deal had been a remarkable triumph, and his second, Trump Tower, seemed likely to do even better. But as his star continued its meteoric rise, that of his older brother, Freddy, kept falling. Fred Trump "didn't like wimps," his nephew, John Walter, said later. "He thought competition made you sharper." But it made Freddy so miserable that he left for Florida before Donald came to work at the Trump headquarters on Avenue Z. After Freddy failed as an airline pilot, a fishing-boat captain, and a husband, he returned north to live in his parents' home on Midland Parkway and to work on one of his father's maintenance crews. He was unable to stop drinking, and reportedly his father found closets stuffed with empty liquor bottles. Neighbors spoke of seeing someone so thin and frail that he seemed a wraith.

In September 1981, Fred Trump Jr., 42, a man who had long been living in the shadows, died from a massive heart attack caused by alcoholism so acute that it verged on the suicidal. Donald appeared shaken by his older brother's death and would speak over the years of his sense of loss as well as his guilt for having benefited from seeing his brother's mistakes. He would also speak, in a manner reminiscent of his reaction to the dedication of the Verrazano Bridge a quarter century earlier, of his renewed determination never to let people treat him as they had his brother. "Freddy just wasn't a killer," he told one reporter. To another he said, "I saw people really taking advantage of Fred, and the lesson I learned was always to keep up my guard 100 percent."[51]

As THE TAX ABATEMENT LITIGATION dragged on, Donald plunged into the construction of what he liked to call "the world's tallest concrete structure." In point of fact, Trump Tower (700 feet) was shorter than Chicago's Water Tower Place (850 feet) and the MLC Center in Sydney, Australia (751 feet).[52] But the sawtooth edifice was the tallest such building in New York City, where it was unusual to use concrete rather than steel beams to support a skyscraper.[53]

On paper, using concrete made sense. Because this material, made of sand, cement, and gravel, is poured on site and thus can be reconfigured up until the last minute, it offers maximum flexibility. This made it a highly desirable building material at Trump Tower, which was being designed while under construction. But in New York this choice seemed dubious for the simple reason that the local concrete industry was notoriously corrupt. Because city concrete firms could ship their ingredients by barge instead of truck or train, their overhead was actually low compared with that of other northeastern cities. But somehow New York concrete cost 70 percent more than it did in, say, Boston. According to reports in the *New York Times* and a later state investigation, a principal cause of the excess cost was the union whose members operated the cement mixers: Teamsters Local 282, led by John Cody.[54]

A broad, burly man of 60 with a receding hairline and Coke-bottle glasses, Cody had an arrest record stretching back four decades. By the time Trump Tower was finished, he was under indictment for labor racketeering, and two years later he would return to jail yet again. But while at the helm of 282, he had only to nod his head to slow down deliveries of a material that would be ruined if not on site within an hour of being mixed. The mere mention of his name brought developers to heel.

Curiously, Cody seemed disinclined to make the Trump Tower job go slower. Perhaps it was because, as he later told a reporter, he knew

Donald "quite well" and considered Roy Cohn "a pretty good friend." Or perhaps there were other reasons. "A lot of the time it cost money under the table," recalled one Equitable executive closely involved with the Trump Tower construction process. "Donald made a deal with those concrete guys in New York. None of us could figure out why or how he did it, but somehow he conned them into building with reinforced concrete instead of steel." Sometimes the executive wondered if the project was on the right side of the law, but he could do little other than trust that whatever the developer was doing was okay. "You'd hope that he was a magician or walked on water," the executive said, "but the reason was that he made arrangements."

Among those arrangements, in the view of many people involved in the construction, was a comely blonde from Austria named Verina Hixon. Although she had no visible income or assets, she managed, with Donald's help, to get mortgage financing for three duplex apartments at Trump Tower worth about $10 million. Then she ordered a staggering list of alterations and additions, including the installation of the building's one swimming pool, which the developer seemed oddly willing to provide. Although she was often seen in Cody's company, she emphatically denied being his mistress. She was not—repeat, not—the reason that the concrete deliveries to Trump Tower flowed smoothly.

Perhaps. In any event, Cody, who was planning a citywide strike in the summer of 1982, actually speeded up the Trump Organization's shipments so as to avoid potential problems. In July, after Local 282 had shut down construction sites across the city, Donald invited 700 guests to Trump Tower for a topping-off celebration. Before the champagne brunch, a small number of dignitaries rode a hoist to a rooftop press conference. Standing next to an American flag and a few dozen of the 10,000 balloons scheduled for release over Fifth Avenue, Donald, Fred, Mayor Koch, Manhattan borough president Stein, and Governor Carey hailed each other, the building, and the future.

THE INITIAL ARCHITECTURAL COMMISSION at Olympic Tower went to the firm of Morris Lapidus, creator of the flamboyant

Fontainebleau and Eden Roc hotels in Miami as well as the more pedestrian Brooklyn apartment complex Trump Village. Done in conjunction with his son Alan, fresh out of Columbia University School of Architecture, the Lapidus design featured a glassed-in tower that looked a bit like a harmonica—or possibly a radiator—balanced on end. What it did not look like was anything else in Manhattan.

On the morning of Thursday, October 15, 1970, the *New York Times* editorialized that the new building was a "tinsel" mishmash and "a glassy death." Among the readers was the former Jacqueline Kennedy, the new wife of the owner of Olympic Tower, Aristotle Onassis, and an ardent preservationist. Onassis canned Lapidus the next day and hired the highly respectable firm Skidmore, Owings & Merrill. Noted for its many modernist structures, most of them variations on big glass boxes, the company obligingly provided yet another one. When it opened, the *Times* noted its "ice-cold dignity."[55]

But the builder of the successor to Olympic Tower was not married to the high priestess of good taste. He was married to Ivana, whose appetite for the spectacular was, if anything, greater than his. She never objected to anything as too showy. And just as at the Grand Hyatt on 42nd Street, neither she nor her husband had any interest in rescuing Fifth Avenue from the march of time. Instead they wanted to use that march to their advantage. Even more than the Grand Hyatt, the new building would embody the developer's awareness of the newly emerging market segment that real estate brokers called "high net worth individuals": people who were not just rich but super-rich.

When condos at the only competing new luxury building, the Museum of Modern Art Tower, went on the market at lower prices, Donald wasn't worried. He relished the prospect of selling the city's most expensive units and creating a new high-water mark in conspicuous consumption.[56] Trump Tower would be for people who took pride in paying the most, who wanted to live in a building so aggressively different from its neighbors that it would have looked more at home in Houston than limestone-lined Fifth Avenue. Above all, it was for people who never seemed tired of hearing what Donald never tired of saying, that they were getting "the very best, not second best, the very best."[57]

In order to make it the best, the developer dragged Equitable executives across town to look at bathroom fixtures and filled his conference room with tile samples. He spent hours talking doorknobs. Ivana put weeks into the design of the doormen's uniforms and towering black bearskin hats, custom-made in London. When a scale model of Trump Tower, intended as a marketing tool, showed that it would be shorter than the nearby GM Building, and Louise Sunshine pointed out that it would be illegal to make the Trump Tower model taller for sales purposes, Donald told the model maker to reduce the GM building. And, following the Grand Hyatt precedent, the top level of the new 59-story structure would be the sixty-eighth floor.[58]

Der Scutt had suggested the use of a sensuous rosy-peach marble called breccia perniche to help create the buy-buy-buy and spend-spend-spend atmosphere of ultimate consumption that Donald craved. But to make sure that the lobby would have only the choicest slabs, Ivana went to the quarry in northern Italy and, despite being seven months pregnant with her second child, Ivanka, climbed up and down the walls on rope ladders. When much of the stone still proved too blotchy to use, her husband discarded half of it, later boasting that he had gone through an entire mountaintop and used up the world's supply of this particular material. Similarly, when he decided on the eve of the opening that the $75,000 worth of ficus trees planted in the atrium hid the marble, he ordered them chopped down with a chain saw and hauled away.

Such efforts paid off. Ice-cold dignity was nowhere to be found; instead, Donald had created a dazzling, glamorous beehive that *New York Times* critic Paul Goldberger found, perhaps to his surprise, "warm, luxurious, and even exhilarating." Olympic Tower had an unobtrusive entrance on East 51st Street, but the new building's front door, framed with what was surely the shiniest brass in America, opened directly onto Fifth Avenue. Further unlike its predecessor, this skyscraper bore the name of its builder out front in three-foot-tall brass letters so out of scale with the rest of the building that, Der Scutt joked, tourists could see them before the plane landed.[59] In the public space, which had been given a cavernous appearance by well-placed mirrors, the warm marble covered every surface and an 80-foot waterfall gushed like a mini-

Niagara. Dozens of glittering jewel-box boutiques filled the retail atrium, and a tuxedo-clad pianist at a 12-foot Steinway serenaded shoppers streaming up and down on brass-railed escalators.

Before the building opened, the prices for its condos, already the highest in the city, went up again and again and again. Buyers, lured by a presentation that included views from the building and a recording of Frank Sinatra crooning "New York, New York," put down an unprecedented 25 percent of the purchase price, even though moving in was more than a year away. For months, gossip columns carried items on residents-to-be, including Johnny Carson, Steven Spielberg, and Liberace. Donald inflated the already impressive celebrity quotient by leaking, then refusing to comment on, a rumor that Prince Charles and his new wife, Diana, were considering buying there. As expected, even though the project was neither on time nor on budget, apartment sales paid the construction costs; unexpectedly, because of record prices, doing so required selling only about 60 percent of the units instead of the usual 75 or 80 percent.

Retail rents, too, were the highest in the city, even though most atrium visitors were only window shoppers and many of the ultraluxury stores did poorly. "Donald was able to sell those merchandisers the idea that if you're not in Trump Tower, you're not in New York," said a knowledgeable Equitable executive. "One retailer told me he just takes three-quarters of his rent out of his advertising budget and tells himself that he's buying a billboard on Fifth Avenue."

Crowning the top of what would become the biggest tourist draw in New York City was Donald's own personal Fontainebleau. Inspired by the palatial digs of Arab billionaire Adnan Khashoggi in Olympic Tower, the developer carved out a sprawling, 53-room triplex, described by John d'Alessio, one of the many designers who worked on it, as "Louis XIV on LSD." The 80-foot living room featured phenomenal views, a waterfall, a frescoed ceiling Donald compared to the Sistine Chapel, and massive columns, newly carved because he found antique architectural elements too used-looking. In the dining room was a two-story, carved ivory frieze, and elsewhere there were walls covered with onyx, a translucent, multihued quartz that the developer liked to note was more expensive than marble. Everywhere, from chairs and moldings to column capitals and bathroom faucets, there was gilt.[60]

From bottom to top, from the retail stores to the extraordinary penthouse château, Trump Tower was one humongous, sawtooth advertisement for Donald. What was a triumph for the developer, though, was a problem for his partner.[61] "We were in this to make money, not to serve as a marquee for the Trump Organization," said Doug Healey, who had recently taken over Equitable's investment operation in New York City. With the building done, the condos gone, and everything else leased out, Equitable was ready to sell its interest and move on. "We'd been to the altar, had a nice marriage, and made a lot of money," Healey said. Now it was time for a divorce.[62]

When Donald resisted the idea of putting Trump Tower on the market, Healey and George Peacock had the delicate task of persuading him to buy Equitable out. Bad cop Healey fussed about the cost of the pianist and the constant cleaning and polishing of the lobby; nice cop Peacock nodded sympathetically as Donald complained about the new guy who was nickel-and-diming him to death. Three years after the opening, lawyers for the Trump Organization and Equitable found themselves at another seemingly endless closing, their own. Equitable walked away with a 378 percent return on its original investment; Donald walked away with his own permanent logo.

The Grand Hyatt had been Donald's first significant move away from his father's approach and accomplishments; now, with Trump Tower, the separation was complete. Fred called and grilled staffers about projects, and on weekends his grandson, young Donny, would accompany his father to construction sites and pick up used nails, just as Donald had done with Fred years before in Brooklyn and Queens.[63] But now it was Donald who was calling the shots.

Fred respected his son's success, but there was little in Donald's latest project that made sense to the older man. To someone who had made his reputation and his fortune putting up square buildings, to whom extra corners meant extra leaks, the very idea of a sawtooth building was incomprehensible. Equally mystifying was his son's refusal to rent the empty Bonwit Teller building over the Christmas season to

Strawberry's, a down-market women's clothing store temporarily displaced by the Grand Hyatt construction. To Fred, this was a chance to use vacant space and turn a profit. But to Donald, the mere presence of a working-class store at this location would erode its appeal to a luxury market his father had never dreamed of pursuing.

When Fred visited the building site and saw an expensive glass curtain wall going up, he tried to rein in what he considered a waste of money. "Why don't you forget about the damn glass?" he told his son. "Give them four or five stories of it, and then use common brick for the rest. Nobody is going to look up anyway."[64] The idea of leaving lights on at the site all night to draw attention was similarly problematic to someone who still routinely checked that even the lowest-watt bulbs were turned off in his own buildings in Brooklyn and Queens. Still an outer-borough man at heart, he would find little use for the sixty-third-floor apartment Donald had reserved in his name.

ALTHOUGH THE SKYSCRAPER at 58th and Fifth was the most famous building in Manhattan to bear the developer's name, it was not the only one. While Trump Tower was under construction, Donald had built a second luxury building, an elegant East Side co-op called Trump Plaza, which also received a 421a tax abatement.[65] And much as the idea of a tax giveaway to either building galled Ed Koch and other city officials, there was justification of sorts. Trump argued that he was putting people to work, attracting tourists to New York, and, on a more facetious note, saving the outer boroughs by pushing Manhattan prices so high that even the relatively well-to-do would have to move to Queens, the Bronx, and Brooklyn.[66] More important, fully three-quarters of the sales at Trump Tower were to wealthy nonresidents and out-of-town corporations—exactly the people who would bring with them the high incomes, spending, and taxes that could help galvanize the city's revival.[67]

Or so the argument went. Meanwhile, though, the city was rebounding, and the ground around Donald was shifting. His brash, steamroller style, welcome and even refreshing when the city was on the ropes, began to appear in a different light, particularly after he became involved in a bitter battle to raze 100 Central Park South, a large limestone apartment house thrown in with his purchase of an adjacent hotel. As soon as he could empty the apartment building, he planned to replace both structures with a new luxury hotel and shopping arcade.

But the more than 100 tenants had no interest in leaving this prestigious address, and when the relocation firm hired by Donald tried to hasten their departure by removing lampshades from hallway lights and seats from the lobby, they hired a lawyer and called the press. Frustrated and furious at what he saw as tenant intransigence, Donald complained that arcane city rent regulations were allowing affluent residents, about a quarter of the total, to pay bargain rents; what he didn't mention was that building demographics included an equal number of people who were far from affluent.[68]

In a pro-tenant town like New York City, it was inevitably a delicate and problematic situation. But whatever sympathy Donald might have tapped disappeared after he offered to turn over vacant units to the homeless, a group that included schizophrenics and drug addicts. The tenants saw this as a blatant attempt to scare them; Donald insisted that the invitation had been simple altruism and, digging himself in deeper, noted that the tactics he had used so far were nothing compared with what he could have done.

After five years of threats, suits, and countersuits, Donald folded. Scrapping his plans, he left 100 Central Park South a rental building and surrounded it with a Y-shaped luxury condominium tower named Trump Parc. But just as with the 60th Street yards and the Bonwit Teller sculptures, he refused to acknowledge anything that smacked of defeat. Instead he claimed that the tenants had done him a favor. Because he had been forced to hang on to the building, he said, he would now benefit from market changes that made it more advantageous to renovate than to demolish.[69]

Perhaps. But the honeymoon he had enjoyed in the New York press was over. He was no longer the boy wonder, the hyperactive hero. He was still the New York real estate wizard, the man who had helped rescue 42nd Street and created the shiniest, showiest new building on Fifth Avenue. But he was also a breaker of promises and an art vandal, an anti-tenant landlord and an exploiter of immigrant labor. Back in the mid-1970s, his first *New York Times* profile compared him to Robert Redford and intimated that his worst defect was talking too fast. Now the same paper said that he would be a shoo-in for "a stupendous new unpopularity prize." *New York* portrayed him as a tasteless vulgarian, the *Daily News* portrayed him as a sorehead, and the *Village Voice* accused him of being a conniver, a racist, and a liar.

In short, he was a major player, part of the city's power elite. No longer his father's protégé, he had earned his own place at the table, and he would draw all the attention, praise, and fire to which it entitled him.

CHAPTER FIVE

Gambling on Atlantic City

Donald worked almost as hard on his public image as he did on real estate development. His father had sent out occasional press releases about his buildings and, once in a while, his opinion on public affairs; Donald issued a steady stream of news about his every move. He returned every call from the press, and when the calls weren't coming in, he made them himself. No longer the awkward young man who had embarrassed himself at the '21' Club with investment banker Ben Lambert in the mid-1970s, he had permanent claim to one of the most visible spots in the restaurant, which allowed him to see and be seen by everyone coming and going. As he ate, he would jump up to greet those passing by and then sit down again to answer the phones being brought to the table, sometimes two at a time, for urgent calls.[1]

In classic American huckster fashion, on every occasion he pronounced his projects and himself as the best, the brightest, the greatest. Trump Tower didn't have a good address; it had "the Tiffany location." The Grand Hyatt wasn't a successful hotel; it was "incredible, gorgeous, gleaming." His deals, he told the New York Times, "would have taken an older man a lifetime to do, if he could ever get them done." To New York magazine he confided, "No one has done more than I in the last seven years."[2]

Such efforts bore fruit. In the fall of 1983 Town & Country featured a full-length article on Donald and Ivana Trump. A national showcase for the rich and well connected, the magazine presented the couple as healthy, wealthy, and blond. That same year People gave the developer its American Image Award for business. The next spring he appeared on the front of the New York Times Magazine as the subject of a story entitled "The Expanding Empire of Donald Trump."[3]

A month later he gazed out with the same self-satisfied look from the cover of Gentleman's Quarterly, then the hottest men's magazine in the country. The 10-page profile ragged him for his glitzy aesthetic and penchant for exaggeration, but also labeled him "a remarkably deft dealmaker" and featured half a dozen photographs of his newest purchase, a cozy 11-bedroom, seven-fireplace family hideaway on six acres of the tony Connecticut shore.[4]

Real estate and fame had not usually gone together in New York. When developers like Fred courted press attention, it was for their projects, not themselves. They did business under faceless corporate pseudonyms and hired Howard Rubenstein to keep their profiles low. "You didn't know who built your building or even who owned it," said Jerry Schrager. "But all of a sudden, you lived at Trump Tower, Trump Plaza. It was unique."

Even more unusual, a public that ordinarily hated landlords and developers couldn't seem to get enough of Donald. "I was constantly astonished at how people received him and his projects," Schrager said. "The man on the street, the cabdrivers, everybody wanted to touch him and shake his hand." But the developer did not become a national celebrity until he had his first large-scale failure.[5]

Seven months after the opening of Trump Tower, he paid $9 million (which he rounded down to a more favorable-sounding $6 million) for the New Jersey Generals. A second-tier professional football team, the Generals belonged to the fledgling United States Football League (USFL), a loosely organized group of clubs owned by land developers and shopping-center czars. Playing in the spring off-season to avoid direct competition with the immensely popular and profitable National Football League (NFL), the USFL was following a prudent strategy of low player salaries and a slow start-up.

Too low and too slow, in Donald's opinion. He wanted to challenge the NFL immediately. Within weeks of his purchase he launched a campaign to move the USFL to the prime fall season and dangled big bucks to snag gridiron stars. Taking the USFL big-time fit neatly with his own game plan: building and managing a huge new city- and state-backed stadium in New York City, naming it after himself, and making the Generals the home team. Doing so would raise his own profile and put him in line for the real money in professional sports, the hefty profits from leases on private boxes and lucrative fall television contracts.

There could be an even bigger payoff. Years earlier the NFL had faced a rival, the American Football League (AFL), which played in the fall season. To the immense profit of the AFL's owners, the two leagues had merged. If Donald could force a second merger, he could end up owning a first-tier team for a fraction of the current asking price of $70 million. But the situation would be win-win even without a merger or USFL entrée into the networks' fall market, for the upstart league could then take the NFL to court for monopolistic practices and rake in a huge settlement.

Seizing the initiative, Donald told Roy Cohn to file a USFL antitrust suit against the NFL in October 1984, asking for $1.32 billion in damages. Although Cohn was ill with AIDS and would be dead by the final verdict, he remained combative. At a press conference, he claimed that a "secret" NFL committee had plotted the USFL's demise. But the

USFL was nowhere near ready to handle either its newest team owner or the NFL and collapsed almost immediately, $150 million in the red. Although Donald claimed to have sold 30,000 tickets for a debut fall season, none were seen and no games were played.

The USFL made its final tackle a year and a half later in Manhattan federal district court, where the NFL was found to be a monopoly. But the jury saw little deleterious economic impact on the USFL and awarded it the token sum of $1. Donald had reportedly sunk about $22 million into the deal, but characteristically he refused to acknowledge a defeat. Instead he called the outcome "a moral victory." The jury acted as it did, he later wrote in *The Art of the Deal,* not because his case was too weak but because it was too strong. He had been such a compelling witness and his lawyer so powerful a litigator that the jurors had simply taken pity on the NFL.

Although the developer's "explanation" of the jury finding was cheerfully wide of the facts, he had scored a victory of sorts: the publicity he received for being associated with a professional sports team. His name, already seen in the news, business, and gossip columns, now became a regular feature in the sports pages, the most-read part of every paper in America. Aggressive, arrogant, often amusing, and always ready with a plainspoken zinger of a sound bite, he made great copy.[6]

From now on the name would be an integral part of every project in which he was involved.[7] So would a certain style of deal-making. As former Prudential vice-president Brian Strum recalled, during negotiations Donald, dressed in an expensive tailored suit, would give his side while patting his interlocutor on the shoulder and saying, "You know," or "You know what I mean." Although his facts were often wrong, those present, most of them individuals of modest net worth, were flattered at being addressed as insiders and did not want to interrupt him. "But if he says you know, and you don't say you don't know, you've sort of agreed," Strum said. "The next time you meet, he'll say, 'But we talked about that!' You must be obtrusive to hold your own, and this isn't a style most people take to naturally. Most people are too polite."

BEING THE OWNER of a professional football team brought Donald the media attention he had sought. But he had to go elsewhere for the money. He still did not have the financial wherewithal his lap-of-luxury style suggested and was essentially marketing himself with bluster. The uncomfortable truth was that he remained heavily dependent on his father's resources and fortune, which meant that his father remained a questioning presence, in there kicking the tires on the deal even if he didn't understand it. This chafed his son, who loved his father but did not want anyone reading over his shoulder. To become truly independent, Donald needed his own source of cash flow.

He had an idea about where to look. Ever since he had learned that the 150-hotel Hilton chain made more than one-third of its net profits from its two casino hotels in Las Vegas, he had been toying with the idea of owning such a money machine himself.[8] Now, just 125 miles from Trump Tower, a tidal wave of cash was washing over Atlantic City, the second place in the nation to permit games of chance for money.[9]

Gambling was not new to Atlantic City, founded as a health resort on a small barrier island off the coast of New Jersey in the 1850s.[10] But along with prostitution and bootlegging, games of chance had been backroom entertainment in a town whose public face consisted of modest family boardinghouses, elegant hotels, and a four-mile-long boardwalk along a wide white beach. By 1900 Atlantic City attracted a quarter of a million visitors on hot holiday weekends, and the town's kitschy creations, which included picture postcards, the Miss America Pageant, and saltwater taffy, became part of mainstream American culture. So did Monopoly, the most popular board game in the nation's history, which copied Atlantic City's street names.[11]

After World War II, air-conditioning and cheap airfares to more exotic destinations cut deeply into the Atlantic City tourist trade. When the resort played host to the 1964 Democratic National Convention, its sad decay was revealed on national television.[12] In the mid-1970s local legislators, desperate to reverse the town's steady losing streak, embraced legalized gambling as the way to bring the tourists back. The first effort to pass the necessary statewide referendum failed, but it did get the attention of Resorts Inc., which had launched a casino hotel in the Bahamas and wanted to set up shop on the mainland. Noting that Atlantic City was only a few hours' drive from nearly one-third of the nation's population, Resorts bankrolled a second, successful referendum in November 1976.

Determined to keep organized crime out of Atlantic City, state legislators then drew up enabling legislation. Among other provisions, it established the Casino Control Commission, which would monitor and regulate casino operations, and the Division of Gaming Enforcement (DGE), a permanent investigative body in charge of policing the casinos. When Governor Brendan Byrne signed the act, he shook his fist and warned the Mob, "Keep your filthy hands out of Atlantic City and keep the hell out of our state!"

But none of these efforts even remotely prepared the city or the state for what having casino hotels would actually be like. "It was like the scene in *2001: A Space Odyssey* where the cavemen are standing around looking at the monolith and not knowing what to do with it," Jim Whelan, city council member and later mayor, told one reporter.[13]

Before most people in Atlantic City knew what had hit them, the economic forces unleashed by the casinos had taken over the town. Because little land was available, speculators immediately bought up whatever they could lay their hands on, enriching a fortunate few but driving prices, taxes, and rents beyond the reach of small-business owners and forcing local residents to leave.[14] Worried about competition from other states and impatient to get the casinos up and running, officials did not spell out how casino taxes would translate into city renewal, an oversight that delayed meaningful improvement for years. Instead the newly appointed commission waived one shiny new regulation after another. After a hasty makeover of an old Boardwalk hotel, Chalfonte-Haddon Hall, Resorts slapped on neon lights and opened for business on Memorial Day weekend of 1978.[15]

Long before Governor Byrne cut the ribbon, the lines stretched down the Boardwalk and out of sight. Inside, the 30,000-square-foot casino area was packed, and customers could not move in the aisles. Competition for slot machines was so fierce that gamblers reportedly peed in their pants rather than surrender a seat at a one-armed bandit.

All day long and into the night, thousands of people waited to lose money. Overwhelmed by the volume of business, Resorts was unable to count the bills and coins it was hauling in or even to fit all the money into a safe.[16] At the end of the first year, gross revenues of $224.6 million made it the most profitable casino in the world.[17]

Even the most optimistic casino advocates had not grasped the public's appetite for gambling. Although many people objected to it as unproductive, immoral, and possibly addictive, others saw casinos as a place where they could safely take risks. Filled with glitter, crowds, and noise, casinos were a special realm, without clocks or windows, where customers could set ordinary caution aside. Whether they were putting quarters into a slot machine or dollars into a hand of blackjack, the result was an adrenaline spike that could be repeated from ten o'clock in the morning until four o'clock the next morning. For a small number of people that experience was habit-forming and dangerous; for most it was a relatively inexpensive, exciting, and totally legal way to feel a fantastic buzz.

SHORTLY BEFORE New Jersey citizens voted to legalize gambling in Atlantic City, Donald had driven down for a look. But he had not been impressed by the shabby old beach town. Rather than pursuing opportunities there, he opted to reconfigure the Grand Hyatt floor plan so that it would be possible to carve out a large casino space if gambling became legal in New York.

After seeing the phenomenal success of Resorts, he flew down to Atlantic City by seaplane for another look. He quickly decided that the Tiffany location was the 2½-acre Boardwalk site where the major expressway into town crossed the main street. Meeting with a local broker named Paul Longo, he offered several million dollars for one of the leases on the property. But speculators had already driven prices higher, and his bid went nowhere.[18]

In February 1980 Donald called Longo again and said that he was ready to make a deal. With the Grand Hyatt finished and Trump Tower under way, he was ready for a new project, and now that the federal probe into the West Side rail yards was over, he could pass muster with the DGE. Moreover, New Jersey's hunger for casino revenues seemed to be cooling its initial regulatory passion, for the Casino Control Commission had recently awarded Resorts a permanent license despite vehement DGE objections.[19]

But the main reason for Donald's renewed interest was ABSCAM, an explosive, casino-related federal sting operation in New Jersey that had implicated that state's senior U.S. senator and a host of local politicians. In its wake, casino gambling seemed too tainted an endeavor to gain legal status in New York. If the developer wanted gambling dollars, he would have to go to Atlantic City.

On a gray Saturday in February, Donald made another visit, this time with Ivana.[20] After a Frank Sinatra concert and dinner, he left her and a friend playing the slots and took a stroll up the now-deserted beachfront with Longo. The broker, who had grown up there and at one time or another had managed most of the stores along the Boardwalk, pointed out the four casino hotels that had opened and the five then under construction. Although it was bitterly cold, they stopped and looked at the same site the developer had tried to lease two years earlier. It consisted of three separate properties, held by 30 separate owners, details that did not seem to discourage Donald in the least. "This is the best location in Atlantic City," he said. "I want to be right here."

He began hammering out leases with holders of major parcels, and Longo filled in the missing pieces, one postage-stamp-size lot after another. "We were paying the highest price per square foot in the city at the time," Longo recalled later. "But these people weren't selling real estate, they were selling part of their lives."

He found Donald to be plain-talking and direct, which made him easy to work with, but oddly insistent on maintaining a formal, businesslike image at all times. In early July the developer arranged with Longo to spend a day scoping out recent developments along the Boardwalk. It was blisteringly hot, but Donald wore his uniform of dark suit, dark shoes, and red tie. Longo, who was wearing cutoff jeans and sneak-

ers, told the developer he was surprised that he wasn't dressed more in-
formally. "I came down here for business," Donald said, "and in New
York this is the way we dress for business."

It was a formula that worked, for he seemed to get even the most
unpromising situation to go his way. "He will say things like 'Why don't
we just remain friends and forget the deal,' " Longo said. "He is able to
make you believe this is the best deal you're going to get from him—if
you don't like it, talk to the next buyer—and he makes you wonder if
there is going to be another buyer."

Preparing to make his move on Atlantic City, Donald had added
to his small staff two key players. One was attorney Harvey Freeman, a
brainy veteran of Olympic Tower whom Donald nicknamed "Harvard"
after seeing how quickly he whipped through the *New York Times* cross-
word puzzle. Known for his dry humor and poker face, Freeman was a
teddy bear–like figure in his early forties with curly salt-and-pepper hair
and crinkly eyes. Donald's lead negotiator and investment adviser, his
most important role was saying no. Whether alone or in concert with
Donald's other chief naysayer, Jerry Schrager, Freeman made it his job
to spell out the downside of potential deals. "Harvey was always negative, gloom and doom," said architect Alan Lapidus, who had worked
with Freeman on Olympic Tower and would do so again on Donald's
first Atlantic City casino. "He would unearth every pitfall."[21]

The other addition was Donald's younger brother. Like Donald,
Robert was tall, blue-eyed, and heavy-browed, but he had an altogether
different personality. As one former Trump employee put it, on an intensity scale of 1 to 10, Donald would be 15 and Robert 5.[22] Soft-spoken
and unassuming, the baby of the family drove a 10-year-old Oldsmobile
Cutlass and lived in a hand-me-down apartment, Donald's old bachelor
pad on East 65th Street. After graduating from Boston University,
Robert became an investment banker and showed no interest in the
family business. But as his representative in Atlantic City, Donald
needed someone whose loyalty was beyond question, and to him that
meant someone named Trump.

As it turned out, Robert would do far more than stand in for Donald. As Fred's son he was comfortable on a construction site, and as a

former banker he could handle number crunching and detail monitoring. He could also talk tough when he had to but did not have the same need to win every time that fueled his brother. "Robert was the good Trump," said Alan Lapidus. "Donald would come on and do the hard negotiating and be the tough guy. Then you'd need the good guy to come in and make everybody feel like his best buddy."[23]

In mid-July there was a marathon closing. In part because the property was still being assembled, the session stretched out nearly 24 hours and involved more than 100 participants, including Fred Trump. Privately he was not enthusiastic about this venture into new and unfamiliar territory; publicly he was at his son's side whenever he was needed. Because Donald had to draw on the same Chase line of credit he had obtained through his father and used for cost overruns on the Hyatt, Fred signed documents as vice president of the new entities created for each transaction.

At the time, the definition of high-profile casino design in Atlantic City was what Skidmore, Owings & Merrill had done for the new Bally's Park Place, a large glass box reminiscent of the firm's earlier work at Olympic Tower. Rejecting that elegant but austere vision, Donald had instead selected an architect whose sense of design was, if anything, anti-Skidmore. In 1970, Alan Lapidus's flashy and obtrusive plan for Olympic Tower had turned Jackie Onassis off. But in Atlantic City, his taste for arresting and unusual shapes that jutted up above the horizon was exactly what Donald wanted.

Within the industry, it was axiomatic that casinos had to be on the ground floor. But on Donald's narrow site, the hotel's front desk and concierge booth would take a large bite out of the available floor space, a serious problem given that a casino's profitability is directly linked to the size of its gaming floor. To gain more room, Lapidus made the heretical suggestion of putting the casino one flight up. Donald agreed but decided that even the second floor was not large enough. With Lapidus he proceeded to lay out an alternate plan. An obscure city regulation required passageways between neighboring hotels so that even in bad weather visitors could go from one hotel to the next. Other hoteliers had built narrow, utilitarian tubes across adjacent streets, but Donald suggested expanding the passageway into a huge plaza that hung over the street. By doing so, he would create a 60,000-square-foot casino— the largest in Atlantic City and one of the biggest in the world.

At ground level, the extra floor space would have cost Donald a fortune, but he unilaterally declared the street overhang an enhanced public amenity, paid a token $100, and had a building with every guest room angled for an ocean view.[24] Like the Grand Hyatt and Trump Tower, the structure was not quite as tall as he said it was—it was only the second-highest building in Atlantic City—but there was no doubt that it would have the town's oddest silhouette.[25] Looking like two giant Edsel radiator grilles set end to end, it would be the one casino hotel no one could possibly miss seeing.

Donald had learned from his father the value of going along with the powers that be. He had done it in New York, and now he would do it in Atlantic City. Rather than sending lowly minions to the endless regulatory hearings, Donald made sure that either he or Robert was present to answer every question. He would hire local attorneys, he would do everything in his own name, and he would be prompt, polite, and respectful. "Donald's attitude was, I'll do anything," Lapidus said. "You want me to stand on my head, fine. You want me to get undressed, I'll get undressed."

But at the same time, Donald would keep up the hard sell. When state regulators or casino officials came to New York, the visit would start with a Trump Tower promotional film strip that heaped praise on the developer and extolled his visionary powers. After he applied for a casino license, he kept up a drumbeat of telephone calls to those in charge. "He'd say was there anything he could do to help, could he make someone available," said Bob Sturges, a former prosecutor then serving as deputy DGE director. "The real message was always 'Don't forget about me, keep pushing this thing along.' " Asked for character references, obviously a request for business colleagues, the developer listed Norman Vincent Peale. "It seemed typical Trump, hit-you- between-the-eyes-with-a-sledgehammer style," said a close observer of the licensing process. "You know, you want character references, I'll give you a character reference."

In the end, Donald would get what he wanted. Once again a city was in distress, and the tall, blond entrepreneur would play the white knight, experienced enough to build a casino but too new to the gaming industry to have problematic entanglements.[26] With the first wave of casino applications over, anxious regulatory officials eagerly catered to this rich New York developer who promised to bring "some pizzazz" to the Jersey shore. They interpreted his lack of casino experience as an asset—it meant he was untainted by the Mob. When he failed to record in his application that he had been charged with racial discrimination in Trump-owned buildings in Brooklyn, the regulators noted the lapse in a footnote but excused it because he mentioned the incident during an interview. And they evidently ignored the fact that he had been investigated in connection with more than one federal probe. "We were a little shell-shocked at getting so many applicants with licensing problems," Sturges said. "With Donald, it was a pleasure to be looking for skeletons in the closet and for once not finding any."

DONALD TRUMP was still a real estate developer. Unlike everyone else who had started a casino resort in Atlantic City, he would not open for business, hire staff, or begin construction until he had permits and money in place. It would not be easy, for the stigma attached to gambling meant that banks and institutional investors were wary. Further, he had no experience actually running either a casino or a hotel. There was also the ever-present worry that an infraction could shut down a casino hotel overnight. As a result, the man who was arguably the hottest name in New York real estate had to go around the country begging financial institutions to put in even relatively small participations of $3 million to $5 million.

Discouraged after months of knocking on doors and having to borrow money from his father to keep going, Donald began looking for ways out.[27] At one point he went to see *Penthouse* editor and publisher Bob Guccione, the owner of the adjacent casino site, at his lavish East Side town house. Walking past beefy security guards and half a dozen

Rhodesian ridgeback hounds, Donald made his way to a walnut-paneled study lined with Impressionist and Postimpressionist paintings. There the king of glitz proposed that the king of soft-core porn take over his Boardwalk property. But Guccione's own casino was a rusting pile of girders because his financing had dried up mid-construction, and he passed.

Donald also made a pilgrimage to Los Angeles to visit Drexel Burnham Lambert bond trader Mike Milken, who was heavily involved with another casino operator, Steve Wynn. The owner of casinos in Las Vegas and Atlantic City, both named the Golden Nugget, Wynn had a background not unlike Trump's. He had grown up in Utica, New York, attended a military academy, and been a fiercely competitive athlete. After graduating from Wharton, he worked in the same field as his father, a manager of bingo parlors, and had achieved remarkable success at a young age with his Las Vegas Golden Nugget.

Wynn had been drawn to Atlantic City early on, showing up for Resorts' Memorial Day opening and within days scooping up an old motel property along the Boardwalk. In part because Wynn put up his Las Vegas holdings as collateral, Milken floated a $160 million bond issue to finance Wynn's East Coast expansion. The junk-bond guru was willing to consider a similar deal with Donald, but he balked at the terms. More a developer than a casino man, Donald would not use his own resources or provide a guarantee that the project would be completed.[28]

Then, in June 1982, in walked the man who would make it all work out, a six-foot, seven-inch Harvard-trained lawyer named Mike Rose.[29] The chief operating officer of Holiday Inns, he had already established the most profitable casino in Atlantic City. Located at a marina across town from the Boardwalk, it was operated by Holiday's newly acquired gambling subsidiary, Harrah's.[30] Now Rose wanted to try his luck on the Boardwalk itself, but because Donald already had a license, an excellent Boardwalk site, and a hole in the ground, it made sense to come calling.[31]

Earlier Donald had tried and failed to get Harrah's attention; now Rose was like Santa Claus, bringing a sack of goodies right to the developer's front door. Through Harrah's, Rose would put up $50 million, out of which Donald would be reimbursed for what he had spent so far. In addition to paying Donald a fee as construction manager with a bonus for staying on budget and on time, Rose would operate the facility at no cost, cover all losses for five years, and split any profits. Not batting an eye, Donald, who until that moment had been faced with deep-sixing the whole project, said that he wasn't sure he wanted a partner and would have to think the offer over. His dumbfounded staff wondered whether Rose was simply setting the developer up.

He wasn't. To Rose, combining Harrah's casino expertise and Donald's construction savvy seemed a no-brainer. But as soon became apparent, nothing could have been further from the truth. The contrast between Mike Rose, corporate man, dedicated to making money for shareholders, and Donald Trump, entrepreneur, dedicated to making money for himself, created a gap too wide to be bridged. The perhaps inevitable result was a near catastrophe.

Rose had made his mark by bringing modern management techniques to Holiday Inns, a large Memphis-based motel chain. Established in the 1950s, when Americans began crisscrossing the country on interstate highways, Holiday had once been an industry leader. Plucking its name from a Bing Crosby film, it had opened company meetings with a prayer and constructed chapels next to its motels, but by the time Rose arrived, in the 1970s, it had become a disorganized collection of haphazardly assembled properties. After dumping the money losers, he began looking for investments that fit with Holiday's core business of food and shelter and quickly zeroed in on casinos.

It was hardly a whim, for his father was a slot machine manager in Las Vegas. More recently he had watched as legitimate investors and professional managers transformed the once sordid gambling business. First Hilton, one of the top names in the hospitality industry, bought two casino hotels in Las Vegas. Then Harrah's, the classiest casino operator in Nevada, received approval from the Securities and Exchange Commission to go public. Wall Street kept its distance, but the first issue of stock sold out immediately and soon Harrah's had the industry's first institutional investor, a major insurance firm.

Like Donald, Rose saw legalized gambling in New Jersey as a

golden opportunity and began scouring Atlantic City for a site as soon as Resorts opened. Unlike the developer, however, Rose went through a methodical decision-making process. After commissioning a study to find out whether current guests cared if Holiday got into the casino business (they didn't), he used the results to override the antigambling faction on Holiday's board of directors and buy Harrah's. Once in Atlantic City, he continued in the same deliberate fashion, ordering studies, writing reports and memos, then slowly steamrollering ahead.

But what worked at Holiday was anathema to the Trump Organization, which had no studies, no reports, and no layers of authority. "There was just Donald," said Jeff Walker, who worked for the developer for more than a decade and never wrote a memo. "You went to him for every major decision." When Donald was asked what sorts of marketing surveys and other homework he did before deciding to go into Atlantic City, he simply pointed to his nose. "There," he said. "That's all the study I need."

Not only did Rose and Donald have radically different styles, they also had significantly different markets in mind. Because Rose wanted a consistent earnings picture, he preferred the same middle-class, middle-aged slot players with whom Holiday had done well at the marina; Donald was willing to take on high rollers with winning streaks because he was after the more glamorous image of table games and assumed that the house would come out ahead over time.

Long before the property opened, the relationship had turned sour. "Donald would say something like 'Let's use Cadillac limos, a friend of mine does a great job, so-and-so from the U.N. uses his limos, so let's strike a deal with him,'" said Darrell Leury, a Harrah's executive at the jointly owned facility. "His decision-making style was, Let's do it." But other executives from Harrah's would insist on a cost-benefit breakdown that compared lease prices from Donald's friend with buying vehicles and hiring drivers, and when the developer found out about the time-consuming delay he would blow up. "There were two different approaches," Leury said, "and they were at loggerheads all the time about everything."

Donald was partly to blame. As he later bragged in *The Art of the*

Deal, when Rose first brought his board of directors to Atlantic City to examine the property, the developer faked construction on the site, instructing bulldozers to drive back and forth so as to impress the suits with his progress. Then, during the actual construction, the developer refused to make much-needed changes, such as adding more elevators, because the costs would eat into his fee.

Harrah's executives compounded the problem by insisting that they were the experts and acting so disdainful toward Donald's employees that one top executive said he felt like a construction worker with a dirty undershirt. Then Harrah's made its name noticeably larger than Donald's on the official logo of what was to be called Harrah's Boardwalk Casino-Hotel at Trump Plaza. When the developer saw the logo, he was furious—and with good reason, for his ownership of the New Jersey Generals had brought so much attention that his name was arguably better known than Harrah's.[32] Apparently agreeing, Harrah's emphasized the developer's name in advertising and later agreed to shorten the casino hotel's name to Trump Plaza.

By the opening, both sides were doing their best to undermine each other. Donald did not come through with the parking garage stipulated in the partnership agreement, which cut into business but would lower the price tag if he managed to buy Holiday out. In turn, Harrah's tried to avoid its contractual obligation to sell out to Donald in the event of low revenues by setting its performance goals so low that it could not fail to meet them.

Less than a year later, the relationship between the two partners collapsed. The immediate cause was the Casino Control Commission's totally unexpected refusal to grant a license to the Hilton Hotel Corporation only three months before the scheduled opening of its new $320 million casino. The stated reason for the denial was the unsavory record of a former Hilton attorney, Sidney Korshak, who was a legendary force in the entertainment industry; the unstated reason was the refusal of Hilton Hotels and current owner Barron Hilton to be sufficiently obsequious to commission members. Without any discussion with Holiday, Donald immediately began negotiating with Hilton to buy the new casino, which was located on the marina next to Harrah's.

The deal had gotten its start when Ben Lambert, then a Hilton board member, told the developer of licensing difficulties.[33] As Lambert knew, Donald's antitrust lawsuit against the NFL did not sit well with Barron Hilton, part owner of an NFL team called the San Diego Chargers. Playing peacemaker and matchmaker, Lambert held a dinner party at his elegant Manhattan town house and introduced the two men. During the course of the evening, the developer and the hotelier, heir to hotel chain founder Conrad Hilton, had a private conversation in the garden. But Barron's financial transactions were severely constrained by his father's will, and he was still too enraged at being barred from Atlantic City to start figuring out an exit strategy.

Soon after the chat in the garden, Golden Nugget owner Steve Wynn made an unsolicited takeover bid for the whole Hilton chain. To fight him off, Hilton would need cash; suddenly, Donald's overtures were welcomed with open arms. But because the opening of Hilton's new Atlantic City facility was imminent, everything was on a take-it-or-leave-it basis, with no time for the master negotiator to employ his bargaining skills or even to inspect what he would be buying. Instead he would have to hand over $320 million, trusting his guess that what Hilton considered the finest structure it had ever built would be good enough for him.

First, though, the developer would have to obtain the $320 million. Ordinarily the last place he would have looked for help was a big New York bank, for such institutions still had deep reservations about the gambling industry. As it happened, however, Barron Hilton had a seat on the board of Manufacturers Hanover, the bank that had given Donald his first construction loan for the Grand Hyatt. In the past, Manny Hanny president John Torrell had stoutly insisted that he would not loan money for Atlantic City and that he required collateral he could see out his window—that is, New York real estate. But after the developer sent him a sheaf of casino reports, circling the profits with a fat green felt-tip pen, Torrell began to see certain virtues in faraway New Jersey.

After making sure that seller and buyer were willing to overlook the NFL-USFL fracas, Torrell held his nose and pushed through what would be New York banking's first casino deal, arranging the details so as to avoid public notice. "I lent him three hundred on the phone," Torrell said later. "But there were two conditions, that he and Barron were in love and that he and Ivana would sign the note personally."

There was also a third condition: The developer had to look for long-term financing immediately. This meant Wall Street, but Drexel Burnham, which had been the only investment firm willing to underwrite projects in Atlantic City, turned Donald down. Until recently, this would have sunk his new project, but another Wall Street firm, Bear, Stearns and Company, drawn by the fees Drexel had earned on casino deals, jumped in and floated its first issue for a gambling enterprise. It was Atlantic City's first privately placed bond issue and the first for an individual rather than a publicly traded company. The result was a $353 million mortgage-bond issue that gave Donald 100 percent financing and a $5 million fee. He would have to meet a higher interest rate than with the bank, but he would be out from under the personal guarantees. In case of default, the holders would have no claim on any other assets.

Harrah's executives were furious to find their supposed partner in direct competition with their flagship casino. In May, just one year after the doors opened at what was now Trump Plaza, the sniping became open warfare. On the opening day of the developer's new casino, Trump Castle, Harrah's filed suit against his use of his own name. The developer retaliated with what might be called his personal trump card: the media. In the tightly regulated, corporate environment of Atlantic City, his breezy, flamboyant style had made him a favorite of the local press. When reporters called, he had one story after another about Harrah's supposed incompetence and mistakes.[34]

Doing so was business as usual for Donald, but for Rose this created a nightmare situation. The chief executive officer of a publicly held company and answerable to stockholders, Rose found himself going toe to toe with an antagonist answerable only to himself and for whom there was no such thing as bad publicity. At the same time, Donald's team launched a direct offensive through long, bristling letters; reportedly Robert was particularly skillful at composing them. Soon nasty missives filled with purple prose were shooting back and forth.[35]

Ultimately Mike Rose was a guy who colored within the lines and followed the rules, and Donald was not. He liked fighting in public, he liked dragging his partner through the mud, and most of all, he liked winning. Rose sued for peace, and Donald bought out Harrah's interest in Trump Plaza the next March, using the same financial methods he had put together to buy what would be Trump Castle from Hilton.[36]

TWO YEARS AFTER OPENING one casino hotel, of which he owned only half, Donald Trump was the sole owner of two casino hotels in Atlantic City. He controlled 120,000 square feet of casino floor space, slightly more than two football fields and double the casino floor at Resorts, the second largest of the city's 11 casinos. Together, his two properties were grossing about $30 million per month, or 19 percent of the market, the highest market share of any casino company in town. By just about any index, he was the most powerful person there. It was time to start doing things his way.[37]

On March 14, three days after becoming sole owner of Trump Plaza, Donald held a press conference to announce that he would begin construction on the very object over which he and Holiday had parted ways, the long-postponed garage. He also told the assembled reporters that he might change the name of Trump Plaza once again, to Trump's Palace. Although Caesars, which had a second casino in Las Vegas named Caesars Palace, had sued to protect the word *palace*, Donald expressed confidence his use would not be a problem. "You have the palace and you have the castle, hence you have the kingdom," he said, sounding like a little boy playing with his favorite toys.[38] Then he denounced a project tied to the new casino. In order to prepare for future development, the state had required Hilton, and now Donald, to participate in an ambitious and expensive effort to widen and upgrade marina-area roads, a plan that the developer refused to follow and dismissed as "ridiculous."

Theoretically, Donald's refusal should have triggered the loss of his license. But at license renewal hearings three months later, he defended his behavior by claiming that Hilton attorneys had not fully informed him of the obligation. Although Hilton heatedly denied the charge and even presented the bill for the hundreds of pages of photocopied materials the attorneys had provided to the developer, the Casino Control Commission voted to renew. "I think they knew full well that this man hadn't told the truth," said deputy public advocate David Sciarra, who opposed renewal. "But they really wanted his money in Atlantic City."[39]

Donald had won the battle and the war. From now on, he could write his own ticket in Atlantic City. This meant approval for a $30 million, eight-floor addition to the Castle, even though he had refused to pay for traffic problems caused by the Castle. It also meant quitting the Atlantic City Casino Association, an industry trade group. Supposedly he did so because it failed to get a legislative okay for 24/7 gambling, but in reality it was because he did not need it any more than he had needed the Real Estate Board of New York, which he had also scorned. He did not want to recognize the other members as his equals, and he did not want to have anyone else—an individual, a corporation, or a trade group—make decisions for him. He would take care of himself, by himself.[40]

He would start by using his gaming license as a hunting license.[41] His first target was Holiday, parent corporation of Harrah's, where he purchased stock and started making loud takeover noises. Unlike ordinary corporate raiders, who tend to keep quiet, he was actually empowered to run a casino property. This meant that when he talked takeover, the market listened, the stock appreciated, and he could almost automatically count on a quick profit. And indeed, after takeover rumors pushed up the price of Holiday's stock, Donald sold his holdings for a profit of $12.6 million, which he inflated to $35 million when talking to the press. Nor was that his only gain; to make itself less desirable, Holiday swallowed a so-called poison pill, a $2.6 billion junk-bond issue that put it heavily into debt and left it too strapped to spend much on the Castle's most direct competition, Harrah's Marina.

Encouraged by such easy pickings, Donald tried the same maneuver again, this time buying stock in Bally's. Like Holiday, Bally's loaded up on debt—in this case, purchasing another Atlantic City casino, the

Golden Nugget, from Steve Wynn for an eye-popping $440 million. By so doing, Bally's became the second holder of two casinos in town. As such, it was the one outfit the developer could not take over because state regulations prohibited ownership of more than three casinos, and he already had two. But Donald was scarcely the loser, for he made $15 million, which he publicly rounded up to $21 million, from Bally's repurchase of his stock, and Bally, like Holiday, was now too debt-laden to compete effectively in Atlantic City.[42]

Presumably to avert unwelcome shareholder suits, Holiday and Bally's avoided calling the developer's actions "greenmail," the industry term for buying large blocks of stock with the intention of selling them back to the issuing company at a premium. But the Federal Trade Commission filed a two-count complaint against Donald for stock manipulation, and he eventually paid $750,000 to settle the case. Aside from a little modest throat clearing, the Casino Control Commission, charged with monitoring possible predatory behavior among casino operators, remained silent.[43] But even if its members had spoken up, they could have done little to prevent the ultimate outcome of these events. The take-home lesson for the casino industry was how easily it could float huge offerings of junk bonds. In less than a decade, New Jersey executive assistant attorney general Anthony Parrillo told one reporter, Atlantic City's casinos went from "a cash-rich and soundly capitalized industry" to "a debtor business hooked on junk." Donald had enriched himself by $27.6 million, but he had also helped open a financial Pandora's box. In the years to come, he would be among those most deeply affected by the consequences.[44]

———◦———

DONALD DID NOT VIEW his success as reason to relax. If anything, he worked harder. Whatever he had done, he wanted to do something more the next time. The exaggerations for which he was known and often ridiculed in the outside world were meant to impress, but they were also a way of challenging himself, of setting up a remote and imaginary benchmark in the sky and then pushing himself to achieve it.

Almost any time was potential work time, and he had a strong

aversion to wasting it. In practical terms this meant that he had an extremely short attention span. "He gets bored really easily," said Vivian
Serota, an acquaintance who first met the Trumps back in the Le Club
days. "If you talk to him and he isn't interested in what you have to say,
his mind is somewhere else. He isn't there, even though he's standing in
front of you."

He spent every day at his desk and then, in the evening, took a pile
of papers upstairs to his apartment to read over. "He never really re-
laxes," said his sister Maryanne. "We're all like that. You can be sitting
watching TV and the mind is going a hundred miles an hour. That's the
way Donald is, and the way Dad was." For both men, life was about making deals, and when the action was the busiest and the tension the highest, Donald later wrote, he felt the way other people do on vacation.[45]

A man who slept little, Donald expected employees to be on duty
round the clock. "I woke up every morning at five or six, when he'd call
with his first idea or his first complaint," recalled Blanche Sprague, a
Trump executive whose roles included construction supervisor, apartment broker, and hatchet woman.[46] "Donald would say, 'I just drove by
the site and something needs to be taken care of.' " Even an empty soda
can in front of a building site would bring a predawn call expressing severe disappointment. "Until I met him," Sprague said, "I thought I was
the most hyper, intense, almost unbelievable perfectionist, but then I
realized I was very low down on the ladder."

The organizational model on the twenty-sixth floor of Trump
Tower was perhaps closest to a wheel. At the center was Donald, constantly pressuring everyone to give their all and more. At his side was
executive secretary Norma Foerderer, a former foreign service staffer in
Tunisia who answered a classified ad in the late 1970s and had been
working for Donald ever since. An elegant presence in designer business suits and spike heels, she filtered the constant flood of invitations
and requests and tried to nudge Donald back on track whenever he had,
in her estimation, gone too far astray.

Radiating out from the center of the wheel were spokes connect-
ing Donald to each top staff member. Although these key executives,
fewer than a dozen in all, had considerable leeway, the developer did
not surrender any actual power. He signed checks, read documents, in-

terrogated everyone about assignments, and did not hesitate to call the people they were calling, just as his father had always done.

There was no formal business plan, no development strategy. Instead Donald would come up with ideas, do the preliminary calculations in his head, then tell someone to get moving on it. Usually there was a conversation about the idea with Harvey Freeman; sometimes the developer heeded what Freeman had to say, other times he ignored it. "It didn't make any difference that you had never done something before," Jeff Walker said. "You got an assignment, you went off and did it, didn't let anything get in your way. Move it, knock it down. He wouldn't tolerate it, neither should you."

Most of the time the developer sat behind an imposing burled-rosewood desk in his big corner office and talked on the telephone as people walked in and out of the room. "They'd stop by my desk and I'd say green light, red light, or amber, depending on his mood," said executive secretary Rhona Graff, who sat outside the developer's door and maintained his schedule. "But even if it was green, they knew they would have only a minute." When things weren't going as Donald thought they should, or fast enough, or both, he might erupt like a volcano, screaming, yelling profanities, hurling accusations of laziness and incompetence; those who lasted were those who learned not to argue back. Or he might dispatch someone, most often Sprague, to irritate staffers and stir them up. "He used me to annoy other people," she said. "He really believed that having people fighting and in conflict for approval made them work harder."

He was in control of almost every situation from the start. One way was to turn on the charm. "When he wanted to be attractive, it was like he just pushed a button in his body and became a matinee idol," Sprague said. "People walked in with a very specific idea of what they wanted and walked out doing just what he wanted and feeling lucky as could be." Another was to hire those who had dared go toe-to-toe with him, for he wanted people willing to face challenges. A third was to include a high proportion of women within his inner circle. An enlightened move, it was also smart, for they worked hard to prove themselves in what was still a man's world.

"There was nothing sexual in those relationships, but it was more than employer-employee," said Alan Lapidus. "They all needed Daddy's approval." The way to earn it was to be aggressive, competent, and tough. But Donald would be a rare man if the calculus of placing so many women in top slots did not include the notion, however unconscious, that it might be easier asserting authority over them than over men.

There were two exceptions to any assumption of female pliability. One was Louise Sunshine, whose years of service had earned her a 5 percent share of the profits in the Trump Plaza cooperative apartment building in Manhattan.[47] In late 1985 she quit abruptly. According to Donald and Sprague, Sunshine left because she and Sprague loathed each other. Sunshine said that she left because Donald had saddled her with a $1 million tax bill on her share in Trump Plaza and then told her to sell out to him in order to pay it. "I think this was his way of telling me 'I'm still the boss around here,' " Sunshine later told *Vanity Fair*. She sued and the case was eventually settled for $2.7 million, enough to cover the taxes and give her a tidy profit.

The other exception was Ivana.[48] She had not intended to be an exception; indeed, she had spent years attempting to mold herself into the perfect consort. An early adaptation was speaking Donald-style, dotting her heavily accented, ungrammatical sentences with expletives. "The first time we met, she was saying things like 'It's so incredible fucking party,' and 'Look at it, it is fucking wonderful,' " said Chicago writer Sugar Rautbord, who subsequently became a close friend. "She was so beautiful and glossy, and she spoke in such a soft, silky voice, and then out came these words that she had obviously borrowed from her husband's business vocabulary."

Like Donald, Ivana seemed to run on multiple tracks, always mentally checking off an endless list of tasks—the suitcases unpacked, the phone calls returned, and, especially, everything kept cleaner than clean. Obsessed about cleanliness and worried about germs, Donald avoided shaking hands whenever possible, and when it was not possible, he washed his hands afterward. Perhaps in part because of his father's meticulousness and his own years in a spit-shined military school, he also demanded that his environment be constantly cleaned and polished. Accordingly, Ivana was fastidious, insisting that carpets be vacuumed immediately before she or her husband stepped on them, that sheets be changed daily, and that guests remove their shoes so as not to scuff marble floors.

Her sense of discipline extended to family life as well. In January 1984, when she had Eric, her third child, she kept a full schedule until the last minute, arranging an induced labor late on Friday so as not to interfere with Donald's business day. According to a close friend, society reporter Nikki Haskell, Ivana lunched at Le Cirque, was in the delivery room promptly at six, and by nine was walking around in a black peignoir being toasted with Dom Pérignon champagne.[49] For Donny, six years older than Eric, and Ivanka, three years older, Ivana provided complete schedules; their lives, supervised by nannies, were full of lessons and sports and the elaborate, expensive birthday parties children of the very rich tend to have in Manhattan. At every school function a parent or, more often, a nanny was present, and on Halloween the costumed children paraded around the twenty-sixth floor of Trump Tower as the staff oohed and aahed. Before Christmas a nanny would take them over to FAO Schwarz and note which toys they liked, and those that received high marks would be purchased, wrapped, and placed in readiness under the tree.

Ivana did her homework. She knew the names of the maître d's, the wine waiters, and the photographers, and she knew the names of their wives and which ones had just had children. She learned the names of party guests and thumbnail sketches so that she could make introductions and small talk. Whatever the occasion, she would play the appropriate role. One summer she held a number of ladies' lunches and hired musician Christopher Mason to entertain guests at each one with the same specially composed parody. "Ivana was great," Mason said later. "Every time I'd sing, she'd open her eyes wide and look totally surprised and say, 'Vot! I pay heem money and den he insults me!' " During dinner parties at Trump Tower, Donald would vanish as soon as he'd made whatever contacts he considered useful, while she would play gracious hostess all evening, cementing business connections and extending social neworks.

But her efforts were in vain. At one time, the aggression that Donald and Ivana had in such abundance had seemed to prove that they were made for each other. Both reached automatically for challenges; both seemed to operate only in high gear. They seemed true partners, in work as well as at home. But they were not; they were mirrors. They both wanted to be winners. For a while that was a bond, but eventually it became an obstacle—two people can't both be first.

No matter whom he was with, Donald had to compete, and he had to come out ahead. The primal rival was his father, and in every sphere Donald seemed to be reenacting this ongoing Oedipal contest. Throughout his life, his second wife, Marla Maples, later told a reporter, all Donald really wanted was "to impress Daddy, to show Daddy what Donald can do." As a kid, he broke all the rules Fred had laid down, gravitating to the toughest kid in the entire school and the raw competition of sports; as an adult, he went into his father's same field and far outstripped his accomplishments. "I'm lucky Manhattan wasn't his thing," Donald said. "If he had come to Manhattan, he would have been very successful, but to do my own thing I would then have had to go somewhere else."[50]

Even when the contest was wildly uneven, he still had to win. One such occasion occurred when he played catch with his sister Maryanne's son, David, in the senior Trumps' backyard on Midland Parkway. "David was good, and Donald was superb," Maryanne recalled. "Donald kept throwing it faster and faster, harder and harder, until I hear this crack and the ball hit David's head. Donald had to beat the seven-year-old." A close source said that on another occasion Donald played golf with Robert's father-in-law, who was still recovering from hip replacement surgery. When the older man, then in his mid-seventies, hit the ball into a sand trap, Donald walked in and buried it.

"He likes to deal with people who are tough," Maryanne said. "But he also likes hearing about how he's the greatest—not just the greatest, but the best of the greatest." Perhaps if Ivana had been willing to spend her life telling him that, the marriage would have flourished. But the strength that her husband had welcomed when he was starting out at the Grand Hyatt did not disappear. Instead it had grown, and she had become more self-confident and more competent. Initially her unfamiliarity with American ways and her poor English had held her back, but now she was a rival, at least in his mind. Now he had to take control.

"Donald plays head games with people," Blanche Sprague said. "He looks at you and knows within five minutes where your buttons are." Ivana's button was her competitiveness, and her husband pushed it for all it was worth, constantly setting the hurdles higher so that she had to be harder and more combative. "He'd say, 'Ivana, I want you to go from there to there, from east to west, don't let anything stop you,' " Jeff Walker recalled. "Then he'd say to one of these other women, 'Go from west to east and don't stop,' and he'd sit back and watch the fallout. It could be called creative conflict, but it doesn't work with your wife, whom you have to get into bed with at night."

After a while even this grew old. Sexual passion between the two had apparently waned early on and, for him, given way to indifference and periodic hostility. He made disparaging remarks about her in public, as well as suggestive and sometimes lewd comments about other women. He suggested an open marriage, but she scornfully rejected the idea. Another man might have pursued a divorce, but this would cause his children and his parents great pain.

But now he had an offer Ivana couldn't refuse. He would make her the chief executive officer of Trump's Castle. That she had no experience at anything other than modeling and interior design didn't seem to bother the developer. Presumably he considered it more important to have a member of his own family in charge of this vital asset. More to the point, he wanted her to be out of New York City. He had already established the fact that he could do what he wanted in his business life. Now it was time to do what he wanted in his personal life as well.

CHAPTER SIX

The Tallest Building in the World

Although Donald had been rich all his life, his assets had not been liquid—he could gain access to his own wealth only by selling holdings. His illiquidity, to use the jargon, was a frustrating limitation. No matter how famous he became, he had to approach bankers with his hat in his hand to put together a project. And because his buildings, though profitable, did not rapidly generate huge sums of cash, bankers were cautious in lending to him.

His acquisition of the two casinos in Atlantic City changed everything more than he had dared to imagine. With an annual cash flow in the neighborhood of $60 million and only $30 million in interest payments to cover, one knowledgeable source said afterward, the casino business seemed to the developer literally the greatest thing on earth. Shareholders might have pressured him to use the excess cash to retire his growing load of debt. But because the Trump Organization was private, the developer did not have to worry about whether his balance sheet looked attractive to outside eyes. Instead he could plunge casino proceeds into new ventures, trusting that they would generate enough money to pay off his debts when they came due.

The only drawback for Donald, the source said, was the need to keep quiet. If the public had any idea how profitable the gambling industry was, everyone would want in on it. Then the developer would face more casino competition, pressure for higher taxes, unionization, and interest from the Mob—a possible scenario that often forced him to poor-mouth it and complain about the licensing process and the number of poor people in Atlantic City rather than brag about his success.

With the casino money washing in at the same time that New York was in the midst of a real estate boom that would greatly increase property values, Donald had become extremely wealthy—the fiftieth richest person in America, according to *Forbes*, which in 1986 estimated his fortune at $700 million.[1]

Whether this evaluation was accurate was impossible for anyone to prove, including the developer himself. In part this was because traditional accounting rules do not fit well with the real estate business. As a rule, accountants value assets at their cost or their market value, whichever is lowest. This means that a balance sheet registers only a decrease in the value of a building, not a rise. Further, because the depreciation of improvements reduces the book value of real estate, it is worth less on the books each year even if its market value goes up.

But there was another reason for the difficulty in checking the magazine's numbers: Because Donald's assets were privately held, he did not have to make his balance sheets public. The only figures he released were his own estimates of the market value of his holdings—estimates that tended to be high.

There was no doubt, though, that Donald was now rich in his own right. He had money and access to more money. So far, every action and every purchase in his luxurious life had been highly strategic—part of a plan to make him appear richer and more important. Now, though, he was in a position to buy himself a trophy. Although he did not know it, the object he would choose would provide a distant link to the enormous assets that had bankrolled Monte Cristo, the remote mining town northeast of Seattle where his grandfather, Friedrich Trump, had his first mining adventure.

DONALD CHOSE a spectacular mansion in Palm Beach, Florida, called Mar-a-Lago. Built at the height of the 1920s boom, the house owed its existence to the novel quandary facing the very richest Americans: how to handle their unprecedented affluence. The wealthiest of them all, John D. Rockefeller Sr., agonized over what to do with the enormous sum he accumulated at the helm of Standard Oil. A devout Baptist, he lived relatively moderately and donated vast amounts to philanthropy.[2]

Henry Flagler, Rockefeller's second in command, had little urge to give away his wealth. Nor did he spend it underwriting friends' get-rich-quick schemes, as Rockefeller had done with Monte Cristo. Instead Flagler moved to Florida and created a new opportunity for conspicuous consumption: Palm Beach. In 1893, when he first came to this barrier island off the east coast of Florida, Palm Beach had one hotel, a small population of year-round residents, and 20,000 exotic palms grown from coconuts washed ashore after the wreck of a cargo ship. After constructing a rail link to the North, Flagler built two exclusive resorts and imposed a strict social code requiring formal dress even on the beach. Soon Palm Beach became WASP society's most fashionable winter gathering place.[3]

In 1927 a beautiful blonde cereal heiress named Marjorie Merriweather Post created an $8 million fantasy there, naming it Mar-a-Lago because it stretched from the ocean side of Palm Beach to Lake Worth, the inland waterway between the island and the mainland.[4] A monstrous structure built of Italian stone and fifteenth-century Spanish tiles, the Moorish-Romanesque mansion had 58 bedrooms, 33 bathrooms, and 27 servants' rooms.[5]

From this grandiose citadel, chockablock with antique furniture, frescoes, porcelains, and silver, Post ruled over Palm Beach society, filling the house with rich and often famous guests for the entire winter season. By 1973, when she died, the era of such unstinting excess was over and the estate had become an enormous white elephant. In her will she donated Mar-a-Lago to the federal government, but it could not afford the upkeep and gave the mansion back. It went on the market for $20 million and languished there for the next decade, too expensive for old money types but too old-fashioned for most new money. But as soon as Donald saw it he made a bid, and in December 1985 he bought it for $8 million, the same amount it had cost Post to build the house in 1927.[6]

He now had bragging rights for the Tiffany resort's Tiffany property, an estate that he touted as being even more superluxurious than William Randolph Hearst's San Simeon in California. Being able to buy what Establishment types could no longer afford should have been a moment to savor. So should the lavish 12-page cover story on Ivana, Mar-a-Lago's new mistress, which appeared in *Town & Country*.[7] Perhaps best of all, thanks to banker Conrad Stephenson, the $10 million Chase mortgage had gone unrecorded, which suggested that Donald had forked over the entire purchase price in cash, even though he had paid only $2,811 out of his own pocket.

But it was stultifying to play lord of the manor in a place so genteel that merchants could not display sale signs in store windows and quality tended to mean old and a little worn—a Persian carpet that had been in the family for decades, say. And it was positively galling to have to be polite to people who scorned his skyscrapers as too glitzy, who were still grousing about the Bonwit Teller sculptures, and whose welcome was decidedly cool. Donald wanted to fly down on his own plane on weekends and bring along people like Yankees owner George Steinbrenner and actor Don Johnson, not settle in for the season and cultivate the doyennes of local society. He wanted to wear his usual dark business suit, not the Palm Beach uniform of crested navy blazer and white linen pants. He wanted to tell people his opinion, not stand in little clusters at cocktail parties and chat about gardening and polo.

Like Jay Gatsby, Donald had surrounded himself with great excess. But unlike F. Scott Fitzgerald's character, the developer had no desire to pass for old money and considered most of those who benefited from it to be phonies. Indeed, he was not at all reticent about how he made his money but took every opportunity to boast about just how clever he had been. Nor was there a Daisy at whose feet he wished to lay himself and his material possessions; he did not for a minute consider Ivana to be made of finer stuff than himself. "I would never buy Ivana any decent jewels or pictures," he told friends. "Why give her negotiable assets?"

So Donald did Palm Beach his way. He installed a large oil painting of himself in a reception area and filled the sterling silver picture frames on side tables with magazine covers featuring him. The former owner had installed a berm on the ocean side of the mansion so as to see water rather than the highway that ran between the estate and the ocean; he removed the berm so that drivers could get a clear view of his newest trophy.[8] Rather than using invitations to ensconce himself in Palm Beach society, he employed them as paybacks for business and political favors and as markers for use in the future.

Ever the savvy entrepreneur, he also sued to have his real estate taxes lowered, claiming in classic Fred Trump fashion that his concern was not the $81,525 under dispute, but the principle at stake. Then he applied for a zoning variance so as to subdivide his property and build mini-mansions. Annoyed by the constant jet traffic overhead, he and neighbor George Petty, a Canadian-born paper pulp magnate, backed two anti-noise local political candidates, launched an anti-noise organization, and sued the county over the issue. In all seriousness, Trump proposed that the newly expanded Palm Beach International Airport pick up stakes and move 10 miles south.

But this was not New York City. The courts upheld his real estate taxes and he never obtained the rezoning he sought. The candidates lost, the lawsuit fizzled, and the airport stayed put.[9] Perhaps heeding the developer's complaints about noise, the airport strictly enforced flight curfews, which meant that Donald couldn't fly in or out on his own plane at night.

Restless, he looked for new projects. Across Lake Worth in West Palm Beach, the separate town founded by Henry Flagler to house the workers at his resorts, sat a huge, not quite finished, and almost empty condominium complex.[10] Not long after it was finished, the builder had defaulted on $94 million in obligations, reportedly the largest foreclosure in Palm Beach County history. Ignoring Jerry Schrager's protests, Donald snapped up the development for $41 million, financing the deal with a $60 million mortgage from Marine Midland. He'd seen his father spot a distressed property that locals had ignored; sweep in, buy it for a fraction of what it had cost to build, and, with much fanfare, lay on the spit and polish; then promote it like crazy until the rent rolls filled up. Now he would do the same. Changing the name to Trump Plaza of the Palm Beaches, he announced that Chrysler Corporation President Lee Iacocca was in on the deal, raised prices, and began a national advertising campaign in upscale publications. At the same time, he bid on hotels in Aspen and Los Angeles, offered to build a $250 million domed sports stadium in Queens, bought shares in Alexander's, a New York department store chain, and talked about opening his own chain of upscale stores, named Trumps.[11]

It didn't matter if he made money on these deals, he told Schrager. "If I get my name in the paper, if people pay attention, that's what matters," Donald said. "To me, that means it's a success."[12] By that measure, these moves were a series of triumphs. Each produced a flurry of media coverage, fanned by the developer's well-placed calls to reporters who then quoted "a source close to the Trump Organization" and, occasionally, Trump Organization "spokesman" John Barron.

———=◉=———

BUT THERE WAS A FAR LARGER TRIUMPH in the offing: Donald's long-deferred dream of developing the old 60th Street Penn Central rail yards.[13] Five years earlier, community opposition and lack of financing had forced him to drop his option to buy the property. An Argentine developer named Francisco Macri had gained control of the site and shouldered a project called Lincoln West through the city's torturous approvals process.

It was a pyrrhic victory, for the approval came only after Macri agreed to a staggering collection of amenities, including $30 million to repair a nearby subway station.[14] Because these concessions drove the project costs to stratospheric levels, Conrad Stephenson, the Chase banker attached to the project, began to express doubts. Eventually Stephenson started pushing to bring in a New York developer to cut tougher, more financially sound deals. In the spring of 1984, after on-and-off negotiations with Macri and Donald, the banker abruptly called for repayment of Macri's $75 million debt.

To Macri and many community activists, it seemed clear that Stephenson was trying to deliver the site to his favorite client, who was now ready to pick up where he left off in 1979.[15] Stephenson, who was famous for his rapport with clients and accustomed to intervening when he saw someone making a misstep, had a different explanation. Macri walked in with a big entourage, Stephenson said, and insisted on doing things his way. When the banker objected, Macri threatened to back out of the deal, and Stephenson called his bluff. "We had run to the end of our court," Stephenson said later. "We'd just had enough."

In January 1985 Donald bought the 74.6-acre site, of which 18.5 acres were underwater, for $117 million, which he immediately rounded down to a better-sounding $95 million. It was, perhaps, a forgivable display of vanity, given the achievement involved. Forced by circumstances to relinquish the yards, he had built his fame and fortune through other projects; now, in a near miracle, he had control of the property once again, and this time he appeared to have sufficient wherewithal to proceed. Unable to get to first base with the community or the banks a decade earlier, now he could simply take over Macri's deal.

This meant taking over the huge amenity package as well, but Donald evidently believed he had the solution: his newest lawyer, Allen Schwartz, who had never handled a development deal but happened to be Mayor Ed Koch's former law partner, former corporation counsel, and closest friend. For insurance, Donald, Fred, and the Trump Management Corporation donated a total of $33,250 to the mayor's re-election campaign.[16] As soon as Koch won his third term, Schwartz convened a meeting at the mayor's office and managed to have the amenities put on long-term hold. In effect, Donald had won the game once again. The amenities remained in limbo for years and eventually underwent big reductions under a different set of city officials.

Meanwhile the developer began laying the groundwork for a brand-new design.[17] Unlike the complex he had planned back in the 1970s, essentially a greatly expanded version of what his father had built decades earlier, the new buildings would not be brick or midlevel, but towering skyscrapers sheathed in luxury materials. Because underwriting from public sector housing programs was no longer available, these buildings would be products of the private sector, with rich tenants paying market-rate rents. But Donald was still the son of Fred in one crucial respect: He would somehow find a way to get the government to pick up a major portion of the tab.

He had often mentioned how terrible it was that New York didn't have the world's tallest building, and this was presumably a lament over the fact that *he* didn't have it. Once he had even floated a proposal to erect such a building in lower Manhattan and slapped a *Chicago Tribune* critic who called the idea "one of the silliest things anyone could inflict on New York" with a $500 million defamation suit that was quickly thrown out of court.[18] Now that he had the West Side yards in hand, it was time to hire the architect perhaps most closely associated with extreme height: Helmut Jahn, the Chicago-based designer who was already working on the tallest building in Europe.[19] Told to create a project that would be two and a half times as large as Macri's, the German-born Jahn, once dubbed Baron von High-Tech because of his futuristic glass-and-stone towers, was all excitement.[20]

Donald used a 60 *Minutes* interview with Mike Wallace, broadcast on a Sunday evening in November, to announce plans for what the developer described as "the greatest piece of land in the world." At a packed Grand Hyatt press conference the next day, he unveiled a model of a massive 18.5-million-square-foot development he called "Television City." Sandwiched between the West Side community and the elevated highway on the western edge of the site, the huge complex included the world's largest television studios, the world's biggest shopping center, and, of course, the world's tallest building.

"Do you guys love it?" he crowed exuberantly to then–City Planning Commission chairman Herb Sturz and other officials.[21]

The statistics for the 13-block-long project were mind-boggling: a huge 15-story technical center, seven skyscrapers taller than almost every other building in the city, 7,900 apartments, and 40,000 construction jobs. In the center would be a tapering, triangular, 150-story monolith that looked like a rocket ship and was nearly one-third of a mile high. At 1,670 feet (with a spire and antenna, 1,910 feet), it would restore to New York the world's tallest building title, which had been lost to Chicago's Sears Tower (1,454 feet) in 1974. The whole humongous complex sat on a vast platform, beneath which were the TV studios, the shopping mall, and parking for 8,500 cars.

The largest project in New York City since Rockefeller Center, built in the 1930s, Television City would have to make its way through the same tortuous approvals that Macri had barely survived. Officially titled the Uniform Land Use Review Procedure and known by the inelegant acronym of ULURP, the process included evaluations from the local community board, borough president, City Planning Commission, and, ultimately, a vote by the Board of Estimate. Not wasting a minute, Donald got things rolling that same evening at a two-hour local community board meeting.[22] Appearing before an overflow audience, he enthusiastically pitched the project as "a spectacular city within a city," pledged to "work closely with the community," and responded to comments and questions.

"It looks like the quintessential phallic symbol," said one woman. Another suggested that Donald might have to use helicopters to get any more people into the already overcrowded area. A third declared, "You better prepare yourself for a hell of a fight." The developer smiled at each speaker. "Of all the neighborhoods in New York, this is the one I get, right?" he joked. Then he tried charm: "You folks are not known as pussycats, I can tell you." He walked out grinning and waving his hands in the air like a fighter who's just scored a knockout punch. "I don't expect any trouble from the community," he said later. "I expect they'll be very supportive."

During the months that followed, Donald insisted that he would not make a profit on the world's tallest building and was planning it only because New York needed such a monument. The local residents, he said, would have the benefit of better television reception, a huge new upscale shopping center, and architectural distinction, sorely lacking in adjacent moderate-income brick buildings. This last claim was notable, given that the family fortune came from his father's construction of just such buildings in Brooklyn. But this was Donald, not Fred, and in his view the fact that his project did not fit into the architectural context of Manhattan's Upper West Side was an asset.

"The surrounding area is garbage," he said. "Does that mean everything's got to look like this?"

The press was even less welcoming than the neighborhood.[23] *Time* called the project "screwball," and influential *New York Times* architecture critic Paul Goldberger said that the main rationale for the ugly 150-story building was to distract the eye from Television City's other ugly towers. Firing back, Donald complained to "Page Six," the *New York Post*'s widely read gossip column, that Goldberger had poor taste in clothes. At the Television City press conference, Goldberger later recalled, Donald had complimented him on his investment-banker-style suit. "I think he concluded I cared about clothes and so I'd be vulnerable about it," Goldberger said. "He's good at going for people's weaknesses."

When a study revealed that at certain times of year the shadow of the 150-story building would reach 30 blocks north and all the way across the Hudson River to New Jersey, the complaints grew louder.[24] By June, City Planning Commission chairman Herb Sturz had told Donald that the city would not look favorably on a project that seemed utterly disconnected from the rest of the West Side. To the developer the subtext seemed obvious: "I thought I'd better get rid of the German and get a Jew," he said later. "It'd go over better with Sturz."[25]

Within a week he fired Jahn and went after the anti-Jahn: architect Alex Cooper, whose humane design for Battery Park City, the other major Manhattan development project of the era, had earned universal praise. Unlike Jahn, an autocrat who jetted from one high-profile commission to another, the soft-spoken, easygoing Cooper had spent much of his career in the public sector. There he had earned a reputation for focusing on "the urban fabric"—that is, the scale and feel of whole neighborhoods—and for a design philosophy of thinking smaller instead of larger. Now Donald challenged Cooper, who had denounced Jahn's plan as "too damn big," to come up with something better. "Goddamnit, Cooper, you have to change your image," Donald said. "It's about time you got associated with something huge! And something not so bloody civic!" The arrow hit its target. Shrugging off the horrified reactions of colleagues, Cooper set about trying to make a project big enough for his new client but small enough for everyone else.

Having made end runs around the amenities and design problems, Donald tried to do the same with ULURP and the government subsidies he wanted to underwrite Television City.[26] Back in the mid-1970s the threat of a boarded-up Commodore had produced zoning variances, a leaseback arrangement with the state's Urban Development Corporation, and an enormous tax abatement. This time he hoped to achieve the same results with a different catalyst: the potential loss of NBC, the nation's top network. Although it was the largest tenant at Rockefeller Center, it had long since outgrown its space. Outdated wiring and mechanical systems made routine operations difficult, and major shows like *Saturday Night Live* had to build sets in Queens and then break them up for transport back to Manhattan. Although NBC's lease would not expire for another dozen years, the network was already hunting for a new home. There was plenty of space across the Hudson in New Jersey, but the only alternate New York City site on NBC's short list was on Cooper's drawing board.

If Television City could retain NBC and its 4,000 jobs, the developer reasoned, the city would have no choice but to facilitate zoning approvals and a tax abatement. To get the city to see things his way, he launched a high-pressure campaign that was vintage Donald. At one point he called Deputy Mayor Alair Townsend and gave her a two-hour deadline to decide. In another phone call he pushed Koch to make up his mind that day and added, "I can taste the deal in my mouth."

But it was not the 1970s, and obtaining City Hall endorsement for a project as large and controversial as Television City would require

considerable dexterity. Although Donald continued the family tradi-
tion of large financial contributions to political campaigns, he no longer
had the same network of connections Fred had nurtured so carefully.
Not only did Donald and Koch dislike and distrust each other, but then-
governor Mario Cuomo did not automatically favor the developer's interests. After Cuomo took office, Donald had attended a small dinner
party for major contributors and complained about a 10 percent tax
Cuomo had levied on gains from real estate deals of $1 million or more.
"Donald, it's one of my favorite taxes," Cuomo had replied. "I call it 'the
Trump tax.' "[27]

In the spring of 1986, after months of searching for ways to build
the case for Television City, Donald found the perfect occasion. For six
years he and the rest of New York had watched the city's hapless efforts
to renovate Wollman Memorial Rink. Opened in 1950 in the Central
Park's southeast corner, the large rink was a gift from Kate Wollman, an
80-year-old banking heiress who lived in the Waldorf-Astoria Tower
and had never been on a pair of skates. A much-loved institution that
offered ice-skating in winter and roller-skating in the summer, the facility had closed in 1980 for a two-and-a-half-year, $4.9 million overhaul.
Six years later the tab was up to $12 million and Wollman was still
closed. Worse, the latest prediction was that it would take at least two
more years and another $2 million to finish. To the Koch administra-
tion it was a source of frustration and embarrassment; to Donald, it was
a golden opportunity.

On May 28 he sent a "Dear Ed" letter to the mayor. "I and all other
New Yorkers are tired of watching the catastrophe of Wollman Rink,"
he wrote. "The incompetence displayed in this simple construction
project must be considered one of the greatest embarrassments of your
administration." The job should take four months, he declared. He offered to do it at cost and to manage the rink and its adjacent restaurant
thereafter. In a response dated the same day, the mayor said that he
would be "delighted" to accept the developer's offer to fix up the rink,
although it would not be renamed and the developer could not operate
it. Koch closed by saying, "With bated breath, I await your response,' "
and released both letters publicly. Presumably to his surprise, instead of

hooting at Donald's chutzpah, New Yorkers embraced the idea, and Koch reluctantly green-lighted the makeover.

Now the developer had to live up to his own challenge. After wangling an interest-free construction loan from Chase, he pushed contractor HRH to avoid construction delays and used his newest hire, former city commissioner Tony Gliedman, to get through bureaucratic hurdles. Each morning Donald scrutinized the rink from the high-powered telescope mounted in his sixty-fifth-floor Trump Tower apartment, which was really on the fifty-ninth floor, and throughout the day he monitored progress from the huge windows in his office. Periodically he hiked over to the park for unannounced inspections, after which he often called on-site press conferences.

At the first, in a gesture reminiscent of the huge TRUMP banner he had flung over Grand Central nearly a decade earlier, he posted next to the rink a large sign that made the bold but inaccurate claim "Owner: Trump Ice Inc." Among the numerous press conferences that followed, highlights included the laying-of-the-pipes press conference one day, followed by the pouring-of-the-cement event the next day.

Although the rink would lack Donald's signature mirrors and gilt, it did have one luxury touch: instead of using pedestrian pine for railings, he employed burnished teak. "See this railing?" he pointed out to reporters. "Same railing Onassis had on his boat." The redone rink opened in mid-November, two months ahead of his announced schedule and $750,000 below his announced budget. Like the original benefactor, he was a nonskater; the reason, he said, was that so many people would love to see him fall down. As grateful New Yorkers glided by, he stood in the crisp, sunny weather in his usual dark topcoat, a businessman even on an ice rink.

He had stuck to his word. So did the city. Because he did not pay for the restoration, the city did not budge on the renaming—an idea, the developer insisted, that had never crossed his mind. Instead the city awarded him the contract to operate the rink and dedicated a young Japanese Saphora evergreen to the developer. Although the city considered the tree "appropriate donor recognition," Donald was outraged. "He wanted a sequoia, something huge," said New York City Parks

Commissioner Henry Stern. "He didn't want his name on anything like that [sapling]—he thought of it as the 'Trump stump.' "[28]

The renovation was an impressive accomplishment, although perhaps not quite the superhuman feat it appeared. Donald had given himself a six-month deadline for what he initially called a four-month job, and as a private contractor he did not face the burdensome regulations imposed on public construction to eliminate corruption.[29] But unnoticed by the press and the public, there was also another factor: What the developer did was far easier than what the city had attempted to do.

In the initial design of Central Park by Frederick Law Olmsted, the spot where the rink now stood had been a delicately balanced panorama, with a fanciful gray stone structure known as the Dairy up on a hill and a graceful lawn sloping down to a lake and an adjacent pond. A century later Robert Moses had plopped Wollman Rink and several large, squat buildings square in the middle of Olmsted's vista. When the city closed the rink for repairs in 1980, then–parks commissioner Gordon Davis set out to restore what he could of Olmsted's original contemplative ambiance by making the rink a reflecting pond in the summer. Unfortunately, no engineer could come up with a workable design for both functions, and a supposedly energy-efficient refrigeration method based on Freon instead of the usual brine was a flop.

"We really screwed this up," Davis said later. "It was our version of making the movie *Apocalypse Now.*"[30] When Donald came in, he jettisoned the reflecting pool, poured a new slab over the old rink, and went back to brine. His plan was uglier, more expensive to maintain, and less environmentally conscious—but it worked.[31]

———◦———

THE RESTORATION OF THE RINK was a moment of great triumph for Donald. Although he exploited it for publicity to a degree remarkable even for him, being the can-do hero of Wollman Rink gave him the kind of popular support that could help make Television City happen. Under fire because of political scandals and the departure of Mobil and JCPenney corporate headquarters, Koch seemed disposed to push through the deal.[32] NBC appeared unenthusiastic about relocating in New Jersey and sent technical experts to help design Television City's studio space. The press, primed by the developer's frequent calls, put out story after story emphasizing the import of the situation. Meanwhile, Donald kept all his options open and tried to play the different parties against each other. "We thought we had an opportunity for a quick hit," said Jerry Schrager. "It would have been a grand slam home run for Donald."

But this time, keeping himself at the center of the deal would be Donald's undoing. Instead of negotiating through him, the various parties spoke directly with each other and used him to their advantage. For NBC, the press attention generated by the developer was a great boon. "He was in the forefront, saying that New York cannot afford to lose NBC," said Henry Kanegsberg, the NBC vice president charged with finding a new location. "He was doing it for his own benefit, but it helped us." Alerted by Donald's alarums to the magnitude of its potential loss, Rockefeller Center elbowed its way back into the negotiations and made the case for NBC to stay and remodel—a case that was greatly strengthened, one Rockefeller Center official said later, by city officials' annoyance at Donald's constant leaks to the press.

Koch was already put off by Donald's incessant gloating over the Wollman reconstruction and his coercive tactics. Then the mayor learned that the developer, citing new accounting methods, had slashed his payments to the city from Grand Hyatt profits. Unwilling to take on further profit sharing with Donald or to provide implicit endorsement of zoning approval, Koch rejected the Television City deal at the end of May. Instead of handing the developer the largest tax concessions in city history, he offered a far smaller incentive package that could be used anywhere. Furious, Donald blasted the mayor as "a moron," called for his impeachment, and demanded an investigation of Koch's involvement in his appointees' misdeeds.

"I think I must be doing something right if Donald Trump is squealing like a stuck pig," Koch shot back and referred to the developer as "piggy, piggy, piggy."

Eventually NBC chose to stay at Rockefeller Center.[33] As usual,

Donald shed no public tears. Instead he insisted that he had pulled the plug on the deal because the network "would add nothing to my project" and stepped up his attack on the mayor.[34] His anti-Koch comments and the mayor's responses became regular press features, along with the developer's repeated protests that he would never, ever think of running for mayor himself. In the months to come he made an insult-laced offer to finish the stalled renovation of the Central Park Zoo, noisily volunteered to fix a major bridge that had been closed, talked about spending $2 million on anti-Koch television advertisements, and, after a young woman was brutally raped and nearly killed in Central Park, ran full-page ads in city dailies spurning Koch's call for understanding and instead demanding the return of the death penalty and more police.[35]

＝◎＝

THE LOSS OF NBC at Television City had been a stinging defeat, but Donald quickly bounced back. Three weeks after the mayoral no, the developer put himself back on the sports pages by promoting the first of many lucrative Atlantic City boxing matches.[36] The fight between Michael Spinks and Gerry Cooney, staged on a Monday night in the city's Convention Hall, attracted a bumper crop of high rollers. Afterward they strolled across the aerial walkway to Trump Plaza and wagered six times the average take for that night of the week. The precedent-setting event spurred boxing promoter Don King to coin a new word. He declared Donald to be "telesynergistic," which meant "progress ingeniously planned by geometric progression, the capability to translate dreams into living reality in minimal time at megaprofits."

Continuing his telesynergistic rebound, Donald flew to Moscow on his own jet and talked with officials there about building a capitalist-style luxury hotel. He offered the use of the West Side site for the 1988 Olympic Games, scheduled to be held in strife-torn Korea. Repeating his pattern with Holiday and Bally, he purchased shares in Pan Am and Steve Wynn's Golden Nugget casino in Las Vegas (followed later by Federated Department Stores and Gillette), talked takeover, sold off his holdings, and then exaggerated his profits.[37] As usual, he talked—and talked—to reporters about each of these activities. Each conversation seemed to produce a story, another conversation in reaction to the story, a second story, then a third. "He loves the press," said Edward S. Gordon, a major New York real estate broker. "Whenever anyone calls him, he's talking, he's on stage. He can be in his own room, but he sees the lights go on and he's rolling."[38]

Two months after the biggest defeat of the developer's career, *BusinessWeek* carried his picture on the cover with a caption that read "Donald Trump has conquered New York real estate."[39] *Newsweek* soon followed; its tag line was "Trump: A Billion-Dollar Empire and an Ego to Match."[40] The day after the stock market crash on Black Monday, October 19, 1987, Donald boasted loudly that he had seen it coming, had sold his entire portfolio, and had made $200 million. In fact, he had hung on to certain shares, including those in Alexander's, and had taken a paper loss of more than $22 million.[41] Soon afterward he cheerfully smirked on the cover of *People* under the headline "Too Darn Rich."[42]

IN THE FALL OF 1987 Donald extended the Trump brand in the form of his own book, *The Art of the Deal*, written "with" *New York* magazine staffer Tony Schwartz and published by Random House. Schwartz was not an obvious candidate; two years earlier his article about Donald's efforts to oust tenants at 100 Central Park South had helped turn public sentiment against the developer. But once again Donald hired someone he considered a worthy opponent. Audacious and egotistical, the first-person account is a highly selective retelling of the developer's most successful deals, larded with the same faux frank asides and energetic exaggerations that had served him so well at the negotiating table. Apparently Donald did not care that his grandfather was not, in fact, Swedish; that he had not actually given his elementary school music teacher a black eye;[43] or that he had paid top dollar, not below market, for his land in Atlantic City. Instead he was concerned with being engaging and entertaining. And indeed, the combination of astonishing brashness and relentless optimism that bowled over so many in person had the same effect on the printed page.

At 10 P.M. on Saturday, December 12, klieg lights played over the front of Trump Tower, and a red carpet covered the sidewalk from the curb to the shiny brass entrance. Inside the pink atrium, waiters in white jackets stood at attention, ready to pour champagne. Violinists wearing red sashes played a medley of waltzes and serenades, and disco music blared from the lower level. Christmas lights, red balloons, and red poinsettias were everywhere, and buffet tables were heaped with elegantly arranged platters of food.

As declared at the top of the invitation, it was "The Party of the Year," held to celebrate the publication of The Art of the Deal.[44] At the head of the receiving line stood the tuxedo-clad author, flanked by Ivana and Si Newhouse, close friend to the late Roy Cohn and then-owner of Random House. Filing past them were a gossip column's worth of celebrities: Michael Douglas, Jackie Mason, Cheryl Tiegs, Barbara Walters, Phyllis George, Liz Smith, Joan Rivers, Norman Mailer, Don King. Alongside them came the politicians: Senator Al D'Amato, former governor Hugh Carey, Manhattan borough president Andrew Stein, New York City controller Harrison Goldin, New Jersey governor Thomas Kean. Plus the bankers, investors, lawyers, architects, contractors, and everyone else in the greater New York area who had managed to cadge an invitation. The event, planned by Studio 54 co-founders Steven Rubell and Ian Schrager, supposedly cost $160,000. When it was over, an estimated 2,000 people had celebrated the print debut of one of the most showy, self-involved, and seductive voices of the era.

Also one of the most marketing-oriented. In the months before publication, the developer plugged his upcoming tome at the annual convention of the American Booksellers Association and flew his helicopter up to Connecticut to push the book to regional executives at Waldenbooks, the country's largest mall-based bookstore chain. Then he took Barnes & Noble chief Leonard Riggio to lunch at La Cote Basque and trotted out the same hard-sell tactics he'd used 15 years earlier during his lunch with investment banker Ben Lambert. "[Donald] gets in touch, tugs you by the collar, and pats you on the back," Riggio told the *Wall Street Journal*. Once again the personal touch paid off, for both chains had special displays.

Then Donald and one of Howard Rubenstein's top publicists, Dan Klores, came up with the idea of launching the developer as a presidential candidate. His first foreign policy foray had been a deadpan public offer a few years earlier to serve as an arms negotiator with the Soviet Union. Now he paid $94,000 to run a full-page open letter in the *New York Times*, the *Boston Globe*, and the *Washington Post* that began, "There's nothing wrong with America's Foreign Defense Policy that a little backbone can't cure."[45] As the press speculated energetically about his political aspirations, he insisted on his noncandidacy but gave a speech in New Hampshire, distributed "I ♥ Donald Trump" bumper stickers, and commissioned a telephone poll.

When the findings proved promising, the developer's staff deluged reporters with the numbers: Donald had a 75 percent recognition factor, would be competitive in Republican primaries, and might take more than 20 percent of the votes in a general presidential election.[46] Speaker of the House Jim Wright promptly asked him to host a major Democratic fund-raiser. Although Donald declined, he reaped another publicity windfall—and a best-seller. Within a month of publication, *The Art of the Deal* topped the *New York Times* list and ultimately sold 835,000 hardcover copies, capturing the number 19 position on the list of top sellers for the decade.

Donald had become a superstar, a megacelebrity. His name appeared so often in newspapers that it was impossible to keep count, and he was on the front of so many magazines that the framed covers filled the wall next to his desk. Although *Forbes* continued to place him around midpoint in its list of the 100 richest Americans, the public tended to consider him much closer to the top—possibly number one. Similarly, many assumed that he was the largest landlord in New York, although this was not the case.[47]

But in these matters perception easily outtrumped, as it were, reality. He received payments and media attention for the use of his name on Cadillac cars, Parker pens, eyeglasses, and a board game with his face on the cover of the box. In 1988 he made a deal with Ted Turner for *Don*

Trump: The Movie. "I want a very good-looking guy to play me," he said.[48] He was also the subject—and object—of countless rumors, anecdotes, and jokes, showed up in Gary Trudeau's *Doonesbury* and other cartoons, and played cameo roles on television. Whenever he made a preannounced appearance to autograph his book, lines stretched around the block and across shopping mall parking lots.[49]

He had spent his entire adult life working to this end. In Atlantic City, already drenched in his name, he had erected billboards dedicated to making a word that was a noun and a verb into an adjective, as in "You're looking very Trump today." Nonetheless he managed to look both pleased and surprised every time he saw the crowds waiting for him. "He would seem very cool and collected," said Sprague, "but he would always turn to you and say, 'Do you believe this, do you believe this is happening?' "

Known for being able to sell just about anything to just about anybody, he was selling himself to everybody, and the reason it worked was that he was also selling himself to himself. Thus he would speak of himself in the third person, as in "Trump says this" or "People say that Trump is the only one who can do it." The consummate salesman, he was demonstrating his product, which happened to be himself, and at the same time managing to suggest that he actually identified more with the consumers out there deciding whether or not to buy.

Yes, he was rich and, for the most part, they were not, but that wasn't what mattered. What counted was that both salesman and consumer saw the huge mansions, private jet, stretch limos, glitzy casinos, blonde ex-model wife, and gold-plated everything as the embodiment of quality—that is, what any normal human being who struck it rich would like to have. Refusing to subscribe to the old WASP notion that discretion was the better part of wealth, the developer advertised his possessions and invited the public to admire them with him. Whenever estimates of his wealth appeared, he did not, in classic tycoon fashion, round the numbers down; instead he insisted that he was worth more. After years of boasting and bravado, he had become the people's billionaire. Although his means did not approach those amassed by John D. Rockefeller, the developer rivaled the oil magnate as the touchstone of wealth. Instead of aspiring to be "rich as Rockefeller," people wanted to be "rich as Trump."

Wherever he went, whether it was down the street or to a Michael Jackson concert, he was automatically the center of attention, regardless of who else was present. At one charity function in Los Angeles, Jerry Schrager recounted, the VIP room was wall-to-wall Hollywood greats, including Gregory Peck, Bob Hope, Ronald Reagan, and George Burns. "Who was the center of attention?" Schrager said. "In this room, where everybody was a celebrity but me and my wife, Donald was the one person the press engulfed."

He had become the celebrities' celebrity. When people who were household names themselves came to look at apartments in Trump Tower, they would invariably ask if Donald was in. "I'd say he was in his office," Sprague said. "They'd say, 'Why don't you give him a call, I'd love to meet him,' and they'd sound a little anxious."

Inevitably that megawattage affected the responses he received. It was hard to have a different opinion, much less a debate, with a man who presented such an impenetrable, invincible image, who spoke from on high and seemed touched with gold. Although he constantly asked others what they thought, if he heard something he didn't like he reacted strongly and sometimes explosively. "Everyone was afraid of his tirades and his power to get things in the press," said a key staff member. "To influence him you would need to be a combination of Machiavelli and Mike Tyson, shrewd enough to come up with a clever strategy and strong enough to punch him in the jaw."

Donald's extraordinary strength of mind could function as a shield, allowing him to ignore attacks or distractions and forge ahead to his goal. But it also functioned as blinders and earplugs, keeping out information he needed to hear. On minor matters this was unfortunate; on larger ones it would prove catastrophic.

CHAPTER SEVEN

Spinning out of Control

T he night of his book party, Donald had received the homage of New York City's glitterati and literati, people who showed up in boldfaced type in gossip columns as well as the people who disdained them. But the only person he seemed to show any genuine interest in seeing was a 24-year-old aspiring actress from Dalton, Georgia.[1] Her name was Marla Ann Maples, and her idol since childhood had been Marilyn Monroe. Blonde, blue-eyed, and stunningly beautiful, she had a soft southern voice and a friendly manner. She also had a spectacular body: five feet eight inches tall, 125 pounds, long legs, and full breasts. When she was only 16, her looks had brought her an offer to pose nude for *Playboy*. She refused but did accept first place in a swimsuit pageant, modeled in print ads for airlines and ceramic tile adhesive, and had a bit part in a Stephen King horror movie called *Maximum Overdrive*, in which she was crushed to death by a truckload of watermelons.

Now these same looks brought her Donald's complete and, for once, undivided attention. Over lunch and, soon, late-night dinners, she shared with him her earnest belief that everyone is on this earth for a higher purpose; he courted her with press clips and reviews of his book. Soon he installed her nearby, at the St. Moritz, a hotel on Central Park South that he had bought with the idea of someday turning it into condominiums. When he was in Atlantic City, she stayed at Trump Plaza. He relished showing off her photograph and boasting of her 37-25-37 measurements, and he sneaked away from work whenever possible for a midafternoon rendezvous. He paid her expenses, bought her lavish gifts, and flew her and her family in his jet. When she called she used a special code name, and his staff had standing orders to handle her every need.

Donald's life was already impossibly crowded. Every day he barely made his way through phone calls, documents, urgent requests for attention from his employees, and all the schemes and dreams that were constantly running through his mind. He gave few people more than a moment or two of his time, slept only three or four hours a night, and, reportedly, for an extra boost took diet pills. The prescription, supposedly written by a doctor who had once been investigated by *60 Minutes*, was for an amphetamine-like substance that suppressed a patient's appetite and produced a sense of euphoria and boundless energy—precisely the sort of manic behavior that his staffers often saw their boss exhibit.[2]

Now he was embarking on a second, secret life, with all the claims, conflicts, and confusions that inevitably accompany such a situation. When possible, he dodged his wife; when this was not possible, he became furious at her, setting off hurt feelings, self-justifications, and more dodging. Flitting from one illicit love nest to another, he struggled to keep straight the half-truths, careful shadings, and outright lies he had to tell to keep the two lives going. He began making deals for their own sake, or deals that had no purpose other than self-aggrandizement, or, most worrisome of all, deals that made no sense on any level. And as the deals piled up, Donald lost track of what he was all about—a fatal error.

To blame the disaster that would eventually unfold on the curvaceous blonde from Dalton would be a mistake and also a misconception. For all his adeptness at deal-making and his astuteness at reading other people's minds, Donald seemed remarkably unaware of what was going on in his own head. The man who had made being a winner the most important thing in his life would not acknowledge even to himself that he was in the throes of one of the few truly unavoidable facts of life, which was aging. Reportedly he had nips and tucks to eliminate wrinkles and sagging jowls and, eventually, liposuction to take away the extra pounds from pizza and from his favorite Cakemasters chocolate cake. Acutely aware of his thinning hair, he took to arranging what was left in a careful comb-over and, by one account, hiding the pink skin of his exposed scalp by tattooing it a darker hue. Taking a cue from Fred, who applied a red shade to his locks, Donald dyed his hair a color reminiscent of Tang.[3]

In classic male midlife-crisis fashion, he looked outside his marriage for affirmation that he was still attractive, vital, and potent. Even before Ivana began commuting to Atlantic City to run the Castle, he had pursued other women. Because he was a notorious germ phobe, it seems doubtful that many of these liaisons involved sexual intimacy. Nonetheless, gossip columnists linked his name with those of glamorous actresses and models, and he fanned such rumors with selective leaks and innuendos. As often happens to public figures, other women pursued him, which he lost no opportunity to brag about.

On one occasion he gave real estate broker Jack Shaffer a ride to a party and boasted that every woman in the room would head his way. "You want to throw up when you hear that," Shaffer said later. "But when he walked in, they did all run over. I felt like I was carrying his briefcase." Such attention was thrilling, but it was also wreaking havoc in the developer's head and his life. "He would walk one block and twenty-two women would hit on him," said another colleague. "This availability of other women can be unbearable if you don't have things in balance, and the other women were making him crazy."

EIGHT MONTHS BEFORE MARLA MAPLES entered the devel-
oper's life, when he was still trying to bring off Television City, his
biggest deal in New York, and to unload the unsold condominiums at
Trump Plaza of the Palm Beaches, he made another, unrelated deal in
Atlantic City. It would bring him the largest casino in the nation at the
time and eventually lead to his downfall. Named the Taj Mahal, this
asset became available in April 1986, after James Crosby, international
playboy and owner of Resorts International Inc., died of acute emphy-
sema. Facing a messy squabble over his estate, his heirs opted to sell off
his casino properties, and in March 1987 Donald arranged to buy a con-
trolling interest for an eventual price of $96.2 million. For this sum he
received Resorts' $600 million in junk-bond debt and two gambling fa-
cilities: the tired and by then money-losing Atlantic City casino that
had opened back in 1978, and the half-finished Taj, which would cost
an estimated $525 million to complete.

The three-casino rule would require the developer to sell or con-
vert one of his properties upon completion of the Taj, which was already
over budget and behind schedule. Not only would it steal business from
his other casinos, but it would tie him even more closely to a place that
often seemed worse off than before the 1976 referendum. At this point
Atlantic City had 35,000 residents, 18,000 slot machines, and the highest crime rate in the state. Most of the 40,000 new casino jobs had gone
to outsiders who commuted from elsewhere, half the city received public assistance, the ex-mayor was in jail for misconduct, and other public
officials had set new records for personal greediness. Instead of reviving
the old resort, the shimmering casinos had become almost entirely
white enclaves strung out along the Boardwalk and the marina, and
most of the black-majority city remained a bleak wasteland.

Those were the negatives connected with buying the Taj. The
positives were a gambling resort in the Bahamas, vast amounts of prime
Atlantic City real estate, and the tallest building in the entire state.
"Everything is much bigger than it should be," Donald told one reporter.
"It's built as a dream."[4] Evidently this staggering size, plus the fear that if

he didn't buy Resorts someone else would, seemed to him reason enough to act. Against the advice of both Harvey Freeman and Jerry Schrager, he went ahead.

Two months later Mayor Koch turned down Donald's bid for subsidies for Television City. To salvage his reputation, he quickly produced *The Art of the Deal*. But the same month it came out, he followed his dubious purchase of the Taj with an even more preposterous acquisition: the world's third-largest yacht.[5] Built by arms dealer and financier Adnan Khashoggi in the late 1970s and named after his daughter Nabila, it had cost $30 million to build and another $55 million for superluxury appointments. A decade later, Khashoggi was broke, the yacht went to pay off a loan from the sultan of Brunei, and it became clear that, as with Mar-a-Lago, an extraordinary creation had become a gigantic white elephant. In the fall of 1987 Donald bought the streamlined behemoth for $30 million, minus a $1 million discount he wangled to remove the name of Khashoggi's daughter from the hull.

It was a typical transaction. In a phone call during the negotiations for the yacht, broker Edward S. Gordon had advised him to go with the sultan's final offer, which the developer did. "Donald calls me four days later and says, 'It was worth the $40 million I paid,' " Gordon said. "But that's The Donald." After years of working together, Gordon was used to the developer's numbers games. "He'll double the numbers on me, and it's a deal I did for him," Gordon said. "But he believes it, he's doubled it and believes it. That's his strength and his weakness."[6]

Renamed *Trump Princess*, the yacht had 11 guest suites, two waterfalls, a three-bed hospital, and sleeping quarters for a staff of 52. The one thing the ship lacked was any sense of comfort, and it was so large that few marinas could accommodate it. Although its new owner bragged continuously about his latest "masterpiece," he never spent a night there or showed the least interest in anything to do with boats. "I'm not exactly into them," he said. "I've been on friends' boats before and couldn't get off fast enough."

Then again, the developer didn't buy the boat to sail on it or even to relax there; rather, its sheer over-the-top enormity was one more step in establishing Donald Trump as both symbol and measure of world-class excess.[7] An hour after he took possession of the yacht, he was making plans to sell it and build an even larger craft, and he would later briefly own the Dutch shipyard he commissioned to construct it. In the meantime, the current *Princess* would be a place for returning favors and piling up credits, and it would also serve to spawn a line of *Princess* souvenirs.

Although Donald delegated most details about the boat, he took a direct hand in designing the ship's logo, a voluptuous mermaid who would appear on T-shirts and towels as well as crew uniforms. "My marching orders were to make everything else look the same, just brand-new," said longtime deputy Jeff Walker. "But on the mermaid, we tried contemporary, traditional, big breasts, small breasts, nipples, no nipples, for hours and hours."

By contrast, the developer was truly infatuated with his next purchase: the Plaza Hotel, the elegant Edwardian-era landmark at the corner of 59th Street and Fifth Avenue.[8] Built to resemble a French château, it had a mansard roof faced with green-tinged copper, and its lavish interior was filled with crystal chandeliers, European tapestries, and Oriental carpets. Its guest list had included Frank Lloyd Wright, the Duchess of Windsor, and Elizabeth Taylor, but in recent years its appearance had slipped, as had its occupancy rate.[9] Nonetheless, Donald was smitten. Even though he had not done a careful inspection of the property, in March 1988 he signed on the dotted line for $407.5 million, the highest price ever paid for a single hotel.[10]

"Trump wasn't Trump in this deal," said Norman Bernstein, one of his lawyers for the transaction. "Normally we'd tear a property like this apart." But the developer was himself in one detail: his $425 million loan from a Citibank-led consortium, almost $20 million over the purchase price. "He was like an international superstar who says, 'I want to do a movie, who wants to pay for it,' " said Sprague. "Jerry Schrager would have this fabulous way of presenting it to the bankers, Donald would walk in and shake a few hands and smile, and then boom, there was the money."

This time, though, the money came with a condition: $125 million required a personal guarantee. It was a decisive moment. Within the real estate industry, famous for operating on other people's money, risking your own was seen as folly on such a scale as to be almost a sin. A personal guarantee was something Fred would never have considered, and his son had done it only once before, on Trump Plaza in Atlantic City, and then for only 10 days.[11] Worse, he was taking this momentous step in a deal where the property's annual cash flow, less than $20 million, would not come close to covering interest payments.

"I haven't purchased a building, I have purchased a masterpiece—the Mona Lisa," he declared in another full-page open letter in the *New York Times*. "For the first time in my life, I have knowingly made a deal that was not economic—for I can never justify the price I paid, no matter how successful the Plaza becomes."[12]

Actually, the justification had already begun via this faux confession, intended to underscore the hotel's cachet. And, in fact, the prestige the Plaza Hotel conferred was enormous—so much so that for once, Donald made no effort to put his name on the outside. Even though the hotel would never earn out, buying it was arguably the right move. The problem was that the developer did not stop there.

It could not have helped that he was constantly distracted. For one thing, he was still carrying three as yet unprofitable projects: the rail yards, the Taj, and the West Palm Beach condominiums. And then there was also the unresolved problem of Ivana.[13] Commuting by helicopter, she spent three days each week at the Castle, where she had honed herself into an executive machine and copied her husband's hands-on style wherever possible. She signed every check, reviewed in minute detail everything the managers did, and issued an endless stream of orders that, whatever their ostensible purpose, kept the staff on permanent high alert. Despite her lack of casino experience, she managed to surpass Trump Plaza in monthly revenues, enraging the casino veterans who were her counterparts there.

But with every success she had, her husband grew more alienated. He did not want to be reconnected to her; he wanted out. He had dispatched her to run the Castle because he did not want to be around her in New York, but now it was inconvenient to have her in Atlantic City. Because of his involvement with the Taj, he had to be there himself, and he wanted his mistress with him. Abruptly, he yanked Ivana back to run the Plaza Hotel. The gesture might have passed as a reward, but he publicly belittled her by saying that he was paying her $1 a year and all the dresses she could buy. Once again there were hurt feelings, and inevitably there was even more dodging.

Ivana kept trying. After her husband complained that she looked old and haggard, she had extensive plastic surgery and emerged looking at least a decade younger. He seemed unmoved. He had refused to have sex with her for more than two years and complained that she was flat-chested; after she made her entire body over, he recoiled from the sight of her implanted breasts. Nothing she could do, or say, or not do, or not say, was right.

The reason Donald had to pay more attention to Atlantic City was that the Resorts deal had hit a snag. To complete what would be his first takeover of a public company, he had needed Resorts' other outstanding shares.[14] But not wanting to pay the current share price of 62, he had gotten to work. He had demanded a $1 billion management contract and settled for a still-huge $200 million to $300 million. He had declared that the construction of the Taj would cost hundreds of millions more than current estimates. He had spoken of the whole Resorts situation with uncharacteristic glumness. The share price went to 49 and then, after October 19, the stock market's Black Monday, to 33. Somehow word leaked that he was thinking about putting Resorts into bankruptcy. The share price sank to 22. At state hearings on his new management contract, the developer again painted a bleak picture of Resorts' prospects. The share price hit 13.

Disgruntled shareholders threatened to file suit, and by March 1988 the developer had agreed to settle at 22. But as he sat in his Trump Tower office and glanced down at the St. Patrick's Day parade marching up Fifth Avenue, he got some bad news: The Resorts share price, which had been sinking for more than eight months, had turned around.

"What's going on?" he yelled.

The answer was talk-show host Merv Griffin. Flush from selling *Wheel of Fortune* and *Jeopardy* to Coca-Cola for $250 million in cash, the white-haired, ever-affable entertainer had made a tender offer of 36 for all of Resorts' outstanding shares. In mid-April he flew to New York in his private plane and met with the developer at Trump Tower. Griffin knocked off a few jokes, then nodded in his best ego-stroking host style as Donald, speaking in rapid, impatient bursts, outlined his version of the future for Atlantic City in general and the Taj in particular. "I have all the cards," he declared repeatedly, then interrupted himself with his trademark, "You know what I mean?"

For the next month negotiators hammered away at deal points while trying to talk their respective principals out of what Griffin lawyer Tom Gallegher called "the deal from hell." Undaunted and unruffled, Griffin listened and smiled; the developer, alternately engaging and aggressive, raced ahead, jumping back and forth between general points and seemingly random details. "In many ways [Donald was] a Jekyll and Hyde guy," Gallegher said. "He could be enormously charming and you'd almost think, gee, this is a nice, decent, warm guy, and then the bad twin would come out."

Finally the developer and the entertainer cut a deal. Donald would buy the unfinished Taj for $273 million, less than half of what had already been spent on it, and he would also receive $63.7 million in so-called severance for his management contract.[15] Merv Griffin would get the original Resorts casino hotel, the Bahama resort, and the Atlantic City real estate. Essentially each party got what he wanted, although Griffin also wound up with what he didn't want, Resorts' existing $600 million debt.

For months the press speculated about who came out ahead and by how much. It was hard to make a strong case for Griffin.[16] He had immediately piled on another $325 million in junk bonds—a landmark of sorts, for it was Drexel Burnham Lambert's last Atlantic City deal before a securities fraud indictment caused the firm's expulsion from the New Jersey casino industry. In the months to come, Griffin would take Resorts in and out of bankruptcy twice.

Then again, Donald also miscalculated. He had assumed that he could obtain another junk-bond issue from Bear, Stearns, which had provided the financing for his first two casino purchases and acted as his broker during his greenmail-style forays. But this time he wanted to make the property more highly leveraged than even Bear, Stearns could handle, and he had to accept the far less attractive deal offered by Merrill Lynch.

The developer's second misjudgment was what it would take to get the Taj Mahal open. Under the now-deceased Jim Crosby, its construction had eaten cash and lurched along uncertainly for years. "We didn't even have a plan," said Crosby's top aide. "You just said, 'Keep building that way.' " After Crosby died, the estate left the site exposed to the rain and salt air. In effect, Donald was taking on a vastly larger Wollman Rink, but expanding the job instead of reducing it to the bare minimum. Carrara marble replaced less expensive materials, $250,000 crystal chandeliers from Austria bumped more pedestrian light fixtures, and areas that Resorts planned to leave undone became sumptuous hotel suites.[17]

With Marla, Ivana, the Taj, the yacht, the rail yards project, the still unsold Trump Plaza of the Palm Beaches, and the Plaza Hotel to deal with, a mere mortal might have paused. Instead Donald jumped into yet another folly.[18] It was, in effect, a flying building—or, rather, a fleet of flying buildings: 21 Boeing 727s, plus leases on facilities and landing slots at Washington's National Airport, New York's LaGuardia Airport, and Boston's Logan Airport. These assets, previously owned by the Eastern Shuttle, would now be the basis for a new Trump Shuttle— and for extending the Trump franchise even further.

As usual, the developer's nose for publicity value was on target. "Everybody is fascinated by planes and travel," said Goldman Sachs airline analyst Glen Ingalls. "You didn't know who ran Procter & Gamble, but you knew that Bob Crandall ran American Airlines." The problem was that airlines, a highly competitive business with staggering fixed costs, are a potentially disastrous business proposition, particularly for someone whose field is not aviation.

Ignoring Harvey Freeman and Jerry Schrager's advice against the deal, Donald set up a meeting in early October with Bruce Nobles, the president-designate of the independent shuttle operation Eastern Airlines had been trying to spin off. Nobles, whose father starting working at American Airlines six months before he was born, had gone into the industry after college. He'd worked his way up to the presidency of the other Northeast Corridor shuttle, Pan Am, when Eastern hired him for its new operation. But financial and labor pressure had scuttled Eastern's plans, and now the airline was selling its shuttle-related assets to the developer for $365 million.

At the meeting, which began at four in the afternoon, Donald asked Nobles a number of questions. "He was most interested in how much cash flow the shuttle would throw off," Nobles said. "I didn't know why at the time." Evidently his answers were satisfactory, for at five the developer offered him the presidency of the Trump Shuttle, at six he told Nobles he couldn't leave until he agreed, and at seven Nobles accepted the job. One week later the two appeared at a Plaza Hotel press conference to announce the developer's newest venture.

In the meantime, Donald had a seeming stroke of good fortune when Australian beer baron Alan Bond paid him $180 million for the St. Moritz, the hotel where the developer had once secreted Marla Maples.[19] To hear the developer tell the story, he had paid $31 million for the hotel in 1985 and thus made a profit of almost $150 million; in fact the property had cost $73.7 million, which meant a still-hefty profit of $106.3 million. More important, he took the deal as proof that he had not lost his business touch and thus could continue with the string of deals that Freeman and Schrager kept vetoing.

The following June, after several court suits and one crippling labor strike, the Trump Shuttle finally took off and the developer began bragging about a $1 million-per-plane makeover to make the airline into "an absolute diamond." To his chagrin, marble weighed too much and the need to push refreshment carts down the aisles ruled out plush carpeting. Nonetheless he managed an elegant look, with bird's-eye-maple veneer on the cabin walls, leather seats, and gold-plated fixtures in the bathrooms.

Soon the new airline was close to splitting the market with the rival Pan Am Shuttle. This was all that could reasonably be expected, but Donald needed 60 percent to cover the stiff interest on the $380 million he had borrowed to buy and refurbish the planes. As with the Plaza Hotel, Citibank had provided the lion's share, $245 million, and the developer made a personal guarantee to cover the balance. Nobles, who had never seen such high leveraging in airlines, mentioned his concern. "Don't worry," he was told. "We know what we're doing." Citibank lending officers also seemed uneasy, particularly those who handled airlines, but the real estate side, used to high-risk clients and high leverage, had taken charge. For them, the critical factor was having enough cash flow to cover interest payments, which is why Donald, Freeman, and, later, the banks, had grilled Nobles closely on this very point.

Then, in November, only five months after the Trump Shuttle started flying, a recession hit the Northeast and the shuttle market shrank for the first time in 30 years. It shrank again in December, and fuel costs went up. Nobles had to ask the Trump Organization for funds to cover interest payments.

The request made Donald most unhappy. "He wanted each operation to be independent, to live or die by itself," Nobles said. "He wanted everybody competing against each other and beating their brains out." Nobles had suggested economies of scale and synergies like combining information and reservations systems, but such cooperation apparently violated the developer's basic principle of creative conflict. The closest he would come to letting different operations work together was to have the shuttle give out casino vouchers to its passengers. But they were not casino customers, and of the tens of thousands of coupons that were distributed, few were redeemed. Meanwhile the airline's overhead remained untouched.

BELT-TIGHTENING and pulling back did not fit into Donald's strategy. He had come into the world an entrepreneur, and so he remained, always pushing to see if he could get more, thinking of what lay beyond not just the next corner but the one after that. Every deal had to be not just good, or even great, but unbelievable. Because of a labor strike before the deal with Eastern had closed, he could have dropped the whole thing and taken home a $5 million breakup fee, but he refused. At another point he had a solid offer of $107 million for the share in the Alexander's department store chain that had cost him $50 million. He said yes, then called Robert Campeau, the largest retailer in the United States, who was way over his head in debt but offered to pay $120 million. Shortly afterward, Campeau filed the biggest retail bankruptcy in the nation's history, and Donald, who had let the first offer go, continued to pay interest on his money-losing investment.

By definition, entrepreneurs are deal makers. They look for markets, decide where there is money to be made, and make their move. Donald had an elegant way of describing his deals as his "art form." Others were more blunt and called the developer a deal junkie. But whether he was an artist or an addict, or both, he was constantly on the lookout for opportunities to expand. While still hashing out the shuttle purchase in the spring of 1989, he paid $1 million to get in on a third baseball league,[20] bought stock in American Airlines, Universal Pictures, and MCA, and again talked takeover; put more than $1 million into a pilot for *The Trump Card*, a television quiz show to be produced at Trump Castle; and pledged $750,000 to the Tour de Trump, an 800-mile bicycle race scheduled to end in front of Trump Plaza in Atlantic City.

Even in the field he presumably knew best, he could not seem to say no. In Manhattan, where the real estate market was visibly tightening, he plunged ahead on Trump Palace, a large East Side condominium project, and rejected potential Japanese partners for the project. Reportedly, chief saleswoman Sprague initially came up with a sellout figure of $180 million, $40 million short of the $220 million estimated for construction costs. Supposedly Donald kept after her until she came up with a better-sounding $265 million, but she then refused to endorse the figures and wrote a letter to that effect to Jerry Schrager.[21]

By now Donald had Marla, Ivana, the Taj, the yacht, the rail yards project, the Plaza Hotel, the Trump Shuttle, Trump Plaza of the Palm Beaches, and Trump Palace on his mind. Then, in the fall of 1989, three of his top casino executives died in a helicopter crash on their way back to Atlantic City after meeting with him in New York. Such a loss would have been tragic in the best of circumstances; in the Trump Organization, already stretched paper thin on the management side, the deaths were a disaster and left the developer even more unhinged.

For nearly two years Donald had been living a double life. Although there were near leaks, and the occasional not very veiled references in gossip columns, Marla's existence remained more or less secret from the outside world. But the arrangement was taking its toll, and the person most affected was Donald himself. From the *Trump Princess* to the Trump Shuttle, each new purchase and every new venture seemed another, larger-scale version of a little boy asking to be caught. With each grandiose episode he seemed to be risking not just his own fortune but fate itself. He seemed to be almost begging to have the whole huge edifice come tumbling down.

But it didn't. Instead he went on and on, finally topping every outlandish deal so far by opening a casino that could never earn what it cost to build and would inevitably damage and possibly destroy his other casinos.

Over the years, Donald had pulled off a series of audacious and sometimes astonishing moves, but there was one thing he could not do: tell his wife it was over. "I have to confess, the way I handled the situation was a cop-out," he later wrote. "I never sat down calmly with Ivana to 'talk it out' as I probably should have." His wife was also unable to face their disintegrating relationship squarely. Meanwhile Marla was tired of hiding in the limo and bringing another escort to public events instead of her lover. "I felt there were times I just couldn't breathe," she told a later interviwer. "It was just swirling so, so, so fast."

During the Christmas holidays in 1989, Donald's jet brought his family out to a luxury Aspen hotel and then fetched Marla, who bunked with a girlfriend at more modest quarters. On New Year's Eve, Ivana confronted her on the ski slopes and told her to leave Donald alone, giving her a slight shove for emphasis. "Are you happy?" Marla asked as paparazzi immortalized the confrontation. Soon rumors were flying, and an impressive number of people in New York and Atlantic City were claiming to have known of the illicit relationship for some time.[22]

But Ivana had not, and the revelation was devastating.

Every unhappy marriage is unhappy in its own way. For Ivana, the problem was that although she appeared to have the perfect life, filled with material possessions and near-regal splendor, within her own home she was not free to be a winner and a champion. For Donald, it was that he had made the mistake of marrying the wrong parent. Instead of choosing a mate like his mother, eager to play quiet backup to a towering success, he had selected someone more like his father, a born contender who could not hold back even if she tried. Worse, Ivana did not seem to grasp that the enormous opulence with which Donald had surrounded himself and his family was only a marketing tool. The Trump

Tower triplex, Mar-a-Lago, and the *Trump Princess* were places to be photographed in and used to create an impression; they were not environments that anyone should consider normal.

Although Donald had long arranged his worldly affairs precisely so that he could live and work in this atmosphere of ultimate luxury, his own personality was all agenda, and his sole aim in most interactions was getting himself where he had to go. When he needed help, he could be extraordinarily attentive, but when he did not need anything he had little warmth to spare. He went to charity events because his name would sell tickets and being there sold him, but he did not seem to care much about either the charities or the social acceptance attached to them.[23] What mattered to him was being recognized as a serious player, and he already knew that he could have lunch with any of the business heavies there whenever he wanted to. He insisted on leaving early, and he made it clear to everyone within hearing distance that he would much prefer being at home watching television, eating SpaghettiOs or a takeout hamburger, and drinking yet another diet soda.

But Ivana believed in the lavish image he had created. For her the universe of Trump was real, a thing of flesh and blood. And in a way she was right. As any reader of American newspapers and magazines could attest, although it began as a marketing tool, by now there was a true Trump dominion. Unfortunately for Ivana, however, she was not its queen. "We were working in a kingdom where there was really only room for a king," Sprague said. "He would walk into a room of people all in black tie, [and] suddenly there would be nobody there but Donald."

The developer did not want a queen; he wanted a concubine. He wanted to come home at night and relax. If there was talk about business, it should be talk about his most recent triumph, not questions about how something had been handled or discussions of problems. "Marla was subdued," said Mai Hallingby, then-wife of Bear, Stearns banker Paul Hallingby and a member of the same social set as the Trumps. "Donald would be the star of the group, and she would be a listener. She seemed very willing to take a backseat." Evidently she was also willing to have a relationship that would be not only highly public but filled with spats, breakups, marriage talk, and more spats.

A month after the incident in Aspen, *Playboy* published an interview with the developer in which he refused to say whether or not his marriage was monogamous. Two weeks later Ivana made her move. She consulted a divorce lawyer, hired a publicist, and called gossip columnist Liz Smith. More than a dozen years earlier, Jay Pritzker, off on a long-planned trip to Nepal, had been unavailable for comment when Donald had pushed through the noncompete clause for the Grand Hyatt; this time it was Donald who was unavailable at a critical moment. When Ivana phoned Smith, Donald was flying home from a trip to Japan, ostensibly made to see Mike Tyson fight but in fact a desperate attempt to unload the Plaza Hotel. While he was 20,000 feet in the air, his own wife scooped him. She was a whole news-spin cycle ahead, and he would never catch up. In the world's eyes she would be the victim, he would be the cad, and the man whose access to the press was the stuff of legend would be unable to do anything about it.

The nation's press roiled with she said/he said tales. Ivana demanded a larger share of the fortune her husband had once insisted was over $3 billion; he refused to pay any more than $10 million, the comparatively modest sum named in their most recent nuptial agreement, which had been renegotiated upward three times. Intent on capturing public sympathy and getting in the last word, husband and wife threw selective tidbits to a voracious press.

Meanwhile the mistress donned a red wig, assumed a false name, and secreted herself in a series of hideouts that included a Peace Corps encampment in Guatemala. Journalists dug into her life, and the *National Enquirer* paid a reported $11,000 to her high school and college sweethearts for the mostly banal details of her earlier romances. Hundreds of reporters and photographers followed the bread crumbs, and publishers outdid each other with headlines, including the *New York Post*'s memorable BEST SEX I EVER HAD, supposedly a remark made by Marla to a friend.

Donald was thrilled, his parents were distressed, and his executives were appalled. "Businesswomen won't fly your shuttle with you on the front page of the paper every day [talking] about your sex life," Bruce Nobles told the developer. "Yeah, but the guys love it," he replied. Perhaps, but that admiration did not translate into ticket sales. The airline's market share continued to decline, possibly because passengers worried, like one respondent in a focus group, that someone distracted in his personal life might not be paying attention to airplane safety. The banks were also unhappy about the headlines. The image of a brilliant dealmaker had attracted them, but they were troubled by the idea of doing business with someone whose marriage was in such visible disarray.

Marla's public debut as the developer's mistress was scheduled to occur on April 5, 1990, the same day as the opening of the Taj. For weeks beforehand, stories about her appearance and the different outfits she might wear filled the tabloids. But on the big day, Donald's family prevailed, and he appeared alone. The delay was brief; two weeks later Marla was on *Prime Time Live* and talked to Diane Sawyer about her relationship with Donald. The interview gave the show the best ratings it had ever received.

IN THE END the Taj cost more than $1.1 billion, and Donald personally guaranteed a loan for $75 million. To meet interest payments, he would need daily revenues of $1.3 million, more than any Atlantic City casino had made on a regular basis. Such a sum was impossible unless he could figure out how to bring in stunning numbers of slots players and high rollers—that is, both mass and moneyed customers. His solution: a gaudy seaside palace calibrated to have the drawing power of Trump Tower. A surreal contrast to the original Taj Mahal, a serene and elegant Indian mausoleum, the New Jersey Taj would be neither beautiful nor peaceful. But in its own way, it would be a design triumph, a unique and unforgettable building that drew paying customers by the hundreds of thousands from around the country and the world.

In New York Donald had sheathed his tower with glass so that it would contrast with limestone neighbors and placed his name in shiny brass over the front entrance; here he covered his new casino with candy-striped onion domes and miniature gold-topped minarets, creating a building that looked nothing like the big, boxy casinos next door, and his name blazed from the roof in bright red neon.

Inside the Taj he used the same floor-numbering magic as at the Grand Hyatt and Trump Tower, turning what was the forty-second and highest floor into the more dramatic-sounding fifty-first floor. In much the way that Der Scutt had used rosy peach to set a tone of rich abundance for the Trump Tower atrium, Donald coated the Taj interior in bubble-gum pink to create a carnival-like atmosphere. There was even a spectacle comparable to Trump Tower's waterfall: the noise and lights of 3,010 constantly clanging slot machines.

The record number of slots would be a magnet for low-stakes players; to draw the high-stakes crowd, the Taj offered 160 table games, also a record number, plus special high-roller amenities. Overlooking the baccarat pit, favored by many wealthy customers, a pink-chandeliered restaurant named Scheherazade eschewed menus, instead keeping records of guest preferences and serving them with gold-plated tableware. Upstairs were Lucullan penthouse accommodations named after historical figures; the most opulent was the 4,500-square-foot Alexander the Great Suite, listed at $10,000 per night and boasting its own weight room and white baby grand piano—almost enough to compensate for the depressing view out over the town's abject poverty. Architect Francis Xavier Dumont apologized profusely during one tour. "Unfortunately," he said, "we overlook Atlantic City."

Donald called the Taj the Eighth Wonder of the World; it had to be if he was to recoup his investment and avoid cannibalizing his other properties. As usual, he did everything he could think of to achieve this miracle, including cold-calling veteran Philadelphia casino analyst Marvin Roffman. "I just want to let you know I read your reports and I think you're right on the money and one of the best guys on the street," Donald said.

Unlike many in his field, Roffman was a guy who did his homework not once but twice. "I almost have a curse," he said. "Before I do or say anything I have to do my research, almost to the point of nuttiness."[24] To the balding, gregarious analyst, the Eighth Wonder of the World was compound interest, not a mammoth facility opening in a shrinking market, and he issued a negative report on the Taj in an industry publication. In response, the developer invited him to come and see for himself. "I'll have my brother take you on a personal tour," he said. "At the end, I want you to pick up any phone in the lobby and tell me how thrilled you are."

On March 20, the day Roffman went to Atlantic City, the *Wall Street Journal* had a story in which he was quoted saying that the Taj would do well—but only in warm weather. "Once the cold winds blow from October to February, it won't make it," Roffman said. "The market just isn't there." When he showed up at the Taj, Robert Trump met him at the door and ordered him off the property. "You're no fucking good," Robert yelled and accused him of having stabbed Taj bondholders in the back. After Donald threatened to sue and Roffman refused to apologize, the brokerage house where he had worked for 16 unblemished years fired him. "Marv Roffman is a man of little talent who disagrees with other people," Donald told a reporter.[25]

Two weeks later, on April 5, the Taj had its opening night. The weather was chilly, and despite claims that there would be celebrities by the yard, only a handful of lesser lights showed up. After a brief walk-through earlier in the day, Governor Jim Florio had departed. That evening, the highest-ranking public official to mount the small outdoor stage was the current mayor, then under indictment on corruption charges. He drew a solid round of boos. Then a cheerful Merv Griffin congratulated the developer and joked that he had once owned the Taj for 24 hours. Finally Donald, wearing a wide, bright red tie, touched a large Aladdin-style magic lamp, and an enormous televised genie appeared, followed by green lasers and pink-and-purple fireworks.

As Roffman had predicted, the crowds were huge—too huge for the Taj's slot operation, which was unable to keep track of its cash and had to shut down. The same thing had happened at the opening of the developer's first casino, and he had the same reaction, which was to launch a vicious attack on everyone in sight. When he turned on his brother, Robert quit and went home to manage the real estate their father had built. Soon the slots were up and running, but Donald kept the heat on his executives, demoting, reassigning, and in some cases firing them summarily.

In late April, Neil Barsky, the young *Wall Street Journal* reporter who had written the article quoting Roffman, came to Trump Tower for an interview. Donald was sitting at his desk with the reporter's clips spread out before him. By way of greeting, Donald turned on a tape recorder and said that he had three sworn affidavits from sources stating that Barsky was spreading rumors of a cash flow problem.

"He also said he'd retained [prominent libel lawyer] Martin Garbus and he'd sue my ass if I mentioned a negative cash flow," Barsky recalled later. "Then the interview began." He didn't know that the developer was considering selling, refinancing, or securitizing every asset and that the shuttle was actually on the block. But Donald thought he did, and when the reporter bluffed, asking for confirmation of the potential sale, the developer provided it.

"I really just played poker with him," Barsky said. "I won."[26]

It was a major scoop for the reporter, whose subsequent *Journal* story quoted Donald as saying that he wanted to be "king of cash" so that he could scoop up bargains later. To the financial community, the article was a red-light alert, and the market for Trump casino bonds took a nosedive. A year earlier *Forbes* had ranked the developer's wealth at $1.7 billion, making him one of the country's 20 richest people; now the magazine ran a cover story that estimated his net worth at $500 million.[27] When the numbers from the Taj's first month came in, there was more bad news: Despite the crowds, the casino had failed to break even and it had cut into revenues at Trump Castle and Trump Plaza. The Taj started laying off workers, Trump Shuttle flight attendants began charging passengers for coffee and newspapers, and the Trump Organization's small development office in Las Vegas shut down. The board game named for the developer showed up on the remainder shelf in toy departments, and Turner Broadcasting tabled the biographical film it had planned.

On Monday, June 4, 1990, Barsky had another scoop. It was entitled "Shaky Empire," and it was the lead story on the front page. Less than two months after the Taj had opened, Barsky wrote, Donald was struggling for his financial life. His attempts to sell or refinance the pieces of his empire had failed, and he was holding secret meetings with representatives of New York's four biggest banks, Chase Manhattan, Citicorp, Bankers Trust, and Manufacturers Hanover. In the conference room at Trump Tower, dozens of bankers and lawyers were poring over numbers that indicated a staggering $2 billion in bank debt and more than $1 billion in casino junk bonds. Perhaps even more stunning, Donald himself was on the hook for $800 million.[28]

In less than a decade he had become the Brazil of Manhattan. His annual interest payments, said to be around $350 million or almost $1 million a day, exceeded his cash flow. Worse, only two of his assets, his half of the Grand Hyatt and the retail component of Trump Tower, stood a prayer of making a net profit. "He will have to trim the fat," said one banker, who spoke darkly of selling off the yacht and the mansions and requiring the developer to operate in a more conservative fashion.

It was not the first time that the Trump family had encountered the shadow of bankruptcy. Back in 1934, winning the mortgage-servicing contracts of a bankrupt Brooklyn investment firm, the Lehrenkrauss Corporation, had been the vehicle for Fred's rise. Forty years later the bankruptcy of the Penn Central Railroad had created the conditions for Donald's entrance into Manhattan real estate. Each time enormous sums of money were involved; each time there were long and intricate negotiations over which creditor would get how much and what would happen with the carcass. Now, though, Donald was not an outsider trying to elbow his way to the table; instead he owned the table, the room, and the debt. Just as Lehrenkrauss had been caught short, and then Penn Central, now the party who could not meet over-whelming obligations was a Trump. The debt under discussion was Trump debt, and the assets being picked at by others were Trump assets.

Donald had gotten into this situation by convincing major banks and other financial institutions that his name made any asset worth more and that they could ignore their usual lending guidelines and demands for collateral. In the late 1980s, when the real estate market was so hot that it seemed to be almost smoking, he could have sold or refinanced assets with relative ease and kept his own financial house in order; now, though, the market was contracting. Worse, overexpansion in other areas such as the Third World, where a severe debt crisis was under way, was taking a toll on financial institutions. As a result, banks that until recently had been riding high had to scramble to keep their own operations going. Government bank examiners reportedly visited Chase Manhattan, and there was talk of mergers between banks that were beginning to choke on bad real estate loans.[29]

The events unfolding now were the many times removed consequences of events long past. Back when Fred was building with the help of government programs, interest rates were stable and the pecking order for banks and savings-and-loan institutions, known as S&Ls and a backwater within the financial industry, was a relatively simple matter. Although both charged the same rates for loans, in the low to middle single digits, banks took the most profitable area, real estate and commercial lending, and S&Ls handled home mortgages and passbook savings accounts. At the end of the 1970s, when the cost of the Vietnam War helped drive interest rates up, this arrangement shifted. Banks, free to charge whatever interest rates the market would bear, were able to get more for their loans, whereas the more heavily regulated S&Ls found themselves squeezed almost out of the running.

But not quite. Under Reagan, large-scale deregulation allowed S&Ls to raise rates and invade traditional bank turf. Stripped of their customary prerogatives, banks then had to cast about for new sources of revenue. Competition among banks heated up, and leveraging that would have been unthinkable in the past now became doable. Major banks loaned out not just what was required for a project, but more—in Donald's case, much more. Then they skimmed off hefty fees and syndicated—that is, sold off—pieces of loans to other institutions even more hungry for loans and willing to accept a smaller profit.

The readiness of other banks, particularly in Japan, to buy Trump loans became proof that the name bestowed value on a deal. Donald's lenders then vied to "adjust their own risk/reward ratio," as one Citibank official described his bank's willingness to take on a level of exposure it would otherwise have shunned, and the same cycle repeated itself. In the process, the New York banks put their own assets at what afterward seemed unconscionable risk. But in their rush to loan to Donald, they had also created what might be called a faux moral hazard. In classical economics this term refers to a situation in which a third party is encouraged to undertake risky behavior and is guaranteed against any loss. But in the developer's case, the banks merely encouraged the dangerous activity; they did not insure him against loss. What they did not realize was that he had in effect insured himself by gaming the system—by making himself such a big part of the deals that the financing institutions would have to keep him going to cut their own losses.

Nearly 90 financial institutions would be party to the bailout, and about 1,000 bank executives, lawyers, and accountants would participate in the marathon negotiations. Bankers from New York, Florida, New Jersey, Illinois, and California would have to sign off, along with colleagues from Japan, Ireland, Brazil, Italy, South Korea, and France. The amounts, the collateral, and individual lending practices varied widely, but without each party's approval, Donald stood to lose everything.

As the weeks went by, he missed a $43 million interest payment on Trump Castle bonds and a $30 million loan payment to Manufacturers Hanover. The Ohio-based maker of the Taj's onion domes and elephants threatened to remove them unless he received payment. Citing unpaid bills, Honeywell pulled its computer engineers off the job, leaving the casino's air-conditioning system limping.[30] Negotiations at the separate offices of the lead institutions went round the clock, and exasperated loan officers tried to coax, then coerce, recalcitrant minority lenders to go along. Gradually a plan took shape that reflected the one critical difference between the circumstances facing Lehrenkrauss and the Penn Central and the present situation: In those cases the debtor was done for and the only issue was how to handle the bankruptcy, but this time the debtor was far from finished.

Elsewhere Donald had exhibited a certain strain. He had hovered anxiously when a Japanese high roller who had already won at one of his casinos showed up again. He was gobbling candy and popcorn at an alarming rate, and he had been so abusive to employees that one casino regulator reported, "People are hiding under their desks." But at bank workout sessions, he was positive thinking personified. When he strode into the room, he radiated that indefinable but palpable glow that sets the famous apart from the crowd. Heads swiveled and eyes opened wide to take in his passage across the room, the nod here and the hello there.

The only reason anyone was there was that this man was over his head by an amount that would keep any of a handful of small countries humming for a year, yet everyone in the room still seemed to be a fan.

They had lent him more than they should have because he was a star; now, when he was on the ropes, he was still a star. Outside the meeting room, print reporters and television crews were on perpetual stakeout; when one banker called home to tell his wife that the day's meeting was extended and he wouldn't be home to dinner, she said she'd heard it on the news and then told him what had happened in the supposedly closed-door session that had just finished.[31]

Inside the room, where Donald was coming face-to-face with dozens of people to whom he owed hundreds of millions of dollars, he seemed, of all things, to be enjoying himself. Bizarrely, this may have been the best thing that could have happened to him. Finally, with a gun at his head, he started paying attention. The skillful Donald of old crawled out from under all the wreckage he had made of his life and his business and, once again, found the critical leverage points. His debts were so big that everyone in the room was afraid to see him fall; in addition, they didn't want to admit they had been suckers. He had debtor's leverage, and he played it to the hilt.

When he said the usual pleasantries, the good-to-see-yous and the glad-to-be-heres, he meant them, and when he sat down with the bankers and lawyers, he was the same model of decorum he had been at every regulatory hearing in New Jersey. He had always been what imbued his properties with "quality," and he gave every appearance of still being at the top of his game. "He didn't go around ranting and raving and picking the wrong fights with the wrong people," said the head of one Japanese bank's real estate department. "He acted as a businessman."[32]

No one had wished to resuscitate Julius Lehrenkrauss or the Penn Central's Stuart Saunders, but everyone in these negotiations wanted Donald to keep going. In a period in which the real estate market was turning soft, they had little desire to take over major properties and still less to become involved in casinos, which would require bank personnel to go through the onerous licensing process. Perhaps most of all, they did not want to admit that they had been seduced by parties on the

Princess and lavish receptions at the Plaza Hotel, and that the special "quality" that had attracted them was not the same thing as bricks-and-mortar collateral.

Instead they hung on to their belief that eventually both the real estate market and the value of things named after the developer would recover. During the negotiations, banks occasionally used the threat of a bankruptcy filing against one another, and Donald raised the specter to win a point. But even the most balky parties had no real interest in seeing the problem put in bankruptcy court, a lengthy process that would mean staggering legal fees and almost certain devaluation of the Trump name and properties.

More than a month after they first sat down, the banks finally came to an agreement. Donald, who remained $3 billion in debt, would receive an immediate loan of $20 million and a five-year, $65 million bailout. They would lower the rate of interest and suspend it on nearly half of his bank debt, but not on his mortgages or his junk bonds. He would have to appoint a chief financial officer (CFO), and he would have to live on a budget. Although CFOs were a standard feature in most corporations of any size, and Donald's monthly allowance of $450,000 was hardly draconian, it was the first time in his adult life that anyone had imposed even the appearance of limitations.

But he did not have to surrender ownership of any assets. If the market turned around, he could end up paying less for them than if he were not in a financial crisis and still benefit from any increase in value. As he saw the situation, he had emerged "greatly enhanced" by the agreement. What he didn't say was that he had survived because of his remarkable ability to make whatever he did the center of public attention; instead, he gave a more upbeat message to the press: "When you come through adversity, I think people respect that."

CHAPTER EIGHT

Pulling Back from the Brink

In mid-August 1990, the New Jersey Casino Control Commission posted its statistics for July. Traditionally it was the best month of the year, but this time the numbers showed an ominous slowdown. Total July revenues had dropped from a year earlier, even though the opening of the Taj had increased casino floor space in Atlantic City by 14 percent. Specifically, nine out of the town's 12 casinos had posted losses. Trump Plaza revenues were down 24 percent, those at Trump Castle were off by 30 percent, and the Taj, then in its third month of existence, had again failed to break even.

The same day, over Donald's vigorous protests, the appellate division of state superior court had permitted the release of documents relating to the $65 million bank bailout as well as personal financial information. Among the revelations were the details of how much each bank had lent him, plus a survey of his assets, prepared by his own accountants, showing a negative net worth of nearly $300 million.

Two days later Donald stood in the lobby of commission headquarters in Lawrenceville, a suburb of Trenton, the New Jersey state capital.[1] The commission was in the second day of hearings on the banks' rescue effort, after which it would vote on whether to consider him financially stable. Because a negative vote would mean the automatic loss of his casino license, the hearings were a matter of some urgency. The entire previous day the uncharacteristically subdued developer had sat on a metal folding chair as a stream of witnesses described his financial woes. This morning he was wearing the same suit, dark with white pinstripes, that he had worn the day before, and both he and it were showing signs of wear.

As he spoke to reporters and television crews, he did his best to rally. The reason for his economic difficulties, he announced, had little to do with anything he'd done. Instead the causes included the invasion of Kuwait by "that madman" Saddam Hussein and the major recession—practically a depression—that was gripping the entire country. "It's a great time to buy," he said. "Of course, anyone just starting out couldn't get what I already have."

Warming to the topic, he insisted that his situation was not all that bad. "Overall, we're in really good shape," he declared firmly. The shuttle was "doing really well," and even though the Taj did "cannibalize" his other casinos, it was a surmountable problem. "If one of these properties goes into a Chapter 11 [bankruptcy filing]," he said, "it doesn't lead to Trump. Individual events don't affect Trump, the overall Trump."

As half a dozen flashes went off, he walked into a public hearing room and sat near the front. Arranged around him in the large, anonymous-looking space were his advisers, lawyers, and bodyguards. It was a far cry from the situation three years earlier, when *The Art of the Deal* seemed to seal his reputation as the master business strategist of the era.

Soon afterward he had contracted to write a second installment, but the title, *Surviving at the Top*, now seemed a fantasy to many observers.

At the moment, the real question seemed to be who would pull the plug and when. Some 90 banks had demurred, but whether the Casino Control Commission would do the same remained to be seen. The official watchdog, created to safeguard the legal and financial integrity of the $3 billion casino industry, it faced an inherent conflict of interest in attempting to sit in judgment over someone upon whom the economic well-being of Atlantic City depended. Finding Donald financially unstable and appointing a conservator to run his casinos could create economic panic and shut off the flow of investment capital necessary for casinos to stay competitive in an increasingly crowded field. But to overlook his situation meant flying in the face of mounting evidence, including a scathing 115-page report from the state's Division of Gaming Enforcement, that he was in a financial crisis deeper than anyone ever imagined possible. No one explicitly mentioned this problem during the hearings, but only because there was no need to do so.

Within the hearing room, the mood was highly skeptical. Only two people there seemed entirely confident that Donald would surmount his current financial crisis. One was the developer himself, and the other was a man whom he had grudgingly hired the day before the hearings began. As part of their rescue package, the banks had insisted that he take on a chief financial officer. To the banks it was a routine step in straightening out tangled financial affairs; to Donald it meant breaking the habits of a lifetime. For the first time he would not be able simply to embrace his version of reality. Instead someone else would be looking at his deals from the inside and would see where the facts left off and the exaggeration began.

Still insisting that he would be "the top guy," he had finally bitten the bullet and offered the CFO post to Steve Bollenbach, a financial wizard at Holiday Inns who was regarded by the business community as a straight shooter.[2] A gentle, soft-spoken man with gray hair, a neatly trimmed beard, and dimples, Bollenbach had started at Holiday the day Donald began making takeover noises. "Donald announced that he had bought 5 percent of the company and was planning to clean out its stupid management," Bollenbach later recalled. "I thought, Some welcome!" Forced to defend Holiday by taking on a massive amount of debt, Bollenbach had come to detest the name Trump.

But when the developer tapped him to do a financial reorganization at a salary estimated to be at least half a million dollars, Bollenbach jumped at it. As he later explained, he saw this as an opportunity to make his mark in the ever-growing industry of high-profile "financial workouts"—business-world jargon for figuring out what to do when a company owes more than it can pay. "This is just like the Super Bowl," he told the *Wall Street Journal*.

His first challenge was to persuade the five members of the Casino Control Commission to overlook their deep misgivings and allow the bank bailout to proceed. Even with his easygoing manner and the credibility he had earned during lengthy commission hearings on the Holiday restructuring, it would not be an easy task.

Yes, he told the commissioners, he was familiar with Donald Trump's situation, for he had spoken with Bankers Trust and Citibank.

Yes, he understood big numbers, for he had handled the $2.8 billion recapitalization for Holiday.

Yes, he knew from visionaries and huge losses, for he had been with Daniel Ludwig when the legendary industrialist had tried—and failed—to carve out a billion-dollar timber empire in the Amazon River basin.

Although Bollenbach had just started working for the developer and didn't know the detailed financials, he assured the commission of the Trump Organization's viability. "With good hard work, the business can be turned around," he said firmly. "I don't think of that as dire straits, but maybe some people do." Again and again he struck his central theme: Donald's major assets—the casinos, the shuttle, the Plaza Hotel, half of the Grand Hyatt, and the commercial part of Trump Tower—were sound and simply required consolidation and refinancing.

Evidently this soothing messenger and his calming words were what the regulators had been waiting for. Intent on keeping the Mob away, they had left the door open to Wall Street, and the massive debt loads assumed by the casinos were consuming quarterly profits, currently at their second-lowest level yet. Caught in an impossible bind, the Casino Control Commission met at its Atlantic City office four days after the hearing and voted in favor. "There are no good answers for Mr. Trump or New Jersey," said acting commission chair Valerie Armstrong.

Donald thought otherwise. Dressed in a fresh dark suit, he smiled and called the vote "a great success." Afterward he stood outside and chatted with Neil Barsky. "It's all going to work out," the developer said grandly. As he spoke he eyed a buxom young blonde in cutoff jeans who was strolling along the Boardwalk. She walked over to a souvenir stand, then walked back. Finally he called out, "Hello!" Apparently assuming that she recognized him, he did not tell her his name but instead introduced Barsky. "He's an important reporter," Donald said.

She seemed unimpressed, but he pressed on: "Hey, you look great—have you been working out?" Next to the curb, his driver and his limousine waited. For once, Donald seemed to have all the time in the world.

———◦◦◦———

IN REALITY, he had no time.[3] He had taken care of the banks and the Casino Control Commission, but now he would have to contend with casino bondholders, who were growing increasingly impatient. The day before the commission okayed the bank bailout, institutional investors holding about half the junk bonds sold to finance the Taj had retained Rothschild Inc. as their adviser. As everyone in the financial community knew, this meant Wilbur Ross, who had served as adviser for Resorts investors when Merv Griffin took Atlantic City's first casino into bankruptcy the previous fall.

A Harvard-trained analyst, Ross, then in his mid-fifties, had made a career out of representing the actual owners of public companies— that is, holders of stocks and bonds. Because protecting their interests often meant reviving the companies, he described his work as running "a corporate emergency room [where] when a company gets in trouble, we either fix it and reorganize it, or let it die."

Acting as corporate doctor, he checked debtors' vital signs to see if there was hope, then figured out how to get them working capital to keep going and repay their owners' investment. To come up with a treatment plan for Donald, Ross took a field trip to Atlantic City, flying down with the developer in his helicopter. When they landed on a helipad next to the Boardwalk and crowds surged forward to greet his companion, Ross quickly came to the same conclusion as that reached by the banks: It made no sense to try to take the Trump name off the Taj.

The trick would be getting angry bondholders to agree with this diagnosis. As was usual in such cases, bondholders and company began far apart. What was not usual was Donald's involvement in the negotiations, which focused an enormous spotlight on every move. The media, with its appetite for conflict, played up even the slightest difference of opinion. In turn, because people dislike changing positions they have taken publicly, it was hard to get those involved to be flexible once they had enunciated a stand. "It complicated my life," Ross said of the media barrage. "But it also helped in a strange way—what better proof [of Donald's drawing power] than the fact that he was all over the papers every day."

For the developer's own advisers, there was a similar double edge in representing someone so accustomed to hyperbole. "We kept saying, 'Look, this isn't about getting new money,' " said Ken Moelis, an investment banker at Donaldson, Lufkin & Jenrette who had worked on the Holiday reorganization and had been recruited by Bollenbach to help dig out their former opponent. "It's about restructuring loans, about not having to give it all back." But much as Donald's habit of inflating numbers sometimes caused problems, at other times his characteristic bombast let his bankers seem reasonable by comparison. Likewise his negotiating style, which included grandiloquence, convenient slips of memory, and liberal doses of flattery, could be embarrassing to his advisers, but it also allowed them to keep renegotiating until the end.

A further complication was the appearance of TWA chairman Carl Icahn, a predatory entrepreneur who made a habit of buying up the stock of distressed companies. Over recent months Icahn had scooped up a reported 22 percent of outstanding Taj junk bonds, said to be worth

$100 million, which made him the biggest single bondholder and a major player in the negotiations. Because Icahn insisted on meeting on his own turf, the developer had to get into a limousine and drive 40 miles to the TWA corporate offices in suburban Westchester County. "Driving up there, Donald was crazed," Moelis said. "He had to go see Icahn to try to get his own company back, and he doesn't like to be in that position."

Then, too, there was Donald's personal style. A man of enormous self-confidence, he was both extraordinarily astute and oddly adolescent. As his world teetered close to collapse, he reacted with a combination of petulance, denial, and furious intensity. Sometimes he would focus with such laserlike attention that he seemed about to burn a hole right through his interlocutor; at other times he simply ignored all advice and insisted that everyone do it his way. He would sit at his big rosewood desk hour after hour; then, with no warning, he would disappear upstairs to the three-bedroom Trump Tower apartment where he now lived. Lying on his big bed, he would snack on junk food and watch television with Marla, leaving those in the office to fend off calls and muddle through the day's inevitable crises. On still other occasions, sometimes in the middle of the night, he might be seized with energy. Regardless of the hour, he would call his financial advisers and launch into a lengthy monologue.

In the early days of his relationship with Marla, he had wanted relief from Ivana and her alternating moods of fierce competition and desperate subservience. Now, though, Marla seemed his only refuge from a world spinning out of control. In the middle of conversations he would pull out her picture and rhapsodize about her physical endowments. Sometimes he would interrupt meetings in his conference room and put on a videotape of her for everyone to watch. "There she'd be in a bathing suit, jiggling around," said one participant, "and he'd be making all these comments about 'nice tits, no brains.' "

Part of the problem was that he had lost his reality check. For years he had raced ahead at top speed, relying on the members of his inner circle to act as brakes. But now most of that inner circle had either left or was in the process of leaving. In part this was a simple budgetary move, for he did not have the money to pay them and was scrambling to cover Bollenbach's paycheck. But there was another reason: The developer could not stand being around eyewitnesses. He could not acknowledge his refusal to heed their warnings or accept responsibility for the problems that had resulted from his own actions.

For years he had needed these men and women for their skill and judgment; now he needed them as scapegoats. Blanche Sprague, Tony Gliedman, Howard Rubenstein, Harvey Freeman, Jerry Schrager, Jeff Walker, other top employees and casino executives—one by one he fired them, pushed them out, refused to pay their bills. "He has burned an immense number of bridges in the last six to eight months," one former adviser said at the time. "It's come to be Donald against the world." True to form, however, he refused to acknowledge that the staff departures were linked to his financial problems and at one point threatened the *New York Post* with a $250 million lawsuit for suggesting such a possibility.[4]

Unlike the bank bailout, the settlement he eventually reached with the Taj bondholders and, later, Castle and Plaza bondholders involved filing for bankruptcy. In the 1930s the Lehrenkrauss Corporation had done the same, providing the catalyst for Fred's success, and Penn Central's bankruptcy in the 1970s had jump-started Donald's career. But in 1978 a congressional overhaul of bankruptcy law had ended up favoring debtors, and since then lawyers and judges had refined this step almost beyond recognition. Donald would be using a "prepackaged" bankruptcy, a legal maneuver that had recently evolved to take care of the technical requirement that all bondholders agree to any settlement. When Lehrenkrauss and Penn Central had declared bankruptcy, they had surrendered everything to the courts; when he did so, it would be to maintain his control. He would not have to turn over the asset in question to a bankruptcy judge, and the entire procedure would take only a few months.

Bondholders did have a victory of sorts. As was inevitable in such cases, they had to accept an extension of the maturity date on their bonds and a reduction in their interest rate from 14 to 12 percent, which was still more than the casino might be able to pay. In exchange, they now owned half the casino. But in almost every other respect it seemed that Donald came out ahead. He would be board chairman for the legal entity that owned the Taj and retain an ownership stake of 50 percent, upgradeable to 80 percent if he met certain performance goals. In addition, he would receive an annual management fee of at least $500,000, which, as the *Journal's* Barsky observed tartly, was probably more than he was making from any other assets.[5]

It was an early use of such a prepackage, a device that would soon become commonplace. But this was only one of the many ways that losing money had changed over the course of the twentieth century. At its opening, bankruptcy had been a black hole from which few of those touched by it were able to emerge. When Lehrenkrauss and Penn Central went under, the creditors were so fearful of seeing vast assets swallowed up the way the Jarndyce fortune disappeared in the Charles Dickens novel *Bleak House* that they cooperated on allocating the spoils. Now, though, Donald himself was such a large part of the assets that in order to keep up their value, his creditors had to keep him going.

—◈—

FOR MANY, the hardest struggle might have been to put one foot in front of the other, but this was not a problem for Donald. "He worked 24/7 to get what he wanted," said one participant in the negotiations. "When we agreed to things with the bondholders, he'd say we'll fuck 'em in the paperwork. He's a big-picture guy but he also looks at the details." Donald's modus operandi—always pushing the edge combined with convenient slips of memory—seemed "completely wacky," but it also seemed to work. "He sits there and focuses in, and he's very good at figuring out who is the important person of the moment he needs to flatter."

Whenever Donald talked to the press, he said the same thing: He had not lost a night's sleep; things would work out; two years from now he would be worth more than ever. "He never saw this as a game winding up," Steve Bollenbach said later. "From his point of view, he was simply sorting out the credit overloaned to him." That the debt was much larger than the assets were worth was just another business problem, Bollenbach said, and Donald was taking a rational approach. "He was correct, but that's not the way most people think about it."

Even when he had to auction off Trump Plaza of the Palm Beaches, Donald broadcast an upbeat mood. His father's formula for rescuing failing property hadn't worked, in large part because Fred had gone for sturdy, modestly priced apartments that required little more than fresh paint and enthusiasm, not poorly constructed condominiums starting at $300,000 and still needing significant work. For that kind of money people wanted more than a view of Palm Beach; they wanted to be in a prime residential location themselves. Even after Donald bragged of Lee Iacocca's involvement—the Chrysler president bought three apartments for a total of $1.1 million and resold them almost immediately for a minuscule profit of $41,000—the units didn't move.

Nonetheless, Donald had continued to be optimistic. Whenever he sold an apartment at the complex, he told one reporter, "I'm angry, because I know in four years they're going to be selling, you know, my opinion, for four or five times as much." But after four years, more than half of the units remained unsold. During the first 11 months of 1990 there was one sale. When the developer missed an October interest payment, Marine Midland, which had given him a $60 million mortgage on the property, demanded that he do something.

"Something" turned out to be a public auction. Because it was impossible to move the condominium across Lake Worth to Palm Beach, the location Donald needed to get the prices he wanted, he did the next best thing. He held the sale in the main ballroom of the Breakers, the grandiose hotel built a century earlier by Palm Beach founder Henry Flagler. Once again, elegant advertisements appeared in upscale national publications. Shortly before noon on Sunday, December 16, potential bidders drove up the hotel's long drive and parked in a lot filled with Mercedes and stretch limos. After entering the palatial cream-colored resort, bidders made their way through long hallways hung with crystal chandeliers to the vast, salmon-walled Venetian Ballroom. After local high school cheerleaders performed a rousing if incongruous cheer, a fast-talking auctioneer, whose patter was being broadcast in simulcast auctions in Boston and Chicago, got going on the 35 lots being offered that day.[6]

In novels and films, someone whose property is on the block is instantly recognizable: unkempt, perhaps taking swigs out of a bottle, and almost certainly holding his head in his hands. And, in fact, behind the scenes there were tales of the developer screaming and ranting at the president of the auction house, its sales representatives, and even Louise Sunshine, who had rejoined her former boss for the event. "Sometimes he'd call and be really nice," said Susan Stevens, on-site manager of the event. "The next morning he'd be swearing at us, like someone so out of control he didn't know what tack to take."[7]

But in the Venetian Ballroom, Donald was clean-shaven and immaculately dressed as he stood at the back of the room, smiling and chomping on Tic-Tacs. Conspicuously inconspicuous, the beautiful young woman who had accompanied him sat next to Sunshine and said "I'm sorry" whenever anyone asked her name. By the next morning the press had learned that she was Rowanne Brewer, that she was a model, and that she was the developer's companion du jour during one of his many well-publicized splits from Marla. Graciously Donald accepted dozens of business cards, tossing them after their donors walked away. When reporters wandered over, he launched into his familiar stream-of-consciousness press agentry.

"These are great prices, you know," he said. "You know, this is the wave of the future, it's better than taking two years and schlepping to all the buyers. What you have to remember, though, you have to remember I sold 50 percent of the units in the weakest market in the history of Florida—it's not like these are empty buildings. I'm having a party at the end of the year—not what you think, not to toast the future—to curse the bad year out. It's been a disaster for everyone, look at the airlines, for chrissakes."

He paused to accept another business card, then resumed. "You know what I think?" he asked. Without pausing he answered, "I think there's something very sophisticated and intelligent about auctions."

When the auction ended, all 35 units had sold, at an average of 40 percent below the original asking price—about what they would have fetched before the addition of the Trump name and elevation to the superluxury price bracket. The developer inspected his appearance before a mirror, then strode into a small reception room and struck a commanding pose in front of a huge carved fireplace.

"This has turned out to be a really great event," he declared to dozens of reporters and a handful of television crews. "We've far exceeded our expectations." Pithily he summed up: "Trump Plaza is the building of the future."

FIFTEEN HUNDRED MILES to the north, a second Trump auction took place the same day in a windowless basement room.[8] It was a quiet affair, held at the JFK Airport Hilton Hotel, a white bunker in the wastes outside the airport, and featured one-, two-, and three-bedroom apartments in Brooklyn and Queens. No newspaper reporters were in attendance, and no limousines sat outside.

During the late 1980s the real estate frenzy in Manhattan had spread to the outer boroughs, and Fred had converted a number of properties into condominiums. Anticipating quick sales, he instead ran full tilt into a real estate slump and now hoped to unload 40 unsold units. Unlike the flimsily built condos being sold that day in Florida, these did not have heated towel racks, crystal bathroom fixtures, or ocean views. Instead, as the diagrams taped around the room attested, they were solid, meat-and-potatoes homes for ordinary people, the kind of housing that had been associated with Fred for his entire career and the financial base on which his son had built his own extraordinary career.

Before the sale began, Fred shook hands and answered questions from potential buyers. An erect figure, he wore a dark blue pin-striped suit that was a trifle loose on his 85-year-old body and a bright scarlet tie. When people said they were interested in buying apartments, he reacted with the easy warmth of a good salesman. If he heard the whispers—"You know who that is? That's Fred Trump, Donald's father!"— he gave no sign.

An acquaintance asked him if his son was holding another auction.

"Yes," Fred said, consulting a heavy watch. "We're holding one in Florida right about now. At the end, we're going to see who sold more, Donny or me." He smiled. "Donny'll be sure to tell the reporters he won."

He would have been right. After half a dozen bids for units in Brooklyn and none for the entire borough of Queens, the auctioneer thanked everyone for coming and left the front of the room. Fred had sat stone-faced during the 16-minute-long proceeding. When it was over, he stood and spoke in a low voice to the people seated next to him. The wave of the future had rolled past, leaving him and his properties nearly untouched.

The wave did not rescue his son, either. By April 1991 Trump Plaza of the Palm Beaches still had 70 unsold units, and Donald still had an $18 million Marine Midland loan on the property that he had personally guaranteed and could not repay. Bank and developer struck a deal: In exchange for title to the units, $1 million cash, and the developer's presence at a second auction, the bank would write off the personal guarantee and split with him any eventual profits.[9]

It was Donald's first foreclosure. But instead of appearing devastated, he sounded ebullient. "Talk to Donald and he's happy about this," said Rick Edmonds, a publicist assigned by Howard Rubenstein to handle the event. "He's reveling in how much money he'll make." His optimism turned out to be unmerited; although all the units that were offered sold, the auction revenues did not cover the outstanding debt. "These are the first people in America to take a piece of Donald Trump's empire for as low as sixty cents on the dollar," Edmonds said afterward.

Donald had a more upbeat spin. "It's called 'deleveraging,' " he said. "Everybody's doing it."

LITTLE BY LITTLE, inch by inch, the developer was extracting more favorable loan terms, renegotiating bond obligations, and shedding his most unprofitable holdings. Less than a year earlier he had appeared to be at the mercy of his bankers, but now he seemed to be getting the better of them.

Steve Bollenbach's basic strategy as CFO was to divide the assets between those to which the Trump name added value, principally the casinos, and those to which it did not, such as the yacht, the helicopters, and the block of smaller units in Trump Tower that the developer still owned. "We considered the second group of assets hostages," Bollenbach said, "and every now and then we'd release one of them to [creditors to] get a concession. The whole idea was to end up with the casinos and whatever else we could keep."

Handling what amounted to hostage negotiations took both cunning and brinkmanship. When an insurance premium on the yacht had to be paid, Bollenbach called the bank that had loaned the most money for its purchase, said that it would be a shame if the boat sank without coverage, and then forwarded the bill; on the day it was due, the bank coughed up the money. When the banks were dragging their feet on providing better terms, he drew up bankruptcy papers and sent Robert to file them at federal court in New Jersey. After Robert waited for hours, legal documents in hand, the banks finally cried uncle.[10]

The most extraordinary display of ingenuity occurred on December 17, 1990, the day after the first Palm Beach auction, when Donald had to make an $18.4 million interest payment on Trump Castle bonds. Casino analysts were certain that he was several million dollars short and, because his assets were already pledged to creditors, would be unable to get a loan. But somehow he came through with a check. "We don't need an outside infusion," he told Neil Barsky of the *Wall Street Journal* in a smug voice.

Five weeks later the reporter had another scoop: The reason Donald had not needed any outside infusion was that he had received one from the inside.[11] The day the payment was due, Fred had given his lawyer more than $3 million to buy chips at Trump Castle and told him to leave without playing or cashing them in. In this unorthodox fashion, father conveyed funds to son without actually risking any loss, for state law mandated that chip holders be first in line for repayment in the event of default. Financially the maneuver was foolproof. Legally, however, it was a problem, for lending money to a casino requires a license from the Casino Control Commission.

Knowing that such a tactic was, as one of Donald's colleagues put it, "borderline," one of the developer's lawyers called the Casino Control Commission beforehand and got a verbal okay. Eventually this turned into a not-okay, for the ploy was an unauthorized and therefore illegal loan. But somehow the prior, informal notice, combined with the fact that the source of the funds had been Donald's elderly father, stayed the regulators' hands. Eventually they doled out a fine of $65,000, but they also certified Fred as a casino lending source. As a result, the Castle did not have to return the money that he had advanced right away but could instead repay it over time.[12]

"Sometimes [a confrontation with a creditor] was just a stare-down," Bollenbach said. "I'd say, 'You're right, we should give it back, but guess what, we're not going to.' " At one point, even though Donald had the money, he refused to make mortgage payments on Mar-a-Lago until the bank that had made the loan extended it.[13]

Donald's monthly allowance was a particularly sore point for creditors, who went wild when he wrote a $10 million check for Ivana. "They were screaming, 'That's our money,' " Bollenbach said. "I told them that's the price of keeping Donald from pushing the bankruptcy button." As far as the CFO was concerned, the idea that the developer would ever really stick to a budget was a fantasy. "He wasn't in a Long Island bungalow, and he still had a 727," Bollenbach said. "He never changed how he lived at all." But the mere existence of an allowance provision allowed the banks to save face and Bollenbach's strategy to play out just as he'd planned. Over time Donald ceded his small apartments, yacht, helicopters, shuttle, Alexander's stake, and half of the Grand Hyatt; he retained the casinos, the rail yards, his residences, and a partial interest in the Plaza Hotel.

In turn, Bollenbach had to accept that the developer had an ego as big as the Ritz. "It's part of who Donald is," he said, "like his height and the color of his hair." During one drive to Atlantic City, he recalled, Donald started telling him the same version of his life story that he had already recounted many times. Bollenbach interrupted. "I said, 'Donald, today we're going to do something novel—I'm going to tell you the story of my life.' I began by telling him I was born in Los Angeles, and right away he interrupted to ask if he'd ever told me about the first time he went to Los Angeles."

———◦◦◦———

To BOLLENBACH, the most important asset was the casinos, because of their cash flow. But to Donald, there was another significant asset: the West Side rail yards, which he still hoped to develop.

There had been no shortage of opportunities to get out from under this highly problematic project. In 1986 a Japanese construction firm named Kumagai Gumi had offered to buy a 25 percent interest in Television City for $97 million, a deal that would have paid off most of the land cost at a stroke. At the last minute Donald raised the price to $160 million. "The Kuma people just stared at him," said real estate broker Jack Shaffer, who represented the Japanese firm, and whose own office was across the street from Trump Tower. "Then they walked. By the time I got back to my office, Donald had called and asked me to bring them back, but the damage was done." In 1988, two years before the opening of the Taj and his subsequent near-bankruptcy, the developer came even closer to selling the site to another New York developer for $550 million. But he kept upping the ante with certain financial controls and demands that streets be named after himself, and that deal also fell apart.[14]

In response, Donald launched yet another initiative. Instead of television studios, the West Side project would focus on what he called "the largest and most technologically advanced" housing complex for the elderly ever built in New York City. To promote it, he would tout it as a major contribution to the life of the city and the region, on a par with Rockefeller Center.

The project, now named Trump City, was still enormous and community opposition remained high, but Donald insisted that much of the city was behind him. Because he could outwait any adversaries, he said, he would eventually get the zoning he required. "Whether it's now or later doesn't matter," he said. "All my life, people have been trying to stop me. Frankly, I look forward to the challenge."[15]

Before any real estate development begins its official passage through the various stages of the Uniform Land Use Review Procedure (ULURP), the city's complex zoning approval process, the developer and city agencies usually resolve a number of issues through quiet negotiation. This time, though, there was little pre-ULURP bargaining. Refusing even to consider reducing the size of Trump City, Trump retained zoning genius Sandy Lindenbaum and announced that he would use "underwater zoning"—development rights derived from the underwater portion of the site—to increase the size of what he built on dry land.

On the city's side there was also little movement. In part this was because zoning permits almost always involve last-minute haggling, and everyone tends to save any big guns until then. In addition, said former City Planning Department staffer Tom Glendenning, officials were concerned that it might be counterproductive to try whittling down the size of the project. They decided to let this absurdly huge development get as far as possible through the approvals process before being killed off, because it would then be too late for Donald to do anything else. "We wanted to get Trump going [to] the point where it wouldn't be worth his while to start over," Glendenning said. "That was our strategy to lower the density." [16]

Accordingly, both sides talked about everything except what was on everyone's minds. "No one in City Planning would say anything straight," said a former Trump staffer. "Instead, more subtle signals would come back. City Planning would talk about planning principles, [and] the issue of heights was never really taken on." Donald's office kept mum as well. The former staffer was never sure whether the world's tallest building was simply a chip to be thrown away during negotiations or something Donald wanted so much that he could not admit any difficulties. In either case, the staffer said, such a structure, which swallowed nearly $1 million in preliminary studies, was not worth all the trouble it caused.

"Can you imagine living at the top of such a place?" the former staffer said. "The windows would shake, it would take several elevators to get there, your pizza would be cold by the time it arrived, and the dog would pee in the elevator before you ever got to the ground floor." But following Donald's orders, his staff slogged on through the numerous studies and reviews required before ULURP could begin and, the staff assumed, City Planning would demand major reductions.

In part this reticence was because the staff dreaded Donald's rages. But it was also due to an eagerness to share what still seemed, at this pre-Taj point, his apparently endless triumphs. "Within the office, there was an incredible bullishness," said the former staffer. "It was hard to say there was anything to worry about, because everything he did seemed a success, and people were throwing money at him."

———◆———

ALTHOUGH DONALD CLAIMED to have community support for his rail yards project, the only visible response was the vigorous opposition. Funded by passing the hat at meetings, community organizations handed out leaflets and protested loudly every chance they got. To Donald they seemed a troublesome presence, though not dangerous. But shortly after he first presented what was then Television City at a community board meeting, yet another group appeared. It would cause him considerably more difficulties and, in the end, would change the project in ways he had never imagined.

The new group was born at a small dinner party at the Central Park West apartment of Roberta Gratz, a former urban affairs reporter.[17] "There is nothing right about this project that you can fix with [only] a change in scale," she said to the people around the table. "Everything is wrong." One guest was Arlene Simon, an over-my-dead-body preservationist who had pushed through landmark status for several buildings and forced her neighbor, the broadcasting giant ABC, to curtail a planned expansion on her block. The other guests included Simon's husband, Bruce, a combative labor lawyer for the Teamsters; Victor Kovner, a libel attorney and former law partner of Ed Koch; and his wife, Sarah, a founder of the First Women's Bank and an activist in local Democratic Party circles. To these political veterans, it seemed natural to take on the man they considered only the latest in a long series of threats to their way of life.

Before the evening was over, they had a name, Westpride, and an ambitious strategy. Starting the next day, they would ask 50 families to donate $1,000 each to the cause, and they would solicit the biggest names they could find to join in the effort. Within weeks they had enlisted television journalist Bill Moyers, former mayor John Lindsay, and best-selling writers Judith Rossner, David Halberstam, and Robert Caro. Soon afterward, they had their first benefit, a cocktail party on the roof of the nearby Gulf + Western Building with $125 tickets and a high-profile guest list. Three years and dozens of celebrity-studded benefits later, Westpride had nearly 6,000 members, a $200,000 budget, and paid lawyers, environmental experts, and public relations counsel.

Trying to distinguish itself from other anti-Trump efforts, Westpride insisted that it would favor a project on the rail yards that was in scale with the surrounding community. "We're in favor of development that makes sense," said architect Steve Robinson, Westpride co-chair. The real problem, he explained, was that the city itself had no way to initiate city planning, which meant that real estate projects inevitably ended up designed strictly to maximize profits.

To figure out alternatives, Westpride hired an MIT-trained environmental engineer named Dan Gutman. His solution: Replace the ugly elevated highway at the edge of the rail yards with a ground-level, inland roadway, which would free up a large chunk of the site for a waterside park. Both Robert Moses and Donald had already dismissed this idea as prohibitively expensive, but now the corroded roadway was about to undergo an $85 million rehabilitation. To Gutman, it seemed the perfect opportunity for such a change, and he asked architect Paul Willen to sketch out what it might look like.

A native West Sider, Willen knew the site well, for he had worked on earlier plans for Donald and for Francisco Macri and he had chaired a prestigious American Institute of Architects task force that had, in an unusual move, recommended the rejection of Trump City. But the scheme Willen produced this time was completely different from any of its many predecessors. By lowering and moving the highway, he was able to create a large riverside park and to replace Donald's monoliths with a variety of structures. Designed in the neighborhood's art deco style, they contained 7 million square feet of space, the same housing density approved for Macri and about half that in what Donald now called Trump City. "To our surprise and delight, it worked," Willen said. "Everything fit."

Others agreed. On Sunday, July 1, 1990, his drawing appeared in the *New York Times*. "Everything on Donald Trump's 72 waterfront acres falls into place logically, even elegantly," wrote Paul Goldberger in an accompanying article. The next day Norman Levin, a South African who served as project director at the rail yards site for both Macri and Donald, showed the *Times* to Tony Gliedman, then working on obtaining rezoning for Trump City. "This is a winner," Levin said to Gliedman. "We have a problem."

Levin was right. The plan appeared just as Donald and his bankers were in the midst of negotiating the $65 million bailout he needed to hang on to the rail yards and casinos. Revelations about Donald's financial affairs had spurred Manhattan political and civic leaders to think about wresting the West Side site away from him, and now they had a concrete and attractive alternative to promote. Manhattan borough president Ruth Messinger and other elected officials called for the city to buy the site and take the lead in producing a new and better design. Optimistically, civic groups declared that the proposal to move the highway would cost less than the $85 million already budgeted for repairs and began lobbying transportation officials. In addition, David Dinkins, who had defeated Ed Koch to become the city's first African-American mayor, and his deputy mayor, a preservationist named Barbara Fife, seemed to favor the new proposal.

Publicly Donald continued to plow ahead and to discount the opposition. "You have to understand," he told *Manhattan, inc.* magazine, "they have zero to do with this process. Zero." But the process had changed, and developers could no longer quash problems with a donation, a promise, or a quiet threat. The Municipal Art Society (MAS), a 93-year-old group more accustomed to lifting sherry glasses than picket signs, had recently taken on the huge project planned for the old Coliseum site at Columbus Circle. MAS board member Jacqueline Kennedy Onassis and 800 other protesters had marched into Central Park and on cue unfolded black umbrellas to symbolize the huge shadow the tower-ing skyscraper would cast. A court suit stalled the project and eventu-ally forced its developer to provide a scaled-down version.[18]

Now the "civic alternative," an alliance that included Westpride and the MAS, was pushing the plan Levin had seen in the *Times*. For guidance, the group had approached Richard Kahan, who had worked on the Commodore project and later headed both the Urban Develop-ment Corporation and the authority that built Battery Park City. An amateur wrestler who moved and spoke in a quick, sometimes brusque manner, Kahan had no interest in participating in a mission that seemed to him quixotic at best. "These people were from the West Side," he recalled thinking. "I had heard they were very difficult."

Then he took a look at Willen's drawing. He liked what he saw: a natural extension of the West Side that would let Donald build fewer units and still turn a profit. What he didn't like was that the civic-alternative leaders seemed more set on getting rid of the developer, whom they despised, than having a great project. "I asked what would happen if Donald Trump walked into this room and said, 'I'll build your scheme?' " Kahan said. "It was a very uncomfortable question. Nobody wanted to touch it, but finally Bruce Simon looked at me and said, 'I guess we'd have to do it.' "

Kahan signed on, but even with his help, the civic alternative made little progress at diverting the highway renovation. The day be-fore Thanksgiving 1990, Barbara Fife delivered the bad news: The Dinkins administration had decided that the highway was in such bad shape that the reconstruction had to proceed without delay. "We were devastated," said Kent Barwick, MAS president. "It looked like an op-portunity that had been lost forever." That was not the only bad news. The alliance also learned that Trump City would almost certainly ob-tain approval for a still-too-large 11 million square feet.

Feeling desperate, the civic-alternative groups filed suit to stop the highway renovation. They also began considering the still repugnant idea of asking their nemesis to build their plan. Six months earlier they had found such a notion unthinkable; now, though, it might be think-able not only for Westpride but for Donald, who was in the midst of negotiations with irate Taj bondholders. "He was looking down the barrel at potential foreclosure [and] there were sharks in the water," Barwick said.[19] Talking to Donald directly could be a humiliating failure for the civic alternative, but it also had the possibility of changing the climate of discussion.

MAS chair Stephen Swid, a former co-owner of the '21' Club who was friendly with the developer, volunteered to make the first contact. "I went to him, laid out the alternate plan, and said, 'How about it?'" Swid recalled later. "Donald had only one question: 'Who says the West Side will approve it?'" Swid explained that the sponsors of the plan were the same groups who had been fighting the developer's proposals and again asked if Donald would do it. The developer did not pause to consider. "I'm not going to change my plan publicly," he said. "But the answer is yes if you can get the West Siders to sponsor it."

Donald urgently needed such an opening. Since August, Bollenbach had been maneuvering to retain as many of the developer's assets as possible, but this had been a holding action. Working with groups who had so far done little but castigate the developer would be the municipal equivalent of Richard Nixon's trip to China—a breakthrough with the potential to move this long-stalled project out of the twin quagmires of zoning difficulties and community opposition. While Bollenbach took care of the past, Donald would be able to create something new.

Stunned at his affirmative response, the groups held a flurry of "oh my god, what now" meetings and scheduled a powwow with the developer. On a chilly early morning two weeks before Christmas, about 30 civic and community representatives deliberately scattered themselves around the wood-paneled conference room of Cravath, Swaine & Moore, the law firm of one Westpride board member. When Donald arrived promptly at the agreed-upon hour of 7 A.M., the members of his party had to scatter themselves as well. But it was not hard to distinguish the developer's employees from the activists, many of whom worked in the nonprofit sector. "Some of the men had tweed jackets with leather patches actually covering up holes," Swid said, "not Brooks Brothers jackets with preattached patches."

Donald, who was about to auction off his West Palm Beach apart-ment complex and to get an unauthorized loan from his father to keep the Trump Castle casino from foreclosure, opened with a confronta-tional move. "I want to say that no matter what you read, I'm still worth $1 billion," he declared. As the leather-patches crowd bristled and rus-tled papers aggressively, Swid shrank down in his chair. "If there was one audience who didn't want to hear this," he said later, "it was this one."

Donald went on, talking for half an hour straight. He, too, hated the highway, he said. He had tried to deal with it by hiding it in plain sight. The only reason he had built a huge platform was to act as cam-ouflage; then, because he had space to fill, he had come up with the idea of TV studios and a shopping mall. "He sort of bowled everyone over with his tirade," Dan Gutman recalled later. "He kept repeating himself and making jokes about his financial problems, and he also kept saying that he could get approval of Trump City."

Then Donald picked up a yellow legal pad and a pencil. "Your idea would be better," he said. "It's an exciting design." On the pad he drew a crude oval and bisected it with an arc. "Okay," he said. "Here's the prop-erty. On one side I'll build my development, and on the other side you can build a park."

To Paul Willen, a veteran of so many plans for the site, it was a dra-matic moment. "Donald switched a hundred and eighty degrees," Willen said. "He liked big, repetitive buildings, and never showed any appreciation whatsoever for the history of the city. [But] this project was historic and organic—it was attached to New York City."

By the end of the meeting it seemed as if something could happen. It seemed even more that way during talks with construction leaders to solicit their support for what would now be a new highway, a housing development, and a park. More positive momentum emerged when the groups told city and state officials they would drop the lawsuit on the highway if they could get support for moving it.

Then early in 1991, just after Barsky's revelation that Fred had to cough up the money for an interest payment on Trump Castle, Donald told Swid that he could not move forward after all. The reason, he said, was that he was personally on the line to Chase for the purchase price of the rail yards, plus about $20 million a year in interest, a total of about $220 million. Swid asked an important political contact to make the case to Chase that the best way for the bank to get the money was to allow the project to go forward, and Chase later let Donald off the guarantee. "Donald was very smart, because he didn't tell me everything at once," Swid said. "Until the not-for-profits and MAS agreed, he didn't tell me about needing to get the guarantee lifted."

Keeping Chase reassured would be an important task for Donald's new allies. At his request, Richard Kahan lunched with bank officials, and the alliance's housing expert, Charlie Reiss, who later went to work for Donald, made presentations.[20] Nearly 15 years earlier, when Kahan was a deputy at the Urban Development Corporation, he had seen Donald leverage government support to get the financing he needed for the Grand Hyatt; now he was watching Donald use community and civic organizations the same way. "Donald was the first to understand that the rules had changed," Kahan said, "and that there could be a different way of doing business."

Three months after that morning meeting in Cravath Swaine's conference room, the mayor, the developer, and civic-alternative representatives told a packed City Hall press conference that there would be no Trump City.[21] Instead, Donald would build the activists' plan, an about-face that *Times* critic Goldberger compared to "the news that the Soviet Union had given up on Communism."[22] Smiles and hugs filled the dais; in an expansive moment, Donald even allowed Westpride's executive director to pin on his lapel a button that showed a red circle with "Trump City" written inside and a red cancellation bar drawn across it.

According to the deal struck by the developer and Kahan, the redesigned project would be a little more than half the size of Trump City and cost about half as much. With 5,700 units, it would still be the city's largest private development project of the decade and far larger than anything Fred or Donald had ever done.[23] But there would be no world's tallest building, shopping mall, or public parking garage; instead the developer would donate land to move the elevated highway inland and build a riverside park of 21.5 acres adjacent to the existing 70-block-long Riverside Park.[24] In return, the civic alternative alliance would support what would now be called Riverside South, which would go forward regardless of whether the highway was relocated.

For more than a year the media had provided nonstop coverage of Donald's ongoing financial crisis. *Fortune* kicked him out of the billionaire's club; *Forbes* said he had a negative net worth. Every tabloid and talk show mocked his personal life, and the mainstream press seemed to be licking its chops at the prospect of his collapse. But now the hero of Wollman Rink reemerged as the hero of the West Side rail yards. "This is the biggest turnout I've ever seen here," Donald said happily, and waved an arm at the rest of the dais. "All you folks have persuaded me to do really what was right."

He had not lost his taste for superlatives; he noted that Riverside South would be "one of the greatest developments anywhere" on "the greatest piece of property anywhere in the world." And the compromise was not—repeat, not—a blow to his ego. Rather, Trump City had been a project for the 1980s. "This is a project for the nineties," he told *Newsday*. "The nineties are less obtrusive."

Seated halfway back in the room, Fred watched his son. The older man had just returned from a trip to Miami, where, as usual, he stayed at the Fontainebleau. When asked about his own career, he declined to comment. "I like to keep low and not have a lot of attention," he said. "Other people can have it, I don't need it." He paused, then added, in words he attributed to the Bard but which seemed instead to sum up his own life philosophy, "As Shakespeare said, work is what you do while you're waiting to die."

A moment later he took out a photograph of Donald wearing a tuxedo. "I showed this to people in Florida," he said. "They all seemed to know who he is." He sounded genuinely amazed at something that would not have surprised anyone else in the room. But he had a different relationship with the man in the snapshot. Looking at him, Fred saw a boy in a baseball uniform tagging another player out at first base and a cadet marching at the head of his company. He saw a squash player winning a game and a young man at the topping off of the Grand Hyatt and Trump Tower, and then the same man announcing that he'd bought the Trump Shuttle and Plaza Hotel and opening the Taj by rubbing a big lamp. It did not matter that the man in the photo was a celebrity. What mattered was that he was a champion.

ALL OPPOSITION to the project did not disappear. After a brief sigh of relief that the world's tallest building was history, the original anti-Macri coalition came out swinging. Riverside South was still too large, its members insisted, and the park, cut off behind a wall of tall buildings, was too far away, too small, and too much like a glorified backyard for the new complex. "People formed Westpride because they said we weren't strong enough to fight Donald Trump," said coalition leader Madeleine Polayes. "Then they went to bed with him."

One by one, local elected officials also refused to support Riverside South. "I remember another council member saying, 'Gee, I wish I had this in my district,'" recalled City Council member Ronnie Eldridge, who represented the West Side. "I said, 'That's the point, it should be in another district.'" Jerrold Nadler, who represented the West Side in Congress, flatly opposed development on the site and pushed instead to rebuild rail freight facilities there in order to retain manufacturing jobs in the city and create new blue-collar employment.

In an effort to expand the range of planning options, Manhattan borough president Ruth Messinger sponsored a four-day workshop in late June 1991 at which urban planners and designers from around the country discussed the site and alternative possibilities. Donald himself turned up during one Saturday afternoon session. Dressed as usual in a dark suit and a striped tie, he stood out against the jeans and T-shirts of the other attendees.

As he walked through the lobby, he stopped here and there for brief exchanges with participants. Upon learning that one consultant was from Buffalo, he asked how the project would go over there, and the consultant replied, "It's as big as Buffalo!" Another planner complained about the current proposal's density, and Donald dared him to come up with a way to make money on a smaller project. Then local community board member Ethel Scheffer, a longtime critic of plans for the site, launched into an impassioned plea for a greater sense of social responsibility on everyone's part. The developer listened for a few minutes, then tipped back his head and said in mock earnestness, "Ethel, there's one thing you've got to do, you've got to get more serious about all this! Get more into it!"

As the little group of listeners that had gathered around him chuckled, Donald proceeded to lay out his own prescription for urban ills. "You know," he said, "what New York really needs—besides this project—is to reduce its debt. And let me tell you—this is something I know—it's easy! You just don't pay!"

His listeners grinned at the reference to the developer's most recent failure to pony up what he owed. "There's all these stages people go through," Donald continued. "You know, first there's incredulity, then there's rage, frustration, then grudging acceptance."

The grins became guffaws. "It works every time. You just have to be strong enough not to pay. Look how often I've done it in Atlantic City, four, five times, and each time people said he'll lose the Taj, he'll lose the [Trump] Plaza, he'll lose the Castle, and I haven't at all. For the Castle—off the record, I've just got interest payments for the Castle reduced from 14 to 8 percent. This was the punishment I got for saying I'm not paying!"[25]

Just before Halloween 1992, nearly two years after the developer and the civic alliance first met—the blink of an eye in the real estate world—Riverside South faced the final vote by the City Planning Commission. The alliance still thought that the buildings were too large and there was too much parking in an already congested area, and Donald wanted the towers higher so there would be more high-priced river views. But together they had hammered out a package they could live with.

Alighting from his double-parked limousine, the developer swept into the commission's public hearing room, trailed by the usual gaggle of journalists, three Chase bankers, and a camera crew from *Prime Time Live*. His television makeup giving him an orange glow, Donald worked the room until the last moment. Pointing to a *Newsday* reporter, he effusively praised that paper's favorable editorial. He hugged former foes, squeezed elbows, and put his arm around shoulders. Standing next to the bankers, he said loudly, "They've been great, really great, great guys." Even his most implacable adversaries appeared to blink, if not melt, in the face of this charm offensive; spotting Madeleine Polayes, whom he had faced the previous evening in a televised debate, he yelled out, "You looked good, really good, better than me!" Cracking a smile, she shot back, "I'll send you my hairdresser!"

After receiving unanimous approval from the commissioners, the proposal moved on to the City Council for more tweaking. At one key subcommittee meeting in late November, construction workers, bused in from all over the city, demonstrated outside City Hall, chanting in favor of the project. Inside, lawyers and civic leaders congregated in the lobby, waiting for the meeting to start. City officials dashed back and forth between various offices, and at one point Mayor Dinkins came out, shook half a dozen hands, and then went back into his quarters.

Among those waiting in the lobby was a participant connected with Chase, holder of a large and currently nonperforming loan on the property that would take a big step toward repayment once zoning approval was granted and the property became marketable. En route to the meeting, this participant, who had worked closely on the Riverside South negotiations, speculated that Donald's mother had told him as a child that he was the greatest and he had always believed it. "He will ignore anything negative and he doesn't care about the details," the participant said. "If you spend any time with him, you see that he's always pumping himself up, always. He really believes he's the smartest, the best-looking, the best lay."

In the participant's view, such behavior did not necessarily make for happiness, much less niceness. "He can be mean and nasty, and he has horrible attitudes about women," the participant said. "But he has this gut thing, where he goes ahead on his own gut, and it's why he's a successful entrepreneur." It was also why, although Donald had not made a single interest payment on the West Side site, the participant was there, Chase had not yet pulled the plug, and the civil-alternative alliance had supported the man they once despised and still did not really like.

As the hearing finally began, more than an hour late, Richard Kahan sat up in the balcony and peered down at the scene below, his head whipping back and forth as he tracked key figures. Nearby, Donald chatted with reporters. Down on the chamber floor, the discussion of the project's merits and demerits proceeded in a desultory fashion. As members from Brooklyn and Queens listened, a handful of representatives from Manhattan asked what would happen to the space formerly intended for a television studio, if anything would ever be built given the depressed real estate market, and whether the whole deal was a setup for the sole purpose of bailing the developer out.

This last was a particularly relevant question. Although Donald had reduced his $900 million in personal debt to approximately $150 million, the Trump Organization still owed over $2 billion.[26] But there were few answers on the council floor or up in the balcony. Smooth-browed and smiling, the developer seemed a creature without a care in the world. Roving around the balcony, he munched Tic-Tacs and kept up a running commentary.

"This is going great," he said. "If I want to do anything with the studio space, I have to go back through ULURP, the whole approvals thing—that's fine. What I'm thinking about now is a big sewage plant there that will handle sewage not just for Riverside South, but for the whole West Side. You know, there's lots of money to be made in sewage."

He paused for a handful of Tic-Tacs. "I didn't need to be bailed out, you know. Last year maybe, but not now. Nobody's saying that anymore, are they? This is going to be the greatest job since Rockefeller Center."

At one point a large group of fourth- and fifth-graders on a field trip came in to see where the city's laws are made. Spotting Donald, the students squealed and pointed. He walked over and shook hands. "Do you like my project?" he asked as the teacher snapped a shot. "Yes!" they shouted enthusiastically.

So did the subcommittee, which gave the project its blessing. Three weeks later, on Wednesday, December 17, 1992, the same groups again gathered at City Hall as Riverside South faced its last hurdle in the approvals process. At last Donald was at the final moment of decision on the site that had first brought him to Manhattan nearly two decades earlier.

It was a historic occasion, for Riverside South was the first large project to go through the city's new approvals process. In 1990 a court ruling had eliminated what had been the highest decision-making body, the Board of Estimate, as undemocratic, and handed the City Council the final say on land use. Instead of the old-style horse-trading that had been so beneficial to Fred and to other developers, there would be multiple small-scale deals, in which individual council members haggled directly with developers. In theory, this was a more democratic process; in fact, it meant that decision making was more widely diffused and developers would become relatively more powerful.

Although his project was expected to pass, Donald was still using old-style heavy artillery: registered lobbyists, many of them former city officials, who made a career out of buttonholing and chatting up city officials. In 1992 he shelled out almost half a million dollars to gladhanders working for Riverside South—the highest amount paid to lobbyists that year by anyone in the city.[27] As the council session began, his arm-twisters were still at work, smiling and greeting members as they filed in to take their seats.

It was the first time anybody could remember that a developer and his opponents had jointly asked for approval, a tactic that raised hackles on all sides. Westpride and MAS had lost some members, and even Donald found himself on the defensive. "He got tremendous flak from everyone working for him," Kahan said. "His lawyers, everyone thought it was dangerous to share so much control."

Within the alliance there was shouting, threats to resign, and, occasionally, near-fistfights.[28] There had been moments of incomprehension, as when Donald insisted on defending Mike Tyson, then on trial for rape, to the incredulous women in the alliance, and again when he said, as proof of his dedication to the project, that he had made a very beautiful young woman wait more than an hour late one Saturday night while he answered questions from a member of the City Planning Commission. There had also been second thoughts when, out of nowhere, the developer would suddenly say that he wanted the buildings to be 80 stories high after all or that the banks were really supporting him and things were looking up, so why should the buildings be so small.[29]

And, always, there had been suspicions. Donald wondered whether, even if he compromised, those opposed to the project would litigate, and the civic groups did not know whether he would forget about the relocated highway and park once he had the zoning. "Sincere is an irrelevant concept with Donald," Claude Shostal, president of the Regional Plan Association, one of the constituent groups, said later. "He insisted he wanted to do the right thing, but I think he wanted to be admired for seeming to do the right thing."

Once again Donald sat in the balcony above the council chamber and watched legislators decide the fate of his project. "This will be my most successful project ever," he said. "There's lots of interest in financing it."

Down below, a series of members addressed the council. A large clock kept track of the time, and a bell rang when the three minutes allotted to each speaker expired. Most who spoke favored the project; the most passionate opposition came from Ronnie Eldridge, the member from the West Side, who said that Riverside South was too large and was being pushed through too quickly. She predicted that it would now be sold off piece by piece to bail out the developer. If the project was approved, she said, "The taxpayers of New York [would] be played for small-town suckers."

"That's all just bullshit!" Donald said loudly to no one in particular. "That woman is a fat pig who doesn't know what she's talking about. It's a pack of lies!"

After noting that this was one of the many days he had planned to marry Marla, he mentioned an upbeat report published the previous day on a proposed refinancing of the Trump Plaza casino.[30] "D'ja see the article in the *Times*? A $375 million bond issue—the article said $300 million, but they didn't know the real number—it's 375. I'll be out of personal bankruptcy by the end of the year. I'll have my casinos back by 1995. I didn't lose a thing, I've got it all. What did I lose? I don't have the shuttle and I don't have the boat, but what else?"

In fact, he had also lost his stake in Alexander's, his half of the

Grand Hyatt, part ownership of his casinos, most of the Plaza Hotel, and most of the residential units he owned in Trump Tower. But evidently he found his own answer more satisfactory. "I've got everything else!" he crowed. "Everything!"

As expected, the vote was a landslide in his favor, 42 to 8. Afterward Donald stood on the floor of the council chamber for press interviews. "This could look like just a political payoff, like you just gave political campaign contributions and people paid you back with your votes," said a local television news reporter.

Knitting his brows in concentration, the developer looked straight into the camera and spoke with a sincerity worthy of the young Jimmy Stewart. "Well, that would be a fair conclusion, I guess," said the man whose father had been notably generous to politicians and had profited greatly from their favor, and who in turn had himself been among the highest donors to political campaigns and the frequent recipient of official largesse. "But it wouldn't be true. They supported this because it's a great project and it's good for New York and they know it."

———— ❧ ————

WHAT DONALD OWED on Riverside South could have finished him, but instead he used the project to pull himself back from the brink. In July 1994, a year and a half after obtaining the zoning approvals he had sought for two decades, he sold control of the site and its development to a Hong Kong consortium. Publicly the price was $88 million plus assumption of his $250 million debt on the property. He would earn a handsome salary for building and selling the development (16 buildings were planned, and more would eventually be added on the south end of the site), and he would also receive a share of the profits that could be as high as 50 percent depending upon performance.

Leading the new owners was a father-and-son team, New World Development, with holdings in real estate, power companies, and telecommunications that were far larger than Donald's had ever been.[31] In March 1997, after beating back lawsuits from community groups that had rejected the Riverside South compromise, New World broke ground. By 2005, five buildings were completed, two others were under way and ground-breaking for yet another two was imminent, and the project had obtained a 421a city real estate tax abatement.[32]

According to the noted architect Philip Johnson, whom Donald had hired to do the detailed design for the first four buildings, they were within the guidelines approved by the city. But somehow, the finished structures looked much bigger than many West Siders had expected. In part, this was because many preliminary sketches depicted the project from above, which diminishes building heights; in addition, the most widely distributed drawing, that published in the *New York Times,* had an earlier, slightly smaller density, and almost the entire extra space went into additional height. But Johnson gave a much simpler explanation for the apparent discrepancy: "People just didn't imagine how high forty stories is."

Nearly 90, the elfin, owlish Johnson was the designer of such landmarks as the Glass House in New Canaan, Connecticut; the Seagram Building (with Mies van der Rohe) in New York; and the Transco Tower in Houston. But he had recently been kicked out of his own firm, leaving him in a bind similar to that of the developer: world famous but cash poor. Although the Riverside South commission had helped to relaunch him, his participation had not saved the development from a rather banal appearance. Having the same architect for all four buildings and stripping away Willen's art deco details—an ornamental top here, a stylized triangular pediment there—eliminated the lively variety that distinguished West Side buildings. The ensemble was a far cry from the enormous, arrogant monoliths once proposed by Helmut Jahn, but Johnson's boxy, bulky structures, far larger than their neighbors, seemed bland and institutional.[33]

More disturbing to the civic and community groups that had backed Riverside South, the highway was still in place, covering a wide swath of the park. Probably the most insurmountable obstacle to carrying out the relocation was Representative Jerrold Nadler, who loathed the developer and frequently traded barbed remarks with him. Although Donald's experts pegged the cost of moving the highway at about $120 million, Nadler insisted that the true price would be a prohibitive $350 million on top of the $85 million only recently laid out to rehabilitate the roadway.

Unlike Richard Kahan, who rhapsodized about how the cooperation between civic groups and developer presaged a new urban planning model, Nadler saw something more like colonialism in an alliance that included only one group from the affected neighborhood.[34] "Who the hell gave them the right to do the negotiating?" he said. "Someone in a closed room just decided that it was a good deal."

Perhaps predictably, Donald did not admit defeat, or even disappointment, when the road did not come down. Instead he professed his pleasure when Nadler torpedoed federal funding for moving the highway in July 1998. "The job is a much simpler one for me if we leave the highway in place," the developer said. "Jerry Nadler is my best friend, economically. He's played right into my hands." Given that he was making a profit from the development with the highway in place, Donald bragged, he would just as soon it stayed right where it was so drivers could get a good view. "When the highway remains, everyone sees the great job I've built," he said. "If it goes underground, no one will see what I've done."[35]

Twenty years earlier Donald had taken on one of the most impossible challenges in New York City; now, one by one, actual buildings were rising on the site. Whether the project would ultimately elevate him to master-builder status remained unclear. So did the question of who got the better deal: the developer, who pulled out of the fire something far smaller than he had wanted but still immense, or the civics, who traded a monster for a complex that was still too large and the promise of a park that remained stubbornly unattainable.

What was clear was that although the project no longer belonged to Donald, it would remain linked to him in the public mind. He had dropped the name Trump City and the zoning approvals called the project Riverside South, but the residents of the new complex moved into Trump Place, the name spelled out in large bronze letters over building entrances. By 2004, when Donald had a hit reality TV show, *The Apprentice*, and software entrepreneur Kelly Perdew, the winner of the second season, chose as his prize the chance to work with Donald on marketing Trump Place, the fact that Donald did not actually own the complex was irrelevant. What mattered was that it was part of his virtual empire and as such the perfect spot in which to be his apprentice.

By imposing his name on the project he no longer owned, Donald had completed the process of reinventing himself as a human logo—that is, of branding himself. He would be his own marketing gimmick, charging premium prices for condos and rentals in buildings bearing his name. He was no longer a developer in the old sense, someone who came up with the money and constructed a project. He was the person the public associated with an address. What he possessed was not the project, but the idea of the project. At one time he had made himself into a virtual billionaire, someone whose appearance of limitless resources had taken him surprisingly far; now he was a virtual developer, and this status, too, would have unexpected rewards.

CHAPTER NINE

Trump™

F red Trump died in 1999, at the age of 93, from pneumonia. He
had lived almost twice as long as his own father and left an estate estimated at $250 million to $300 million. For many years he had
not constructed or bought any buildings. Stricken with Alzheimer's dis-
ease, he had his good days, his not-so-good days, and, increasingly, his
bad days. But he still lived with his wife, Mary, in the big house on Midland Parkway, he still had a navy blue Cadillac with the license plate
FCT, and almost every day he still went to Avenue Z, greeted his secretary of the last 59 years, and sat at his desk.

The obituary in the *New York Times* occupied half a page, and the
funeral took place four days later at Marble Collegiate Church. Norman
Vincent Peale had died, but Fred had remained a firm believer in the

power of positive thinking, and Marble Collegiate had remained his church to the end. Filling the pews were more than 650 people, including politicians, developers, a sprinkling of celebrities, and the curious. Sitting near the back was Donald's current girlfriend, a 26-year-old Slovenian model named Melania Knauss, whose plunging neckline would be prominently featured in the tabloids the next day.

After Mayor Rudolph Giuliani offered a brief tribute to the man who had built homes for thousands of New Yorkers, Elizabeth Trump Grau, a banker, recited what she described as one of her father's favorite poems, entitled "Don't Quit." Robert Trump, manager of the Trump Organization's extensive real estate holdings outside Manhattan, recalled hearing his father's whistle when he came home at night, taking two steps at a time because "when you do that, the staircase is only half as high." Maryanne, a federal judge in New Jersey, read a letter she had written to her wealthy father during college asking his permission to wait on tables. "Hiya, babe," he replied and thanked her for doing her part to share the load of supporting their large family.

None of them mentioned their own accomplishments.

When it was Donald's turn to speak, he said it was the toughest day of his life. It was ironic, he said, that he had learned of his father's death just moments after he'd finished reading a front-page story in the *New York Times* acknowledging the success of his biggest development, Trump Place. On this project, as on the Grand Hyatt, Trump Tower, Trump Plaza, the Trump Taj Mahal, Trump Castle, and everything else he had ever done, his father had been totally supportive. When he had been on the financial ropes in the early 1990s, when the press and the public and even his own colleagues said he was finished, his father had insisted he'd come back. Whatever the deal, whatever the project, Fred had always known that Donald would be able to pull it off.

In short, that warm spring day at Marble Collegiate Church did not belong to Fred after all. It belonged to Donald. At his own father's funeral, he did not stop patting himself on the back and promoting himself. The first-person singular pronouns, the *I* and *me* and *my*, eclipsed the *he* and *his*. Where others spoke of their memories of Fred, he spoke of his father's endorsement. Donald had never been defeated in the past, and he was not defeated now. There was to be no sorrow; there was only success. It was the power of positive thinking squared.

———◦———

DONALD HAD BEGUN BURNISHING his name as soon as he got to Manhattan and had always considered it the highest of priorities.[1] He invariably covered his own achievements with a thick coating of superlatives, but sometimes he also attached a string of *-ests*, as in "greatest," "tallest," or "biggest," to other people and their attainments. Doing so served the dual purpose of flattering them while suggesting that the presence of people of such accomplishment was still further proof of his own outstandingness.

But after pulling himself back from the edge of financial disaster in the early 1990s, he went about the task of polishing his name with a special urgency. Because of his still enormous burden of debt and the fact that his assets were heavily collateralized, he could not obtain mortgages on his own behalf. For the foreseeable future he would not be able to put significant equity into deals even if he wanted to. His name was all he had.

Doing a deal meant finding a partner with deep pockets, but it did not take him long to locate one. In the summer of 1993 he once again made a pilgrimage to the provinces. Pulling up at a nondescript suburban office building in Stamford, Connecticut, he paid a call on Dale Frey, chairman of General Electric Investment Corporation.[2] Sitting in Frey's large corner office, the developer made a case that sounded remarkably similar to the one he had once made at City Hall regarding the site for a new convention center and then at Equitable involving the land under Bonwit Teller. He'd heard that Frey had a problem and he was there to take it off his hands.

The problem had to do with a well-known, although not wellloved, New York City landmark, a 44-story skyscraper at the southwest corner of Central Park. Built in 1969 as corporate headquarters for the multibillion-dollar conglomerate Gulf + Western, the silver-and-blackstriped slab now belonged to the General Electric Pension Trust, one of

Frey's many responsibilities. The building's small floors made it ill suited for modern office usage, but the fact that it swayed so much in strong winds that people on upper floors could not have a bowl of soup without getting drenched ruled out conversion to apartments.

The obvious move was to tear down the building and start over, but newer and more restrictive zoning would mean the loss of a dozen floors. Donald had driven up to Stamford because he had figured out a solution: Strip the old structure to the steel frame so as to retain the current zoning, then construct a new and stable building that, for zoning reasons, would be two-thirds condominiums and one-third hotel. "He tried to blow us away with his knowledge of what we should do," Frey said later.

A gruff-sounding fireplug who had spent nearly 40 years working in corporate finance at General Electric, Frey managed $70 billion in assets, of which real estate was a relatively small part. Although he was not about to hire anyone after a brief chat, he was impressed and made inquiries. To his surprise, real estate brokers told him that despite the developer's financial problems, the Trump name was still magic in the target market of wealthy foreign buyers and would bring an extra $150 per square foot in condo sales. Among bankers, too, the developer's name was good, for although he could not borrow money directly, he remained an astute dealmaker. In the rapidly expanding economy of the mid-1990s, the fact that three years earlier many in the banking community had spent the summer digging out from under wildly overleveraged loans to Donald seemed to have little bearing. What mattered was the simple fact that the financial industry makes money off people who do deals, not people who don't. Like any other business, banks would always need new product, which in their case meant new loans, and he could deliver them.

On Wednesday, March 23, 1994, a front-page article in the *New York Times* announced the planned renovation of the former Gulf + Western headquarters.[3] But the real story was that Donald Trump, the man who had been considered a goner only a short while before, was back. He would be part of one of the most prominent projects in the just-reviving construction industry, and General Electric Investment

Corporation, one of the nation's largest corporate investment divisions, was trusting him with its pension fund resources. Unlike any project in which the developer had ever been involved, he would not be an owner of what would be called Trump International Hotel and Tower. He would not control the job, and his share would be limited to the building's restaurant, retail, and roof space, plus a fee for his role on the development team. But it was a golden opportunity to relaunch himself, for without his putting up a penny, another prominent New York building would bear the Trump name.[4]

A few months later Donald obtained a highly attenuated potential ownership stake in the land under one of the world's most famous structures, the Empire State Building. Until the expiration of the current lease, which had another 80 years to go and paid a minuscule rent, he would reap only bragging rights, but that was precisely what he was after. The Japanese owners sold the property in 2002, after Donald's lawsuit to break the lease had been dismissed and many decades before he could exercise ownership in any true sense. But he turned this apparent defeat into more bragging rights by taking credit when the property fetched $57.5 million and neglecting to mention that his share of the profits apparently amounted to a few million dollars at most.[5]

Still further visibility came with the purchase of an office building at 40 Wall Street, just yards from the now-demolished building at 60 Wall Street where his grandfather had once had a barbershop.[6] For once Donald did not have a partner, but he did not need one, for the building, shabby and half-empty, cost him a total of $10 million to buy and refurbish. One more restrained Neoclassical limestone facade on a street lined with them would not seem the sort of exposure he craved. But true to form, he managed to combine conspicuousness and landmark-status correctness by covering the facade's hitherto all-but-invisible rosettes and papyrus fronds with shiny gold paint and affixing the new name, The Trump Building, over the door in bright gold letters.

Suddenly the same building that had been indistinguishable from its neighbors popped out; no one on Wall Street could miss what amounted to a neon sign announcing that Donald Trump was back in the running. The building reopened nearly fully rented, and Deutsche Bank provided a staggering $125 million mortgage. In the summer of

1990 the same bank had sat in the Trump Tower conference room and contemplated the near wreckage of the developer's empire; now it had made The Trump Building one of the most heavily leveraged buildings in the developer's entire career.

It also helped make possible Donald's next bombshell, a structure he proudly described as "the world's tallest residential building." By adroitly buying up air rights around a large site on First Avenue between East 47th and 48th streets, he managed to control enough square footage to begin Trump World Tower.[7] Whether the $360 million as-of-right building would be 90 stories tall, as described in glossy advertisements, or 70 stories, the number given in official documents on file with the city, it would dwarf its neighbors, including the United Nations headquarters. But because no rezoning was needed, protests led by area resident Walter Cronkite and U.N. Secretary General Kofi Annan could do little more than spark a rewrite of zoning rules to prevent such projects in the future. The developer's partner, Daewoo, a huge Korean conglomerate with interests in construction, put up major funding, while in exchange for a relatively modest investment and management of the project, Donald got his name out front and a performance-based profit share.

Further contributing to the luster of the name were three Trump country clubs and golf courses outside Manhattan in Westchester County and appearances in commercials for Pizza Hut. The first ad, shown in 1995, featured Donald and Ivana making double-entendre remarks about sharing a pizza, a tongue-in-cheek reference to their bitter divorce. Four years later, Pizza Hut taped him to introduce their newest pie, the Big New Yorker Pizza, to the 200 million viewers of the Super Bowl. "We only had thirty seconds," said Charlie Miesmer, the BBDO executive who pushed for putting Trump in the spots. "We knew if we chose him, it would generate a lot of attention."[8]

But the name would receive what was literally its most radiant glossing just two blocks from Trump Tower. In the spring of 1998, Donald made a deal to buy the General Motors Building. Like the Gulf + Western Building, this 50-story white marble behemoth was an unloved landmark, designed by Edward Durell Stone and Emery Roth and built in 1968. But because the General Motors Building occupied a square block at one of the city's premier locations, the corner of 59th Street and Fifth Avenue, it commanded a premier price: $800 million, the highest sum on record for a Manhattan property. Donald would put in $20 million and revamp the structure; Conseco, an Indiana-based insurance and financial services company, which managed $100 billion in assets and had been the top-performing stock in the Fortune 500 for the previous ten years, would pick up the rest of the tab.[9]

Because of lease restrictions, the structure's official name would continue to be the General Motors Building, but there would be a new twist: it would be the General Motors Building at Trump International Plaza. Or, at any rate, that would be the official name. From the outside, the first half of the name, which appeared in small letters inside a porch on the Fifth Avenue side, was invisible. By contrast, the second part of the clumsy new moniker, Trump, was impossible to miss. Because there were no contractual arrangements regarding the presence of the developer's name on the building, he promptly mounted it across the front in shiny gold-colored letters four feet high.

In response to complaints from CBS, which had leased the old GM showroom for a broadcast studio for the network's early morning show, Donald replaced the titanium with a duller bronze and told the *New York Times* that the shiny version was "too glitzy" and that "I don't love it."[10] A good thing, because Conseco went into bankruptcy and a company spokesman threatened to sell the giant letters on eBay. In June 2003, after a lengthy court battle, Donald agreed to sell his interest back to his former partner for $15.6 million and an undisclosed portion of any future profits, and his name was stripped off the facade. A few months later, the building was sold for a record-setting $1.4 billion; if Donald received a significant sum, he has displayed unprecedented restraint in keeping this information quiet.

IN ATLANTIC CITY, TOO, Donald continued to protect and promote his name, which loomed over the city in huge red neon letters. In 1995, taking advantage of a long-delayed surge in casino revenues, he began to take his operations public. Starting with Trump Plaza, going on to the Taj, and then finally to Trump Castle, since renamed Trump Marina, he put his holdings into a public company, Trump Hotels and Casino Resorts (THCR), and made enough in a series of public offerings to pay down his own Atlantic City debts. There was a certain amount of controversy over the price he paid himself for Trump Castle, the least profitable of his operations, but he weathered it, in part by his well-timed mention of the fact that the Hard Rock Cafe was considering coming there. It didn't, but bondholders, buoyed by the prospect, backed up the developer.

Like the bankers, they were always in search of new deals and new fees, which meant that after the yelling and screaming of 1990 had subsided, they were ready to sign up again. It had been a bumpy ride for Trump casino bondholders, but in the end most of them had been able to get out more or less whole. True, repayment was delayed, and those who sold—mainly small investors who could not afford to hold on—lost money. But by definition, bonds that yield high rates carry high risks. Indeed, they are referred to as "junk" precisely because, almost inevitably, investors will have to do yet another deal in order to get the principals—in this case, Donald Trump—out from under the current one.

With the Castle deal done and his remaining share of the Grand Hyatt sold to his estranged partner, Donald was in the clear. It was such an unaccustomed situation, one of his lawyers told the *New Yorker*, that Donald could not sleep at night.[11] But the purported insomnia was worth it. In October 1996, after six years of exclusion from lists of the wealthiest people in the land—the equivalent of magnate Siberia—he landed back on the annual *Forbes* ranking of the country's 400 richest individuals. According to the magazine, which ranked him as the 368th wealthiest American, his net worth was $450 million; as usual, his calculations, based on his accountants' estimates of confidential and hence unverifiable figures, provided a higher number, some $2.25 billion.[12] Whatever the total, the virtual developer had restored lost luster to his name, and it shone even more brightly over what was now a virtual empire.

ALTHOUGH DONALD HAD MADE his name into a remarkably successful marketing device, to him it actually represented something to which he was deeply and passionately attached, his own family. Even in the midst of marital collapse, he was a fond, if sometimes distracted, father, allowing his children free run in his office, talking to them on the telephone regardless of whether he was in meetings, taking them with him on trips whenever possible.

Almost ten years after Eric's birth, Donald had become a father for a fourth time. In October 1993, after ten hours of labor, with New Age music playing and scented herbs and oils wafting through the air, Marla gave birth to Tiffany Ariana Trump. Her arrival gave new attention to the question of when, or if, her father would marry the woman who was invariably referred to as his Georgia peach.

Donald had been grateful to Marla for sticking by him. Year after year she had been at his side for marketing pitches and casino receptions, for all the openings and parties that were necessary to polish the Trump name and keep it out there in the world. "If you had a real tough nut to crack, an invitation to have dinner with Donald and Marla went a long way," recalled a Trump casino official. "Before that dinner, it was Mr. Trump and Mr. Banker; afterward, it's Joe and Donald and Marla."[13]

But Marla was more than a helpmate; she was also his lover. "She did something to him sexually that he just couldn't resist," said one close observer. "Deep down, this guy is really just a horny teenager." Six years into the relationship, Donald still could not keep his hands off Marla's curvaceous body; during one business trip in August 1993, when she was eight months pregnant, he was constantly fondling her in the presence of other members of the party. But despite several announcements of engagements and even wedding dates, the two had never gotten close to the altar. Year after year, periods of intimacy continued to alternate with slammed doors and separations.

Now, though, Donald had a pressing reason to reconsider his position: Before he made a public offering on his casinos, he needed to buff his name to the brightest possible sheen. He made no bones about the fact that his second trip to the altar was a marketing decision. Even after he and Marla appeared on the front page of the *New York Times* getting a marriage license, he was still asking family and friends about whether tying the knot would help or hurt his business prospects and whether it might be better for his public image if he reconciled with Ivana.

Instead, on December 17, 1993, he sent Ivana a dozen red roses. The next day, in a lavish ceremony at the Plaza Hotel, before 1,300 guests and with his frail father as best man, he said, "I do." *Entertainment Tonight* had exclusive video rights to the rehearsal, but the groom sold the wedding photos to magazines and newspapers. The proceeds, he declared, would be donated to charity. Prominently featured in news reports was the staggering amount of food and drink and the nine-tier wedding cake. Seven tiers and more than 500 pounds of food were left over and reappeared in the city's soup kitchens over the next several days.

The wedding ring may have helped with the initial public offering for the casinos, but it did not make the man who had always put himself first stop doing so. At one time Marla's lack of high-level involvement in business affairs had been a relief of sorts for Donald, burdened by his collapsing empire. Now, though, when Marla pushed him to balance his time between his work and his new family—that is, to give something of himself back—he had little interest. With his comeback under way, he had reverted to his former workaholic self, totally caught up in his business from the moment he woke until he went to sleep at night.

In April 1996 news accounts reported that a Palm Beach cop had encountered a "rumpled and sandy" Marla on the beach in the wee hours with her bodyguard.[14] Her explanation was that she had merely been taking "a bathroom break." Neither at the time nor a year later, when Donald announced a separation, did he mention the incident. Instead he said that ending his marriage was a business decision. According to their prenuptial agreement, the amount Marla would receive in case of a divorce would soon grow significantly larger. He was, he insisted, simply cutting his losses.

In dollars and cents, the loss to Donald amounted to about $1 million plus child support; in personal terms, it seemed to add up to something far less. His parents, his siblings, and, in recent years, his children were what mattered most to him. They had always been there, and they always would be. Although there would be periodic strains, their relationship to him was constant. They provided a kind of connectedness that he could tolerate, a relationship that was warm and accepting but not intimate or probing. For all the running after supermodels, after women of extraordinary beauty and physical perfection, he was basically a no-touch person, someone who did not, except with his children, engender physical closeness. His insistence on wearing business clothes was only partly for the professional image; it was also the wardrobe of choice because of the distance it provided. Similarly, the security guards who had accompanied him for years were a way of keeping the world at a remove that was psychological as well as physical.

Donald had an enormous number of acquaintances who enjoyed coming to his office for a visit and, maybe, a little business. Sharp and witty, a clever mimic and an engaging storyteller, he could be fun to be around. "He'll be sitting with you and say, 'Let's call Don King,' " said broker Jack Shaffer, who dropped in occasionally at Trump Tower. "Before you know it, Don King is on the speakerphone. I never met Don King, but there I was talking to him." He could also be abrasive or thoughtless, but somehow he would make up for it. "He calls and excuses himself for his jerkiness if he's been majorly bad," Shaffer said, noting that sometimes Donald let Abe Wallach, his chief of staff, smooth things over or take the blame. "He'll say, 'I didn't do that, Abe did.' The whole thing is childish and immature, but most of the time it's fun and sometimes you even make money."[15]

But there seemed to be few truly close friends in the developer's life. It was not hard to see why: He was too busy working, and, like many men, he had little interest in sharing personal thoughts. "He doesn't need that one-to-one," said yet another acquaintance. "He gets along best with people who are very direct—straightforward, unemotional people because it's uncomplicated and you can get straight to the point."

To be a lasting presence in his life, one had to take the long view.

"Keep your eye on the applause meter, because that's where his eye is," said another person who had known Trump since the developer first arrived in Manhattan. "He'll be charming, you'll be the greatest, then he'll say something neutral, then something negative. It will be a whole package. This is understood with someone like this, that everything is marketing."

And control. In any relationship he always had to be in charge, to a degree that precluded the give-and-take that intimacy requires. To be with friends did not mean a long phone chat or a late-night tête-à-tête. Instead, it meant a large private box, filled with celebrities, business contacts, and his children, at the U.S. Open tennis tournament, held in Flushing Meadows, Queens, in late summer. Each year Donald would hold court, eating hot dogs and French fries and watching the world's best tennis players compete only a few yards away.

As at his lunchtime table at the '21' Club, he was exactly where he wanted to be: right in the middle of everything. In the course of the afternoon or evening at the tournament, everyone who was anyone would stop by and say hello. Because the event was televised, millions of others would see this, would nod to him in their heads, would think to themselves, Donald Trump is there, this must be important.

Ultimately, though, he found an even better way to socialize, at Mar-a-Lago.[16] The mansion's builder, Marjorie Merriweather Post, had ruled Palm Beach by inviting the wealthy and well known of her day and providing lavish entertainment. A hostess in the old sense, she had picked up the tab for everything. Now he, too, would invite the most well-connected and well-known people he could think of. He would greet, talk, give a squeeze on the arm and, sometimes, a peck on the check. But he would be a different sort of host, for he would be charging his guests admission. He would be, as it were, a virtual host.

Unable to get the grounds of Mar-a-Lago rezoned for a luxury subdevelopment, he had turned the old estate into a private club. A greatly upscaled version of the Concord, the Catskills resort where Fred and his colleagues had once congregated, Mar-a-Lago would be a place where the nation's highest-net-worth individuals, tired out from the week's wheeling and dealing, could get together and relax with their own kind.

To join they paid an initiation fee, officially listed as $100,000 but waived for those whose names on the membership list added value to the enterprise. The privileges of membership included use of a spa, a three-hole mini-golf course, and a strip of ocean beach, but the real come-on was the opportunity to be part of a social set every bit as exclusive as that which the current owner had found so offensive when he first arrived.

Presiding over it all was Donald. At night, sometimes with his beautiful girlfriend Melania or his daughter, Ivanka, on his arm, he would move through the rooms like a turn-of-the-century grandee, warm and attentive to everyone he encountered. Even among this group, heads turned to follow his progress, and somehow there seemed to be a spotlight on him, although in fact there was none. By his presence and, even more, by his name, he was proof that the men and women there were in the most important place they could possibly be, in the company of the most important people they could possibly be with.

CHAPTER TEN

The Legacy

Donald's constant, unrelenting focus on his own accomplishments alienated many people; others, drawn to winners, found his self-absorption appealing. No matter the occasion, he was always competing, always concentrating on how to make whatever he was doing seem bigger and better than what anyone else had ever done. When he lost, he would say he won; when he won, he would say he won more. A psychologist might call such behavior narcissistic, egotistical, and, no doubt, a sign of hidden insecurity. Donald himself called it "truthful hyperbole." Broker Ed Gordon labeled it "diarrhea of the mouth." But Barbara Corcoran, founder and chairman of one of the largest residential real estate companies in Manhattan, may have put it best: "He's got a gift that's good in good times and really good in bad times," she said. "It's called bullshit, and he uses it unabashedly. We've all gone to high school with someone like that—the only difference is most people have to let it go."[1]

But as Donald would be the first to say, he wasn't like most people. In *The Art of the Deal*, he claims that business deals are what distinguish him; by all accounts, he is indeed an artful negotiator, with his father's skill at walking into a meeting without notes or a calculator because he's got the numbers and deal points in his head. But his most original creation is the continuous self-inflation that has made him a touchstone of excess. Early on, it made him his father's favorite child and treasured apprentice, a choice that sheds a certain light on the journey taken by this family—indeed, this nation—over the past century.

Despite obvious differences in lifestyle and affect, grandfather Friedrich, father Fred, and Donald were similar types. All three were energetic men who would do almost anything to make a buck; all three possessed a certain ruthlessness; all three had a free and easy way about the truth and a wide range of solid, practical skills. But how these traits played out in different eras is, in its own way, a vest-pocket history of America.

During Friedrich's first two decades in the New World, he made a living by providing services that were as concrete as could be imagined. They ranged from haircuts to food to sex, and customers returned because they were satisfied with his work, not because he was the vendor. When he purchased older businesses, he did not change the sign over the door; when he started new ones, he named them after their locations. Even when he moved into real estate, near the end of his life, his intention was to create value not through his name but by buying plots of land and building homes.

Friedrich's son Fred followed in his father's footsteps but created value in his own way. By establishing a network of political contacts, he managed to obtain government housing subsidies, then released a stream of press releases designed to give a special shimmer to what were in fact conventional developments. A man of his era, he gave them innocuous generic addresses, like Shore Haven and Beach Haven. Only on the last, Trump Village, did he place his name, a precedent that his son Donald would expand on in ways that Fred never dreamed of.

Donald shared much with his father and grandfather. He, too, knew how to frame a building and retar a roof. But Friedrich's grandson would not employ this practical knowledge to build anything with his own hands; instead he would use it to hire and fire those who put up his structures and to connect with the construction crews, maintenance men, and retired blue-collar workers who played his slot machines in Atlantic City. Although these skills would be helpful in negotiating contracts, the special value he would add to his projects would be his name. Seemingly the simplest of acts, it was actually quite arduous, for keeping that name going, constantly protecting and buffing it, required vigilance and intensity of the highest order.

By 2005, 11 buildings in Manhattan bore the name Trump,[2] although Donald had provided little or no financing for more than half. To all appearances, he held equity in only three or four, but rather than offering proof of more extensive ownership, he simply insisted, sometimes ferociously, that he owned practically everything labeled Trump. One perennially sore spot involved Trump Place, the vast West Side complex financed by a Hong Kong consortium. When the *New York Times Magazine* asked about Trump's holdings there, the consortium's lawyer delicately described him as "a major partner" who was "not merely receiving a fee"—seemingly a roundabout version of the near-unanimous belief that Trump's portion was a management fee plus a share of the profits.[3]

Donald was less delicate. "I'm not a fucking flunky," he said in response to one person's questions. "I'm a 50/50 owner, owner, owner of the job. Okay, do you have that? I get 50 percent of the profits because I own 50 percent of the job, and it turned out to be one of the most successful jobs ever done in Manhattan." Afterward, in a Trump-style clarification, he added that he did get fees for building and managing the project. "There's nothing wrong with getting fees, and I do get fees, too, but I own that job, can I get it through your head? I own the West Side. I'm the largest owner. I own it. I'm not just a person that works, you know, for a fee. Do you understand? I'm an owner. I own a big chunk of that job, a big portion of that job. Off the record, I own 50 percent of that job. Five-Oh. You said I didn't own it, I got fees, but that's bull-shit."[4]

Such diligence had its rewards.[5] In the early 1990s, when Donald's empire was in trouble, the carefully tended glow attached to his name persuaded holders of the junk bonds underwriting his casinos to cut deals leaving him in place as owner. In 1995, his renown allowed him to take the casinos public and load them with still more junk bonds. But a decade later, the casinos faced stiff competition: neighboring Pennsylvania had legalized slot machines, and right in Atlantic City there was a new kid on the block: the $1.1 billion Borgata, the first casino built since the Trump Taj Mahal. A sleek Las Vegas–style resort with high-end retail shops, celebrity-chef restaurants and a popular spa—the wait list for facials was eight weeks—the Borgata was blowing the doors off every casino in town, but the dilapidated Trump properties were hit especially hard.

The remedy was obvious: refurbishment and more hotel rooms. But staggering interest payments on high-interest bonds had left Donald's public company too short of cash to replace worn upholstery and repaint scuff marks on walls—a serious no-no in an industry that relies on glitz and glamour to lure customers. Worse, there was no money in the till for the expansion that would be required to "right-size" the casinos—that is, to have enough hotel rooms to draw large numbers of overnight customers, who spend on average at least three times as much as those who are there only for the day. "The logic was that if Donald could double the room count, the returns would finally be adequate," said Jacques Cornet, a casino analyst for CIBC World Markets. "It makes sense, but there's a tremendous leap of faith involved."

Evidently, the Trump name continued to give the bondholders that faith. The New York Times described negotiations between Donald and his investors as "a love fest," and in late October 2004, just weeks before another big interest payment that THCR seemed unlikely to be able to make, they took one more haircut. In exchange for the right to keep using that name and likeness, plus an equity stake and a modest cash payout, they accepted a prenegotiated bankruptcy that reduced their rate of return and gave Donald, who would still be the largest shareholder, yet another lease on his ever more highly leveraged financial life.

This time, the man who had insisted that he owned "mostly 100 percent of everything" declared that reducing his own equity by more than half was not such a bad thing after all. "I'll own 27 percent of a great company as opposed to 56 percent of a company that had a lot of debt," Donald said. "Which would you rather own? It's a great deal, no one else has ever done such an amazing deal. The casinos have always been a great deal for me. How much have I made off the casinos? Off the record, a lot. I put a lot of debt on them and I took the money out and I bought a lot of real estate in New York. So I'm very happy at how things have turned out."[6]

It was a remarkable turnaround for a man facing seemingly inexorable death by interest payments. "He has staved off a ticking time bomb," analyst Marvin Roffman told *Newsday*. "He should go home tonight and take out his cashmere Trump bathrobe and crack open some Dom Pérignon and celebrate."[7]

But the difficulties had been postponed, not resolved. According to the terms of the agreement with bondholders, by the following spring, Donald would have to kick in an investment of $71.4 million, including $55 million in cash. Before the ink was dry, there was talk about whether the check would appear. "Will some bank lend him more on a building in New York?" asked one industry observer. "Or against future expected fees on *The Apprentice?* He can get creative—historically, he has."

TO HIS GRANDFATHER AND HIS FATHER, Trump had been a name, a signifier of family and history. But to Donald, it meant something more. When he'd hoisted it on one undertaking after another, it wasn't simply a matter of advertising; he was turning himself into a brand. In turn, when investors backed his ventures and the public patronized them, they weren't merely making financial choices; they were buying into "Donald Trump," the personality brand created by consistently making the same extravagant claims and having the same look—including, apparently, the dark suit, the smirk, and the ever-more-improbable hairdo. "He was an early mover in this kind of personal branding," said brand guru Bernd Schmitt, a professor at Columbia Business School. "Like Bill Gates and Steve Jobs in computers, he became the most well-known brand in real estate—in public awareness and notoriety, no one else even comes close."[8]

It was a strategy that paid off handsomely. In the early 1990s, when he was in his late forties, Donald was nearly $1 billion in the red; by the fall of 2004, when he was approaching his sixties, the Forbes 400 pegged his wealth at $2.6 billion. Along with film director Steven Spielberg and Yahoo! cofounder David Filo, Donald was in a five-way tie for being the 74th-richest American.[9] Such a spot would have been more than enough for others on this exclusive list, who tended to be reticent about their means. But modesty was not Donald's way, and he continued to insist that the real number was far higher.

Indeed, despite the Atlantic City bankruptcy, things had never been better—or so it seemed from the following account: "The primary thing is real estate, you understand, but I make a lot of money from all these different things, you know. Tens of millions. Off the record, this year, between *The Apprentice* and the different things I'm doing, I'll make 55, 60 million dollars cash this year. You can say it, I just can't say it, but I'm making a lot of money this year. And it's only November—I've got another month to go."[10]

As ever, the real numbers were impossible to verify. The *New York Times* suggested that the largest part of his wealth was his inheritance and that his debt-free worth might be closer to $200 to $300 million; he declared that he was worth $6 billion.[11] Ultimately, what anyone believed was unimportant; what mattered was the controversy and the continuous press attention that it sparked.

For years, Donald had looked to such coverage to keep his name in the public eye. But in 2004, there would be, literally, a dramatic change.[12] Producers of the hit reality television show *Survivor* had rented Wollman Rink, the skating arena in Central Park that Donald had renovated nearly 20 years earlier, for the live broadcast of its season finale. When Donald dropped by to watch, a sandy-haired man with a hybrid British-Australian-American accent introduced himself as Mark

Burnett, the show's producer. Back when he'd been hawking T-shirts on Venice Beach, he said, he'd been inspired by *The Art of the Deal,* and now he wanted to talk about a new idea.

Although Donald courted attention every waking moment, he'd already turned down other pitches for day-in-the-life-style reality shows. "Can you imagine 15 cameras in the middle of an important meeting?" he said later. "I don't want to do that, and neither do the people I do business with. It would freak them out." But Burnett, a famously persuasive sort (CBS Chairman Leslie Moonves called Burnett's pitch for *Survivor* the best he'd ever heard), proposed an elimination-style format in which the contestants, divided into teams, would compete on a demanding business task and each week Donald would fire someone. Intrigued at the prospect of a show set not in a remote jungle hideaway, à la *Survivor,* but in New York's real-life business jungle, Trump said yes. Later he explained his decision: "The combination of Mark Burnett, who did *Survivor,* which was the number one show, and Trump, the number one developer in New York, was a great combination. It would be terrific, amazing, totally amazing."

It was a rare understatement. Television right-sized Donald, translating his over-the-top mannerisms and exaggerations into entertainment and turning his sometimes grating behavior into something engagingly camp. "He's a pull-me-in, push-me-back personality," said Michele Greppi, national editor of *TelevisionWeek.* "Seeing the show is like going to the zoo, where there are some things you watch between the fingers of your hand. I wouldn't want to be his employee, but I've got to know who he's going to fire or praise."

Television also seemed to exert a humanizing effect on the developer. As contestants schemed their way to the grand prize, a one-year, $250,000 job with Donald, he consoled a competitor whose mother had cancer, winced while addressing another named Ivana, and made fun of his own hair. In this medium, his much-ridiculed mop and brush with bankruptcy were assets, for they showed that the man who supposedly had everything was mortal. His comeback was also a plus, for it fit into the popular genre, tales of redemption.

On the small screen, his ever-hustling persona seemed refreshingly direct. "You can tell that he's the same way in person as he is on the show," said Charlie Reiss, who appeared on an episode during the first season. "He's not an e-mail person. He's a talker who assesses people by how they react, a salesman who is always selling and needs personal contact to do it."

But perhaps dearest to Donald's heart, the show presented him as he had always seen himself: the most stupefyingly successful man in the world. Contestants gaped with wonder at a Trump helicopter, golf course, and casino, and they turned ashen when he pointed his index finger at one of them and uttered the show's catchphrase, "You're fired." Spending 10 minutes alone with The Donald (and, of course, a camera crew) seemed tantamount to a papal audience. "I show this apartment to very few people," he said grandly when one week's winning team visited his residence in Trump Tower. "Presidents, kings—let me give you a little tour." In fact, his opulent penthouse has appeared multiple times in print, television, and film, but there was not even a snicker from the awestruck contestants.

From the start, the show held an enviable position on the schedule: directly after the hugely popular sitcom *Friends*, then in its last season. But almost immediately after its debut, on January 8, 2004, it was clear that *The Apprentice* was a hit. It attracted an average of 20 million viewers each week, had an audience of 40 million people for the final episode, and scored particularly well with the affluent viewers that advertisers crave. Although the show did not consistently top the charts, such niggling details did not prevent Donald from making the usual claims: "You see the ratings are through the roof, bigger than ever," he chortled. "The show is now number one in demographics and I think in two weeks it's number one overall. It's a big monster. I'm in Los Angeles, I get out of my limo to be on Jay Leno and both Jay and [NBC Entertainment president] Jeff Zucker greet me at the door, and you know they only do that if you're number one in the ratings."

He was equally jubilant about press coverage: "I was on the cover of *TV Guide* last week, and it was their most successful magazine in three years. I was on the cover this week of *Newsweek* and they say you cannot buy *Newsweek* on the stands. So something's happening, right? I don't know what it is, but I just got a call from Rick Smith of *Newsweek*, you know, he's the head guy. He said we cannot put this magazine out there fast enough, there's some crazy phenomenon here."

Evidently the craziness was catching. The *Wall Street Journal* reported that business schools began assigning the show, with some professors endorsing it as a positive example and others pointing to contestants' deviousness as how not to behave in a professional situation. After the first season was over in the U.S., networks in two dozen other countries purchased broadcast rights, and production companies in more than a dozen more began work on their own broadcasts. Ostensibly, there had been just one grand prize for the 16 competitors on the show, but they were all winners: Overnight, they had become celebrities in their own right, netting interviews, magazine covers, job offers, and, in some cases, their own books. "We had a chance at everything from TV to film to business," said Nick Warnock, a Xerox sales team leader who was fired in the next-to-last round of competition. "Modeling ourselves after Donald Trump, we used being celebrities as capital."

At auditions for the first season, some 215,000 people had appeared; at tryouts for the next season, held not long after the show's debut, one million hopefuls showed up. By 8 A.M. on the morning of the New York tryouts, at The Trump Building on Wall Street, there was a line of several thousand, many of whom had camped out overnight despite the frigid winter weather. Among them was Victor Btesh, a high school dropout from New Jersey who owned his own company, Hot Records, which produced and marketed trendy products, including a line of Osbourne family action figures. Btesh had managed to get the name of the casting director and used it to get out of the cold and into a line of only several hundred apprentice wannabes. "All of a sudden I hear all this noise," he said. "Donald Trump was coming up an escalator and there were all these cameras and paparazzi and all this excitement." Outside, when Donald had paused for a moment at the top of the steps, the crowd had started chanting his name; now they began shouting it. "It was like when people were screaming for the Beatles," Btesh said. "These were his people, his fans, people who love the show and just want to be connected to him." [13]

Those who were selected would again be vying to spend a year with the Trump Organization, but the real magnet was public associa-tion with the Trump brand. "Even if I didn't win the job, I could milk this thing," said Rob Flanagan, a Texan who markets mouse pads and pens for trade shows and ended up being the first candidate fired on the second season. "I'd pull on those udders until the powder comes out." For Pam Day, a start-up veteran from San Francisco who made it to the fifth episode, the reason to participate wasn't for the job but "to get PR for the businesses I already run." And for Wesley Moss, an investment manager from Atlanta who hung on until the eleventh week, the goal was to sign up Donald as a client. "It would be really gratifying to get even a small fraction of his portfolio," he said.[14]

For the public, the question was which contestant Donald would finally select as his apprentice. But for the broadcast industry, it was whether the new show could deliver a changed economic model for television advertising.[15] Because of the rise of new technologies like TiVo that allow viewers to skip over conventional ads, broadcasters were eager to find a format that incorporates products directly into pro-gramming. Although Burnett had done so in crude but effective fashion on *Survivor,* where the rewards to weekly winners were sponsors' sodas and snack foods, major marketers were still wary of the concept and hes-itant to tie themselves to an untried new version.

But when Marquis Jet, an unknown company that sells time on luxury private planes, participated in an *Apprentice* episode and became a nationally recognized name overnight, "placement" fees that ranged up to $1 million began to seem like a bargain. By the second season, there were a near-record number of product placements, and familiar names, including Mattell, Pepsi, and Levi's, had moved front and center in almost every episode. Apparently the association with The Donald worked its usual magic; two hours after the broadcast of an episode in which contestants competed to launch Crest Refreshing Vanilla Mint toothpaste, the Procter & Gamble website received a record 800,000 hits asking for samples and offering ideas for how to create more buzz for the new product.[16]

AS SHOWN BY such legendary failures as the Ford Edsel and New Coke, branding isn't everything. In order to last, a brand has to be associated with a product that the public wants to buy. Not what people used to want, or what some marketer thinks they should want, but what they do want right now. For Donald, this product was real estate with the showy, expensive look and luxurious amenities that an elite market segment craved and for which it would pay top dollar. He was successful in this endeavor: Apartments in Trump properties were among the most expensive listings in Manhattan, and he was working on luxury projects in Toronto, Phoenix, Las Vegas, and Palos Verdes, California. Condominiums in his 90-story skyscraper in Chicago, not due to be completed until 2007, were already setting new price records.[17]

Financial arrangements for the Chicago International Hotel & Tower had been protracted, in part because local banks were leery of involvement in the project, the city's largest in 30 years. Ultimately, a New York–based hedge fund, Fortress Investment Group, put up a high-interest $130 million "mezzanine" loan to supplement a $640 million construction loan from Deutsche Bank. "What made the difference wasn't *The Apprentice*," said Bob Horowitz, a commercial real estate investment broker in New York who has handled financing on Trump projects for a decade. "Donald is a very, very sharp guy and he is always financeable. The only question is the price."[18]

But with the success of *The Apprentice*, Donald Trump had once again reinvented himself.[19] Already famous for being famous, he had become the apotheosis of wealth. At one time his name had been synonymous with real estate; now it had become a free-floating brand that could sell anything. Or so it seemed; weeks before the national rollout, the Apprentice Talking Donald Trump Doll was on Amazon.com's list of top-selling new action figures. Other manufacturers were plastering the mogul's name and face on bottled water, men's cologne, a new clothing line, a magazine, and an updated version of the 1989 board game. Meanwhile, Trump kept busy recording syndicated radio commentaries, appearing in commercials for Visa and Verizon, plugging two new insta-books, *How to Get Rich* and *Think Like a Billionaire*, penning forewords for other books by *Apprentice* veterans, and making frequent public appearances with Melania, now his fiancée, and her $1.5 million, 13-carat diamond engagement ring. If he succeeded in efforts to trademark "You're Fired" for everything from booze to baseball bats (he already owns the rights to the letter T displayed on his hotels or associated Trump paraphernalia), there would be yet another avalanche of Donald-related products.[20]

Which raised the obvious question: Could anyone, even The Donald, keep this up? "I'm cautious and skeptical," said Columbia professor Bernd Schmitt. "Even a very successful brand can get diluted by being extended into other products." Taking a more dire view, John Allen, senior partner at the New York–based consultancy Lippincott & Margulies, warned that overexposure could damage or even kill the brand. "If you were managing the brand," he told a reporter, "you'd say, 'No, Don, it's not for you.'"[21]

Other marketing experts were more sanguine. "If your business is exposure, there's no such thing as overexposure," said *Advertising Age* columnist Randall Rothenberg. "Donald is beyond anything like shame or embarrassment. He's created a brand that's about shamelessness and out-there-ness, so why couldn't he keep going forever?"

From the look of his newest logo, a globe with the letter T superimposed on it, Donald would seem to agree. But when he was asked if he worried about overexposure, he seemed almost baffled by the question.[22] He didn't believe there was any such thing as overexposure. As far as he was concerned, the ubiquity of his name, his face, and his voice was as it should be. When, as happened pretty often now that he thought about it—like when he was sitting at a screening of an episode of *Sex and the City* and one of the characters mentioned him, or when he was reading *Parade* one Sunday and learned that he was listed in the *Guinness Book of Records* for having the greatest financial comeback in history, which he didn't even know about, or he saw himself quoted in an article and he had never talked to the writer—in other words, when he saw himself being discussed or heard people talking about him, it was the craziest thing, but okay, that was cool, it wasn't anything to worry about.

"A lot of people sit down and discuss their lives, things like are they happy, but it's not like that with me," he said in one interview. "I don't think positively, I don't think negatively, I just think about the goal. But it's not like I sit down and write goals. I just do things." As for the idea of worrying about anything, he said on a later occasion, it simply never comes up. "I don't worry and I don't give up. My father was a worker, not a worrier. He got things done, like I do. We get things done. Some people worry about things, but I get things done."

ON AN OVERCAST DAY in October, the man who would ultimately determine the fate of the brand stood next to a bridge over the Chicago River.[23] Although his name was Donald Trump and he worked at the Trump Organization, he bore none of the features usually associated with the name. His hair was thick and brown and his eyes were dark, giving him a marked resemblance not to his father but to his mother, Ivana, in the long-ago days before she turned into a blonde.

His manner was low-key and modest, for he was by nature what the family called a Boston Trump, referring to the wing of the family headed by Fred's brother, a physics professor at MIT. Don Jr., as he called himself, did not refer to his bachelor apartment, located on a mid-building floor in a Trump condominium, as a penthouse, nor did he turn every conversation into a checklist of his own attributes and achievements. But as this day made apparent, perhaps his most striking deviation from the path carved out by his father was that instead of rushing to claim the spotlight, he actively avoided it.

The occasion was a press event for the new Trump tower slated for Chicago, and the first speaker before the audience of politicians, local businesspeople, Donald, Don Jr., and hundreds of onlookers was first-season *Apprentice* winner Bill Rancic. For his year on the Trump payroll, he chose assignment to this project, and he had often declared that he was intent on learning the real estate trade. But so far, Rancic, a lanky 33-year-old with a crew cut, seemed more focused on how to exploit his newly acquired fame—like his new master, he had quickly churned out an advice book titled *You're Hired*—and he opened with a crowd-

pleasing reference to his experiences at a different Trump-owned enterprise, the recent Miss Universe contest in Quito, Ecuador.

Then Donald, dressed in his signature black business attire, strode
to the microphone and said that the city planning commissioner, the
mayor, the Trump team, and the architect, Adrian Smith, a principal in
the firm Skidmore, Owings & Merrill, were all amazing. "Chicago is a
truly great city and we're going to make it a little greater," he vowed.
That said, he veered off to a more immediate concern: "Is everyone
going to watch *The Apprentice* tonight?"

The cue was not lost on Smith, a portly figure with a sheaf of white
hair, who spoke next.[24] "People ask me what it's like working with The
Donald," he said. "He's a strong client, who wants the best building, the
best views and the best prices, and you have to give it to him or else"—
a well-timed pause—"you're fired!"

Smith's initial sketches for the Trump project, scheduled for presentation on September 11, 2001, had showed a 2,000-foot-tall monument that would have fulfilled Donald's lifelong dream of erecting the
world's tallest building. But the events of that day had taken their toll
on his seemingly impervious ego, not to mention the potential market
for superluxury apartments, and Smith ended up whittling the design
down to a still-enormous 1,100 feet. It would be the tallest project the
developer had ever done and the highest new skyscraper in Chicago
since the Sears Tower (1,450 feet), built in 1974, but only the fourth-
tallest structure in the city. "As Donald put it," Smith said, "after 9/11,
fourth-highest sounded just right."

After the speeches were over, the crowd trooped over the bridge to
the site, currently occupied by the squat, seven-story former home of
the *Chicago Sun-Times*.[25] Surrounded by workers in hard hats, Donald
nodded his head and the operator of a large yellow backhoe began taking big, noisy bites out of the now-empty building's entrance canopy. It
was a perfect photo opportunity, but Don Jr., who was accompanied by
his fiancée, a model and actress named Vanessa Haydon, stayed out of
the picture.

As might be expected, there were echoes of the father in the son:
"Me and Russell Ticker [a senior Trump Organization executive] have

been pretty well running this operation," Don Jr. declared, passing over the well-publicized involvement of construction supervisor Greg Cuneo. "And I guess Trump Park Avenue [an $85-million makeover of the old Hotel Delmonico in Manhattan] is pretty much my baby."

He seemed even more like his father later on when he invited press to his bended-knee proposal to Vanessa at a New Jersey jewelry store in exchange for a $100,000 engagement ring. Weeks later, on *Larry King Live*, Donald offered a stern rebuke, but it seemed less about what Don Jr. had done than a reminder of who was the family's alpha male. Donald himself copped hefty discounts on Melania's engagement and wedding rings after plugging Graff, the seller, on *The Apprentice*, and he wangled free flowers and food for the wedding, deftly timed to draw attention to the TV show's third season.

Still, what stood out were the differences. At 26, Donald had itched to take over the company, but Don Jr. seemed content to wait his turn. "I'm on my way," he said, "but right now I'm still learning." He worked hard, but not 24/7; he was, he said, "more grounded" than Donald because "I can lay back in my personal life." Even more dissimilar, the one person on whom he lavished praise was not himself but his father. "He's always hands-on and one step ahead," Don Jr. said with evident admiration. "People see him as famous, but they don't know that he knows how to do all this stuff."

Although Don Jr. loved his father, he sometimes found him a stubborn guy with a one-track mind. "I'm the one person who can stand up to my father," he said. "I'm the only one who's not afraid to pull him aside and say here, take a look at the larger picture." In his quiet way, this apprentice was his own man. He might eventually be joined by his sister Ivanka, who had been a fashion model in her teens and was now working for a competing real estate developer based in Brooklyn, or his young brother Eric, a student at Georgetown University. But for the present, Don Jr. had his own plans for where to take the brand next.

He'd experienced its power firsthand—"It's not easy at 12 to walk out of school and see the front page of every newspaper talking about your parents' divorce"—and he'd long since learned the necessity of bracing himself whenever he had to tell someone his name. "It would be nice not to have people prejudge you because they see your father a certain way and there's no chance you might actually be different," he said. "And every time you check in at an airport, it's oh, my god, you're Donald Trump's son."

After working at a minimum-wage job as a dock attendant at the Trump Marina in Atlantic City and on Trump construction sites, he also understood what the brand could do. In 2000, after he'd graduated from Wharton and started working for his father, the company had still been "very New York–centric," but now Don Jr. was working on projects all over the country. "That's not entirely my doing," he said, "but these are things I've helped push. It's such a huge brand, it could be global." Although he was open to almost anything, there was one possibility he'd ruled out: "I have no desire to go on television, so you're unlikely to have *The Apprentice Jr.*"

For the moment, control of the brand remained firmly in the hands of his father. As was so often the case, the Chicago event, meant to be about the soaring silver skyscraper in the large photograph propped on an easel, had ended up being about The Donald. The men and women who stood listening to the speeches seemed to welcome this new addition to their city's skyline, but their real focus was on the man who was building it. They had greeted him with hand-lettered signs; one read "Donald," and another said "Sing Hallelujah, next *Apprentice* challenge." And when he had finished speaking, they crowded around him, waving dollar bills and asking him to autograph them.

Notes

CHAPTER ONE: Born to Compete

1. A key element in the baby boom was the Census Bureau's ability to register it. Until the early twentieth century, high infant mortality rates and the lack of age-related benefits like Social Security made keeping track of births a low priority. But in 1915, growing public health concerns led to a nationwide birth registration system, and by 1933 paper copies of every new birth certificate in America were flowing to a single large room in the Census Bureau. There clerks keypunched the information onto stiff file cards tabulated on the world's only unit counters. Bureau technicians had invented these unwieldy contraptions, which could not add, subtract, multiply, or divide. But they could count, which meant that the nation could know for the first time precisely how many children were born each year.

Until the end of World War II, the numbers were unremarkable, but in 1946 there was an abrupt shift. At midyear the number of births suddenly spiked up by 40,000, more than double any previous monthly increase that year, and over the next 12 months 553,000 babies were born, nearly twice the largest yearly total since the birth-registration system began. What was later dubbed "the baby boom" was under way. Sources include interviews with Jay

Olshansky, 7/1/98; Carol J. De Vita, 7/7/98; Manning Feinleib, 7/7/98; Martin O'Connell, 7/7/98; Sam Shapiro, 7/7/98; Eric Kingson, 7/7/98; I. O. Moriyama, 7/8/98; Howard West, 7/9/98; Frank Sulloway, 7/15/98. Other sources include Leon F. Bouvier and Carol J. De Vita, "The Baby Boom—Entering Midlife," *Population Bulletin*, November 1991; Carol J. De Vita, "The United States at Mid-Decade," *Population Bulletin*, March 1996; "IIVRS Chronicle," November 1991; and *Vital Statistics of the United States, 1950*, vol. I, pp. 1–19.

2. That is, if pre-1946 birth levels had continued.

3. Sources for this section include Frank Sulloway, *Born to Rebel: Birth Order, Family Dynamics, and Creative Lives*, passim; interview with Robert Zajonc, 2/3/00.

4. Audrey Leibovich, Magali Rheault, and Dan Wilchins, "An Amazing Half Century of Progress," *Kiplinger's*, 1/97.

5. Elsewhere Americans were figuring out how to adjust to peacetime. On this same day members of Congress were arguing about whether to draft 18-year-olds; the U.S. was offering to turn over all its atomic warfare information to an internationally supervised commission while at the same time reserving the right to continue atomic bomb tests at Bikini Atoll in the Pacific; and maritime workers, no longer forced to observe wartime prohibitions against strikes, were preparing to walk out at midnight.

6. Sources for this and the following sections include interviews with Robert Trump, 2/3/94; Maryanne Trump Barry, 2/9/98; Louis Droesch, 7/23/98; Nancy Boyd Tickel, 7/17/98; Heather MacIntosh Hayes, 8/10/98; Jan van Heinigen, 6/5/98; Harold Liebman, 4/30/90; Linda Strauss Kearns, 8/3/98.

7. Presumably because they were both engaged in commerce, Fred sometimes seemed closer to his brother-in-law than to his own brother John, an MIT professor who was respected for his academic accomplishments but was considered to have little practical sense. "He had the brains," Fred once said to an acquaintance who had attended the same Queens high school as the Trumps. "But I made the money." Sources include interview with Florence Stelz Spielhouse, 2/90.

8. Donald Trump with Tony Schwartz, *The Art of the Deal*, 1987, pp. 54–55.

9. Sources include Thomas J. Lovely, *The History of the Jamaica Estates, 1929–1969*, and interviews with Bernice Able MacIntosh, 2/90; Dorothea Kuritzkes, 2/90; Heather MacIntosh Hayes, 7/25/98.

10. Interview with Shirley Greene, 3/24/98.

11. Trump, *The Art of the Deal*, pp. 49–50.

12. Sources for this section include interviews with Fina Farhi Geiger, 6/5/98; Peter Brant, 5/11/98; Linda Dufault, 1/27/98; Philip Rogers, 3/24/98; Charles Walker, 2/6/98; Ann Rudovsky Komfeld, 12/01/93; Michael Corbisiero, 11/1/97; Dave Rudovsky, 12/5/93; Joe Sukaskas, 3/24/98.

13. Both men would be high school sports stars and, in later years, keenly

competitive athletes. Donald is a low-handicap golfer; Peter, a newsprint magnate and publisher, is a top-ranked polo player and owner of his own club in Greenwich, Connecticut, which was used during the final competition in the second season of *The Apprentice*. Touted by *Polo* as the sport's "most competitive amateur," he is renowned for a bare-knuckles style that has included brazenly hitting opponents with his mallet and cutting off their horses. Eric O'Keefe, "The Peter Principle in Polo," *Polo*, March/April 1998.

14. Sources include *New York Times*, 1/20/99; interview with Marty Goldensohn, 8/17/98.

15. Brochures described Hilltop as "a summer camp for Christian boys," and religious observances consisted solely of Protestant and Catholic services on Sundays. According to Raymond Hillman, a son of the owners, Hilltop and Hill Manor, like many Gentile camps of the time, discouraged applications from Jewish children and assumed they could attend one of the many Jewish camps in Pennsylvania's Pocono Mountains. Sources for this section include Nancy Boyd Tickel, 7/17/98; Ginny Droesch Trumpbour, 7/14/98; Richard Hillman, 7/9/98; Phyllis Grady, 7/15/98; Stanley Hillman, 8/91; Raymond Hillman, 8/91; Kathy Young, 8/91; Heather Hillman Adams, 7/30/98; Betty Miles, 7/31/98; Brian Goldin, 7/23/98; Fred Briller, 7/23/98; Larry Strauss, 7/23/98; Mary Roche Cossman, 7/14/98.

16. Interview with Mary Trump, 5/17/98. Apparently, even at that time, such close supervision was remarkable.

17. Sources for this section include interviews with Paul Bekman, 4/15/98; Bernie Blum, 1/14/98; John Brugman, 1/13/98; Colonel Anthony Castellano, 4/16/98; Francis Diotte, 4/21/98; Major Theodore R. Dobias, 3/24/98; Warren Goodwin, 3/18/98; Stan Holuba, 2/2/98; Mike Kabealo, 2/3/98; Ted Levine, 1/14/98; David Smith, 8/23/98; Robert V. Ward, 3/18/98; George White, 8/11/98; Mike Scadron, 8/29/98. I am also indebted to Lieutenant Colonel Dan Keenan.

18. Horseplay was a regular feature of life at NYMA, and occasionally groups ambushed one another with, for example, a trash can full of water poised to tip over when a cadet answered a knock at his door. The standard punishment for misdemeanors such as talking during study hours or being late to mess was push-ups and marching back and forth outside barracks. "Donald did his share of walking," coach Dobias said. "The real punishment was that it was so boring." Donald's military career ended with NYMA graduation; despite his athletic prowess, in 1968 he received a medical deferment from the military draft.

19. Although many parents were wealthy, most drove their own cars. According to dorm mate Francis Diotte, Donald once refused to meet his parents because they had, as usual, driven up in their chauffeured limousine. The next time they came in an ordinary Cadillac convertible, with Fred Trump at the wheel, and Diotte was invited to join them for what turned out to be a "kind of harrowing" drive to a local restaurant. "Donald said he had never been in a car

with his father driving," said Diotte, "and after that he allowed his parents to come up with the chauffeur after all." Interview with Francis Diotte, 4/21/98.

20. Trump, *The Art of the Deal*, p. 50; interview with Mary Trump, 5/17/98.

21. Sources for this section include interview with John Meyers, 2/12/99, and with Donald Trump, 12/17/97. The standard joke at Gregory Estates, Trump recalled, was that Seat Pleasant got its name "because that's where they had the largest toilet seat manufacturer."

22. Interviews with Marcy Feigenbaum, 12/24/93; Morris Lapidus, 10/28/98.

23. Sources for this section include interviews with Steve Lesko, 3/26/98; Bob Hawthorne, 7/23/98; Don Robinson, 3/3/98; Artie Storrs, 5/28/98; Rich Marrin, 11/20/97; Peter Shapiro, 3/9/98; Donald Trump, 12/17/97 and 1/12/98.

24. *New York Times*, 8/26/80, 4/16/00, 1/9/05. Ammann also designed the George Washington, Bayonne, Triborough, Throgs Neck, and Bronx-Whitestone Bridges and consulted on the Lincoln Tunnel and the Golden Gate Bridge.

25. Sources for this section include interviews with John A. Cantrill, 2/3/98; Joe Cohen, 4/21/98; Herbert Denenberg, 2/3/98; Peter Gelb, 1/29/98; Marty Goldensohn, 8/24/98.

26. Trump, *The Art of the Deal*, p. 53.

27. Sources for this section include Harry Hurt, *Lost Tycoon*, 1993, p. 13; interviews with Jim Nolan, 3/29/98; Karl Walther, 3/29/98; Homer Godwin, 4/2/98; Maryanne Trump Barry, 2/9/98; Jan von Heinigen, 6/15/98; Louis Droesch, 7/23/98; Ginny Droesch Trumpbour, 7/14/98; David Smith, 8/28/98.

28. "My father was a very formal guy, very proper, with fixed ideas about how things should be," recalled Maryanne. One fixed idea was that business—especially the building business—was the province of men. Although Maryanne worked in Fred's office in the summers (and became a lawyer and, eventually, a federal judge in New Jersey), she never saw herself as a candidate for taking over for her father. "I never tried to get involved in any important way," she said. "But even if I'd been the greatest thing, Dad was an old-fashioned guy, and he thought women were mothers or teachers. If they worked, they worked in a bank. For me to be in line as his right hand wouldn't have occurred to him, or to me, either." Interview with Maryanne Trump Barry, 2/9/98.

29. Glenn Plaskin, *"Playboy* Interview: Donald Trump," *Playboy,* March 1990.

CHAPTER TWO: Manhattan Bound

1. The name Swifton alluded to the fact that the land where the apartment complex stood had been a generous wedding gift from one Briggs Swift to his daughter Eunice back in about 1880. Ian Woodner, a developer in Washington, D.C., completed Swifton Village in 1953 and one year later stood ac-

cused, along with Fred Trump, of windfall profits on Federal Housing Administration projects. A few weeks after Fred Trump sat before the Senate Banking and Currency Committee on Capitol Hill and testified about his FHA-backed construction in Brooklyn, Woodner appeared before the same body and admitted that he had skirted FHA mortgage ceilings on a project in Washington by putting an inch of caulking compound between two halves of a large building and then obtaining a separate mortgage for each side. Sources for this chapter include *Cincinnati Enquirer*, 6/28/90; *Cincinnati Post*, 5/28/51, 8/5/54; *Cincinnati Post & Times Star*, 4/15/64; *New York Times*, 6/7/64; *New York Herald Tribune*, 4/2/64; interviews with Donald Trump, 12/97, 1/98; Murray Feiden, 12/93; Jerry Robinson, 10/26/97; Franklyn Harkavy, 10/10/97.

2. The 1,200-unit complex had 57 two-story, garden-style buildings spread out over 41 acres.

3. *Cincinnati Post & Times Star*, 4/15/64.

4. HOME had received other complaints of discrimination at Swifton, but these were settled by compliance and did not go to court. Sources for this section include HOME records and interviews with Jerry Robinson, 10/26/97; Franklyn Harkavy, 10/10/97; Heywood Cash, 8/21/97; Lee Hereth, 8/21/97.

5. *Cincinnati Enquirer*, 12/23/72.

6. The property being sold was Gregory Apartments in Maryland, where Donald Trump had worked one summer. Sources for this section include interviews with Gerald Schrager, 5/17/99; Brad Zackson, 2/9/95.

7. Interview with Donald Trump, 12/17/97.

8. One of Fred's favorite names for his business holdings was Trump Village Construction Corporation. In Cincinnati alone, the Trump interests were variously known as the Swifton Land Corporation, Swifton Realty Corporation, and Fred Trump's New Swifton Village Apartments.

9. Sources for this section include Trump, *The Art of the Deal*, p. 65.

10. The club was founded in 1960 by society columnist Igor Cassini. Its first board had included his fashion-designer brother Oleg, Italian industrialist Giovanni Agnelli, and actor Rex Harrison, and it still offered a heady mix of exclusivity and glamour to a wide range of socially ambitious New Yorkers.

11. Sources for this section include Nicholas von Hoffman, *Citizen Cohn*, 1988, passim; interviews with Eugene Morris, 12/22/93; Alan Weiselberg, 2/3/98.

12. Sources include *New York Times*, 10/16/73, 12/13/73, 1/26/74, 6/11/75; *New York Daily News*, 12/16/73; Wayne Barrett, *Trump: The Deals and the Downfall*, 1992, pp. 85–88.

13. *Time*, 1/26/68. Sources for this section include *Time*, 1/26/68, 6/22/70; *Saturday Review*, 1/11/69; *Fortune*, 8/70; *New York Times*, 2/9/87; *Corporate Reorganization Reporter*, passim; Eric Posner, "The Political Economy of the Bankruptcy Reform Act of 1978," *Michigan Law Review*, 10/97; Joseph R. Daughen and Peter Binzen, *The Wreck of the Penn Central*, 1971; Robert Sobel, *The Fallen Colossus*, 1977; interviews with Eric Posner, 10/7/98; Fred Rovet,

9/17/98; James Blair, 8/28/98; Cary Dickieson, 9/22/98, 9/30/98; Newell Blair, 12/26/90; Robert Blanchette, 10/5/98; Paul Duke, 9/30/98.

14. The difference in working styles, so pervasive as to be nearly paralyzing from the moment the merger took place, is reflected in this later comment from longtime New York Central attorney Fred Rovet: "At New York Central, we were guys who went into the office and took off our jackets and got to work. But when we went down to this austere Philadelphia office with these big boardrooms, we almost had to genuflect to see their vice presidents." Interview with Fred Rovet, 9/17/98.

15. Estimates of the daily losses vary widely. On 7/6/73, *The New York Times* pegged it at $600,000 a day, whereas *The Wreck of the Penn Central* puts the daily loss at more than $1 million. Daughen and Binzen, *Wreck*, p. 255.

16. Required by government regulations to continue little-utilized routes and to provide money-losing passenger service for which the true cost was more than the market would bear, U.S. railroads were in an impossible bind. Most other industrialized nations maintained reasonable passenger ticket prices and comprehensive services only because they were nationalized. Eventually the Penn Central adopted a modified version of the same solution, with one government-owned corporation, Amtrak, for interstate passenger service and another, Conrail, for commuter and freight service.

17. Interview with Robert Blanchette, 10/5/98.

18. Sources include *Forbes*, 4/17/78; *New York Times*, 7/6/73; interviews with John Koskinen, 8/28/98; Morris Raker, 10/7/98.

19. Central Park comprises 840 acres.

20. Sources include interviews with Morris Lapidus, 10/18/98; Alan Lapidus, 11/6/98; Larry Schafran, 9/2/98; Milton Braveman, 10/10/97; Donald Trump, 12/12/97. By the end of the nineteenth century, the New York Central, like all U.S. railroads, owned immense amounts of property, including rail yards, terminal areas, and, in Manhattan, a wide ditch down the middle of the island used to accommodate coal- and wood-fired steam locomotives. With the arrival of electric locomotives, the New York Central covered the ditch, laid out Park Avenue, and built luxury apartment houses down each side. It also built a new Grand Central Terminal at 42nd Street and hotels and other facilities for travelers. For years income from these properties only partly offset maintenance costs for Grand Central, but after World War II, when Park Avenue became home to new office buildings built on 99-year ground leases with escalation clauses, real estate revenues began to rise. With the 1964 World's Fair, hotel occupancy and income also increased, and the real estate operations previously considered subordinate to the main business of running a railroad began to play a major role. One of the first developers to recognize this historic shift was William Zeckendorf, but he went bankrupt before he could realize his plans for the Penn Central properties. Donald, who also saw this change, got much further before encountering economic reversals and has had a far more successful recovery.

21. Sources for this section include interviews with Peter Martosella, 9/2/98; Victor Palmieri, 9/8/98; Larry Schafran, 11/90; John Koskinen, 8/28/98; Ned Eichler, 9/20/98; interview with Edward Eichler conducted by *Inside Story*, 4/19/89.

22. The subsidiary, Great Southwest, was a land development company gone amok that had been purchased by a rail conglomerate that also went amok. By 1970 Great Southwest owned, among other things, a wax museum, mobile home communities, and cattle ranches. Palmieri's successful restructuring of this subsidiary was key to his later appointment to handle Penn Central's nonrail assets. Sources include *Fortune*, 2/13/78.

23. *New York Times*, 10/29/76.

24. It didn't help the new mayor that the *New York Times*, which would have preferred a Lindsay-style WASP as mayor, viewed Beame as little more than a party hack from the outer boroughs. Sid Frigand, his press secretary, recalled a conversation in which Beame asked why the *Times* was so hostile. "I explained to him that if he worked for the *Times*, he would be known as A. D. Beame because anyone named Abraham couldn't use it as a first name," Frigand said. "Just look at [*Times* veterans] A. H. Raskin and A. M. Rosenthal." Interview with Sid Frigand, 9/1/98.

25. Zuccotti, a liberal Democrat and highly successful real estate lawyer, had his first political experience serving on the Kerner Commission with Victor Palmieri and John Koskinen.

26. Interview conducted by *Inside Story*, 3/19/89.

27. Construction on the highway, a viaduct stretching from 59th to 72nd streets and spanning what was then the New York Central rail yards, began in 1929 and was finished in 1932. Named for Manhattan borough president Julius Miller, the Miller Highway was reportedly the first urban elevated highway in the country. *New York Times*, 2/17/91.

28. After World War II annual traffic at the two yards reached more than 200,000 carloads, but by 1973 it had declined to fewer than 25,000 carloads. Converting the yards to other uses was difficult, however, because the railroad planned to continue running trains through the property. In theory it seemed possible to sell the yards' air rights—that is, the right to build up to a certain size depending on the relevant zoning—with the expectation that any development would be on a platform over railroad operations. (For further discussion of air rights, see the section on Olympic Tower and Trump Tower in chapter 4.) Unable to proceed without knowing how high the platform had to be, Fred Rovet, an attorney who was assistant vice president of the Penn Central's real estate department, went to the railroad's engineers and asked what clearance would be needed for a man hunched over the top of a freight car. After some hemming and hawing, the engineers came up with a guesstimate of 22 feet above the ground, which promptly became the industrywide standard. "When you're in bankruptcy," Rovet said afterward, "you're not surrounded with 8,000 consultants to help you figure these things out. You have to

say to the last guy who hasn't already left to work for a profit-making operation, 'Let's take a guess—what can they do, kill us?' " *New York Times*, 7/30/74; interview with Fred Rovet, 9/17/98.

29. *New York Times*, 11/29/80. Interview with Fred Rovet, 9/17/98.

30. Interview with Cary Dickieson, 9/22/98.

31. Sources for this section include Wayne Barrett, "Like Father, Like Son," *Village Voice*, 2/15/79; "Donald Trump Cuts the Cards," *Village Voice*, 1/22/79; and *Trump*, chapter 4. Apparently Donald had a deep appreciation for David Berger's legal skills, for five years later, in 1984, he hired the Philadelphia attorney to represent him on yet another matter; see chapter 6, note 18.

32. Interview with Herbert Chason, 5/22/89. During the hearing the young developer could barely sit still. "Donald was right next to me," recalled attorney Arthur Arsham. He represented the *New York Times*, which owned a small site on the edge of the rail yards. "He didn't hesitate to make his position known. He poked me with his elbow every time someone said something on the witness stand that he didn't like."

CHAPTER THREE: From Brick Box to Glass Fantasy

1. Sources for the following section include *New York Times*, 11/6/74, 11/3/82, 10/30/98.

2. Appointed to the powerful House Ways and Means Committee in 1970, Carey had forged strong ties with its chair, Representative Wilbur Mills of Arkansas. In the 1972 election Mills suggested to Governor Rockefeller that it would be in New York's best interests if Carey stayed in office. In response Rockefeller told Carey's Republican opponent to decline Conservative Party support, thereby contributing to Carey's victory amid the statewide rejection of the Democratic presidential candidate, George McGovern. *New York Times*, 11/6/74.

3. Interview with Ken Auletta, 10/14/89.

4. Barrett, "Trump Cuts the Cards," *Village Voice*, 1/22/79.

5. Such postelection committees, which real estate developer Richard Ravitch, named to the same task force, summed up as "all b.s.," are usually little more than public opportunities to say thanks and/or to line up contacts for the future. This particular group apparently never met; afterward several members had no recollection of its existence. Interview with Richard Ravitch, 12/11/98.

6. Interview with Matthew Lifflander, finance chair of the Democratic State Committee, 1973–74, on 10/20/97.

7. *New York Times*, 3/10/85.

8. Gruzen and Samton had been fascinated with the yards ever since Leonard Bernstein's *West Side Story* had sparked interest in the area and the new performing arts complex at Lincoln Center had opened the West Side to large-scale development. In 1963 the Amalgamated Lithographers Union hired the pair for the 5,000-unit apartment complex, to be called Litho City.

After it fizzled, a state education agency commissioned them to create a project nearly twice as large, but due to the astronomical cost of air rights and plat-forming, this proposal also went nowhere. Sources for this section include Wayne Barrett, *Trump*, chapter 4, passim; Elliot Wilensky and Norval White, *AIA Guide to New York City*, 1988, passim; interviews with Jordan Gruzen, 11/22/98; Peter Samton, 1/4/99; Paul Willen, 9/13/91 and 9/22/91; Scott Keller, 4/24/90 and 1/2/99; Ned Eichler, 9/20/98, 11/28/98; Stuart Sheftel, 3/7/89.

9. *New York Times*, 6/30/74, 3/11/75.

10. *Westsider*, 3/20/75.

11. Robert Moses, "West Side Fiasco: A Practical Proposal for the Restoration of the West Side Highway and Parkway to Public Use," 11/25/74.

12. *Forbes*, 4/17/78; interview with Richard Dicker, 3/22/89.

13. Interview with Sally Goodgold, 6/5/89.

14. A Gruzen representative complained to a community board co-chair that at one community presentation, shouting, chanting, and "general chaos pervaded the meeting," and "it was effectively impossible to have any rational discussion." Letter from Amanda Burden, community liaison for Gruzen & Partners, to Doris Freedman, Community Board 7 co-chair, 7/11/78.

15. Interview with Jonathan Barnett, 11/5/98.

16. *Westsider*, 5/6/76.

17. Sources for this section include Peter Wilkinson, "The New Fixers," *Manhattan, inc.*, January 1988; *Manhattan, inc.*, 9/88 and 9/89; *New York Times*, 10/3/84, 11/23/92, and 10/6/99; *New York Daily News*, 3/5/89; interviews with Howard Rubenstein, 9/16/98; Breina Taubman, 3/8/89.

18. A classic workaholic, Rubenstein began his 15-hour workdays by rising before dawn, jogging while dictating memos into a tape recorder, then packing in scores of phone calls and half a dozen meetings. But when talking to clients, he spoke in the low, reassuring tones of a psychotherapist, calming outsize egos and restoring self-control to business magnates and political big shots who could never openly admit to having gone off the rails. Even after moving to Manhattan, Rubenstein retained and polished his ties to Brooklyn, helping Abe Beame become mayor and Hugh Carey become governor. "Howard had become someone people called because he could make a call," said former Rubenstein employee Breina Taubman.

19. Sources for this section include Nicholas Pileggi, "How to Get Things Done in New York: A Case History," *New York*, 11/73; Dan Dorfman, "The Bottom Line," *New York*, 11/13/75; *New York Times*, 10/8/75, 10/17/75, 12/12/75, 12/13/75, 12/18/75; *Chelsea-Clinton News*, 11/13/75, 12/18/75, 12/25/75; *New York Post*, 12/18/75; *New York Daily News*, 12/19/75; interviews with Howard Rubenstein, 9/16/98; Mary D'Elia, 2/2/99; Charles Urstadt, 5/14/96; John McGarrahan, 9/23/98; Der Scutt, 9/24/98; Breina Taubman, 3/8/89; Joe Walsh, 2/4/99; Jordan Gruzen, 11/28/98; Dan Gutman, 2/2/99. I am

grateful to Der Scutt for allowing me to read and quote from his private, un-published diary covering the years from 1974 to the present.

20. Area residents had initially opposed the proposal and enlisted Repre-sentative Bella Abzug, the feisty New York congresswoman known for combat-ive stances and large hats, to hold up necessary congressional approvals. They also suggested using the 34th Street yards, but to no avail. But eventually their protests had produced guarantees of neighborhood preservation, and now they had relaxed their opposition.

21. As Eichler recalled the conversation, Donald asked if he was kidding, then said, "You start talking about the convention center on the 34th Street yards and you'll be dead in a month because so many people have put together this whole package around 44th Street." Interview with Ned Eichler, 9/20/98.

22. Lead designer Der Scutt was not a member of the firm but served as consulting architect on this project. *Interiors*, 2/76.

23. Der Scutt diary, 10/4/75.

24. Charles Urstadt, then chairman of the Battery Park City Authority, was driving to work when he heard a reporter saying that Donald Trump had demanded an investigation of Battery Park City. "[Donald] said that putting the convention center there was totally unwarranted," Urstadt recalled later. "This was news to me. It was the wildest thing I ever heard."

25. Donald Trump's 34th Street proposal called for a 540,000-square-foot convention center. The McCormick Place Convention Center in Chicago, built in 1960, had been expanded in 1971 to 644,000 square feet.

26. Then again, with Howard Rubenstein pushing the 34th Street site, there wasn't all that much doubt where the convention center would end up. He had steered the 44th Street plan right up to the finish line, and the only rea-son it stopped short of completion was the city's fiscal crisis. When Beame dropped 44th Street, Rubenstein cut his losses and joined forces with Donald Trump to put the complex at 34th Street. Sandy Lindenbaum, who had also worked on 44th Street, did the same. To those left at 44th Street, such switches were a dire portent. "When Howard left, it was a sign that the center of gravity in this thing had shifted," said John McGarrahan, attorney for the 44th Street project. "The convention center had become a Brooklyn project, that's what happened. Howard's moving over told us the decision had been made."

27. Among the other key players in the Brooklyn network, two of the most important were City Council president Tom Cuite and state assembly Speaker Stanley Steingut, both long-term friends and colleagues of Howard Rubenstein and Fred Trump.

28. Sources for this section include newspaper articles of the period; Tom Shachtman, *Skyscraper Dreams*, 1991, passim; Der Scutt diary; letter from John Koskinen to Wayne Barrett, 2/6/79; interview with John Koskinen, 8/28/98; memo from Mike Bailkin to John Zuccotti, 1/9/76. After making a fortune in shipping, Vanderbilt had gone on to railroads and merged several lines into the New York Central. In 1870, he began construction on what would eventually

become Grand Central Terminal, next-door neighbor to the Commodore Hotel.

29. *New York Post*, 12/12/75. In April 1975 the projected loss for the year for the Commodore was $840,000, but by December the predicted shortfall had grown to $1.2 million.

30. Trump, *The Art of the Deal*, p. 82.

31. Although Donald had a reputation for being cheap, Scutt was unprepared for how hard a bargain the developer would drive on the Commodore. As Scutt recalled, Donald sat across from Scutt and Gruzen and told them he would give them the job for about 10 percent less than they had expected and dismiss the firm he had already spoken with. Then he moved the phone to the corner of the desk and asked for the other firm's phone number, a gesture Scutt found "incredible and enticing." With much discussion, Donald increased the fee somewhat but demanded that they cut the total construction costs and added on more expenses. After they agreed he slapped on one last item, making the final fee only slightly higher than the offer with which he began. Interview with Der Scutt, 9/24/98.

32. Sources for this section include Karen Cook, "Street Smart," *Manhattan, inc.*, 12/86; interviews with Ben Lambert, 8/5/98, 8/7/98.

33. According to Henry Benach, head of the Starrett Corporation, whose subsidiary HRH was the contractor on the reconstruction of the Commodore, Hyatt Hotel Corporation initially declined to invest in the deal and instead agreed to take a management role. After Benach saw the management contract Jay Pritzker had provided, he told Pritzker it was a "very tough document" but he was considering entering the deal because he knew Fred and the Trump Organization. Pritzker said that he didn't know Donald, but if Benach said he and his father were okay, Pritzker would become a third partner. Pritzker and Benach met with Donald and Fred, but soon it became clear that Benach, as owner of a public company, wanted to build and then sell, whereas the Trumps and Pritzker, owners of private companies, wanted to build and hold on, using the tax depreciation as a write-off for other properties. Accordingly, Benach backed off and, after Starrett purchased HRH from Richard Ravitch in 1977, served as the builder, while the Trump Organization and Pritzker remained partners. Interviews with Henry Benach, 4/20/98, 5/29/98, 7/7/98, 1/24/99.

34. *New York Times*, 5/4/75; Der Scutt diary, 5/4/75.

35. Der Scutt diary, 5/4/76.

36. Sources for this section include Shachtman, *Skyscraper*, chapter 14; *New York Times*, 7/19/96.

37. Rudin, head of an old Manhattan real estate family, persuaded large taxpayers, including Consolidated Edison, New York Telephone, and Rockefeller Center, to join his company and other real estate firms (the list did not include the Trump Organization) in this civic gesture. Meanwhile the state established a new entity called the Municipal Assistance Corporation (MAC),

a consortium of banking and financial interests led by investment banker Felix Rohatyn and empowered to sell bonds for the city. But despite the credentials of MAC's directors, its bonds didn't move on the market.

38. Cavanagh, then 61, had been a civil servant for 37 years and was Abe Beame's closest friend at City Hall. One of Beame's first appointments after his election, Cavanagh was a rumpled, plain-talking, old-style Brooklynite, which endeared him to the mayor but not to the financial forces who had gained ascendancy in the midst of New York City's financial crisis.

39. Sources for this section include *New York Times,* 1/6/74, 1/17/75, 7/2/85; *Barron's,* 8/20/79; Barrett, *Trump;* interviews with Mike Bailkin, 2/22/89, 3/7/89; David I. Stadtmauer, 4/11/89; John Zuccotti, 9/30/98.

40. The last had been the New York Hilton, built in 1963.

41. Specifically, the UDC issued $1.3 billion in bonds and in 1975, unable to meet $135 million in short-term obligations, went into default. *Barron's,* 8/29/79.

42. Perhaps Bailkin's tenure at this state agency, to which Louise Sunshine would presumably have access, was yet another reason Donald Trump came back to see him.

43. John Portman, innovative architect of the Hyatt Regency in Atlanta, was promoting another large hotel for 42nd Street, but the project was stalled and would never be built.

44. Sources for this section include interviews with Henry Pearce, 2/3/94; Bill Frentz, 4/6/98; Claude Morton, 3/7/98; Ben Holloway, 11/1/98; Frank Bryant, 3/2/98.

45. Trump, *The Art of the Deal,* p. 87.

46. Interview with George Puskar, 11/17/97.

47. Sources for this section include letter from John Koskinen to Wayne Barrett, 2/6/79, and interviews with Henry Stern, 11/17/98; Richard Ravitch, 9/30/98; Mark Alan Siegel, 10/9/98; Mike Bailkin, 2/22/89; Mario de Genova, 9/18/98.

48. Ravitch did not pursue his interest in the site with vigor. As he later recalled, he was preoccupied with his pending UDC appointment as well as the death in a plane crash of his cousin and partner in the family-owned construction business HRH (which Ravitch subsequently sold and the Trump Organization hired to renovate the Commodore). Ravitch's own West Side project, Manhattan Plaza, was also in serious trouble, a factor that had inclined Ned Eichler to favor granting the option on the yards to the unencumbered Donald Trump. Interviews with Richard Ravitch, 9/28/98; Ned Eichler, 9/20/98, 11/27/98.

49. Dun & Bradstreet Reports, November/December 1978, p. 10. UDC chair Ravitch eventually decided that the UDC was merely acting as a conduit and that a state agency had no standing to veto what was, at heart, a city project.

CHAPTER FOUR: The 28-Sided Building

1. Every year in December, the real estate and construction industries held a dinner-dance to benefit the National Jewish Medical and Research Center in Denver, Colorado. Previous recipients included Samuel LeFrak, who had carved out a development path in Queens parallel to that of Fred Trump in Brooklyn; World Trade Center architect Minoru Yamasaki; HRH partner Saul Horowitz; and Manhattan real estate heavyweights Sylvan Lawrence, John Larsen, James Gorman, and Bernard Rosen. Interview with Lenny Boxer, 11/28/97.

2. The first was Thomas Wilett, elected in 1665.

3. Sources for this chapter include Barrett, *Trump*, passim; multiple interviews with Phil Wolf in 1989 and 1990. Sources for this section include interviews with Richard Rosan, 2/1/99; Richard Kahan, 9/29/98; Gerald Schrager, 5/17/99; Henry Stern, 11/17/98, 11/18/98; Hadley Gold, 10/5/98.

4. Ultimately, Equitable Life plus the Bowery, Manhattan, Greenwich, Lincoln, Dry Dock, and Central savings banks came up with the permanent financing. Sources include "Private Enterprise Breathes New Life into Old Cities," *Dun & Bradstreet Reports*, November/December 1978.

5. Sources for this section include interviews with Ralph Steinglass, 1/4/99; Joe Kordsmeier, 1/22/99; Bill DiGiacomo, 10/16/98; Harriet Economou, 1/12/99; Lowell Goldman, 1/14/99.

6. Hyatt called its atrium-style luxury hotels "Hyatt Regency" to distinguish them from the other lodgings in its chain, known as "Hyatt Hotels." But this practice ran into problems in New York City. The name Regency was already being used by the Tisch hotel chain, whose head, Robert Tisch, a backer of the 44th Street convention center and opponent of the 34th Street site, had complained that the tax abatement given the Commodore was unavailable to other hotels. Hardly surprising, the Tisches did not care to share the name; in addition, Donald objected to using the name because it implied that the former Commodore was merely part of a chain. Thus the Commodore became the Grand Hyatt, reflecting its proximity to Grand Central Station, which was next door. Sources for this section include Der Scutt diary, 5/24/77.

7. Michael Stone, "Clash of the Titans: Business Tycoons Donald Trump and Jay Pritzker," *Chicago*, 10/94.

8. Sources for this section include Marie Brenner, "After the Gold Rush," *Vanity Fair*, 9/90; interviews with Gerald Schrager, 5/17/99; Sugar Rautbord, 2/27/99, 3/6/99.

9. Concerned about underbudgeting, Ralph Steinglass, the on-site project architect, tried to bump up the contract to what he considered a more realistic level. "I've got a Christian project manager architect with a Jewish name," Donald Trump joked. Top HRH executive Irv Fisher shot back, "And we've got a Christian owner with a Jewish head!" Der Scutt diary, 11/23/77.

10. On Fred's large FHA-sponsored Brooklyn apartment complexes Shore Haven and Beach Haven, it had been to his advantage to make actual costs as low as possible. After covering those charges, he could "mortgage

out"—that is, use the balance of his construction loan to pay off the mortgage—then issue dividends out of rental income to the official sponsor of the
projects (that is, himself). He ran into trouble at Trump Village because he was
putting up an unfamiliar building type, high-rise apartment towers, and had to
call in HRH for help. But he had figured in such an ample profit margin that despite having to pay another builder, he still collected a handsome profit.

11. Phil Wolf, the on-site owner's representative, recalled other unpleas-
ant discoveries, including the cinder fill the original builders of the Commodore had used to make up for differences in floor thickness. At that time,
cinders, produced by the locomotives next door at Grand Central, were plenti-
ful and made good filler because they are not as heavy as concrete or sand; however, they are corrosive and thus had to be removed. Another surprise was that
steel beams adjacent to the Commodore's ice-making machinery had been corroded by the salt used to produce the vast quantities of ice needed for iceboxes
and to cool large common areas, where fans blowing over blocks of ice had created a rudimentary form of air-conditioning.

12. Sources include Barrett, *Trump*, p. 161; interview with Margo
Wellington, 4/12/99.

13. Interview with Jeff Walker, 3/17/98.

14. Sources for this section include "The Two Faces of Ivana—Model
and Sportswoman," *Montreal Gazette*, 12/31/75; Marie Brenner, "Trumping the
Town," *New York*, 11/17/80; Jonathan Van Meter, "Ivana! Ivana! Ivana!" *Spy*,
5/89; Glenn Plaskin, "Queen Ivana Approximately," *New York Daily News
Magazine*, 12/17/89; Norma King, *Ivana Trump: A Very Unauthorized Biography*,
1990, passim: Wayne Barrett, *Trump*, passim; interview with Jerry Goldsmith,
3/20/99; Ivana Trump, speech, Church of the Holy Apostle, 11/19/99.

15. Like many people, Ivana tended to look better in person than she did
on film. In photographs her wide smile showed too much tooth and, even
worse, too much gum. A further problem was that at a little over five feet seven,
she fell about two inches short of the minimum requirement for top-of-the-line
modeling work, which meant she would be limited to runways.

16. Carol V. R. George, *God's Salesman*, 1993, passim; interview with
Arthur Caliandro, 10/27/97.

17. *New York Times*, 8/30/79. One of the few personal touches was a small
bedside photo of Donald in the nude, with his back to the camera. "It was like
a secret piece of intimacy in the room," said *Times* reporter Patricia Lynden,
"and it stood out from the rest of the impersonal decor."

18. Sources for this section include Brenner, "Gold Rush"; *New York
Times*, 8/30/79; notes of Patricia Lynden.

19. Interview with Andre d'Usseau, the Hyatt vice-president in charge of
technical assistance, 10/21/98. Thus, for example, Donald retained Der Scutt
as well as Jordan Gruzen as architects on the Grand Hyatt and the convention
center and fanned the competitive flames between them with selective praise,
credit, and payment.

20. Interview with Alan Lapidus, 5/7/90.

21. *New York Times*, 8/26/80.

22. This meant, among other things, an aggressive effort to expel certain on-site retailers. In one instance, Donald insisted on the right to review the display windows of a sporting goods store he considered tacky; in another, he wanted to replace Strawberry's, a moderate-price women's clothing store, with escalators that would serve as place-holders in case casino gambling became legal in New York. Negotiations between the developer and site tenants were long and often bitter and in some cases led to court suits. Eventually, Strawberry's and some, but not all, of the site tenants returned. Sources for this section include Brenner, "Trumping"; interviews with Paul Willen, 11/27/98; Richard Rice, 1/4/99; Peter Samton, 1/4/99; Rich Rosan, 2/1/99; Arthur Emil, 2/25/99.

23. *Dun & Bradstreet Reports*, November/December 1978.

24. HRH had figured the construction would cost about twice as much as the $35 million the Trumps had insisted on. But for those on the job who were used to building on time and on budget, the experience of being constantly behind was dismaying. "It was nerve-wracking and scary," said Joe Kordsmeier, a Hyatt vice-president assigned to the construction site. "It was the first time any of our projects had gone over budget, and if it hadn't been for the tax abatement, it would have been a disaster." Another Hyatt executive, John Nichols, recalled being under tremendous pressure to finish and resorting to a "soft opening," which meant renting rooms in the unfinished building and imposing strict work rules, such as no food or beer on the job, so as to encourage workers to finish the job and move on.

25. This figure includes land costs of $10 million. Sources include Barrett, *Trump*, p. 160.

26. *Dun & Bradstreet Reports*, November/December 1978.

27. "He wasn't the only one promoting himself," Marino said, "but he did it with more flair. Most of the developers were these nice older Jewish guys—we called Donald 'the Golden Goy.' " Interview with Ron Marino, 3/5/99.

28. The new mayor announced in April 1978 that the new convention center would be built at the 34th Street site. Within a week Donald Trump told Der Scutt that he was no longer in the running for developer but wanted a percentage of any architectural fees collected by Scutt's firm on the project—a demand that became moot when the design commission went to I. M. Pei. Perhaps one of the reasons the young developer withdrew so precipitously was that the U.S. Department of Justice was again breathing down his neck with claims that the Trump Organization discriminated against blacks, this time in its Brooklyn apartments. Sources include *New York Times*, 4/29/78; Der Scutt diary; Jerome Tuccille, *Trump*, 1987, p. 131.

29. *New York Daily News*, 11/22/78.

30. Sources include interview with Peter Solomon, 3/29/99.

31. Five years later Peter Martosella, the Palmieri executive in charge of

closing the 60th Street yards deal, sent Donald Trump a note congratulating him on a recent acquisition and saying that the developer had succeeded at everything he tried to do except the 60th Street yards. "Within a second of his receiving the letter," Martosella said later, "he was on the phone with me explaining why he couldn't go ahead." Sources include interviews with Larry Shafran, 9/27/98; Peter Martosella, 9/2/98; Fred Rovet, 9/17/98; John Koskinen, 8/28/98.

32. Artistotle Onassis's partner on Olympic Tower was Arlen Realty and Development Corporation, headed by Arthur Cohen, owner of E. J. Korvette's. To get control of the land on which it was built, Onassis made a deal with Meshulam Riklis, a celebrated manipulator of corporate assets who later leased office space on two floors in Trump Tower for a monthly rent of $100,000. In 1991, after five years as a tenant, he and his wife, singer Pia Zadora, skipped out, stiffing the Trump Organization for many months of rent. Vowing revenge, Donald Trump eventually won a judgment against him for $750,000. Sources for this section include *New York Times*, 10/3/70, 10/7/70, 10/15/70, 2/10/71, 9/1/71, 6/24/73, 10/5/91, 1/10/92, 9/6/74; interviews with Alan Lapidus, 5/13/99; Jerry Shrager, 5/17/99.

33. The size of any building in New York City depends on its floor area ratio, or FAR, which is the ratio of the total floor area to the size of the building lot and is a function of the specific zoning assigned to the lot. At that time, the FAR in most high-density commercial areas in Manhattan was 15. Because Olympic Tower (OT) had public space at the ground level, more than the minimally required retail space, and residential units, the FAR increased to 21.6, the highest permissible ratio of floor area to lot size. As a result, OT was able to maximize its density, or total square footage relative to the size of its building lot. Although the Empire State Building (ESB), 102 stories, is far taller than the 52-story OT, its density is not as large because (1) the ESB spreads out over a far larger building lot; and (2) unlike OT, which is essentially a big rectangular solid sitting on its end, the ESB is stepped back, in wedding-cake style.

34. Interview with Rochelle Corson, 2/25/99.

35. Sources for this section include *BusinessWeek*, 4/5/78, 1/29/79, and Der Scutt diary, 1/22/79, 1/23/79.

36. One day after the appearance of the January 1979 *BusinessWeek* article, planted by an Equitable executive on the Genesco board of directors and the first to describe a possible Genesco sale to Donald Trump, the Equitable board approved Project T. Because it was obvious that the deal hinged on the developer's participation, Equitable took out a $20 million life insurance policy on Donald Trump, payable to the partnership.

37. *New York Times*, 8/26/80; *Los Angeles Times*, 4/7/85.

38. Sources for this section include Barrett, *Trump*, passim; Harry Hurt, *Lost Tycoon*, 1993, passim; interviews with Bill Frentz, 4/6/98; Ben Holloway, 11/9/98; Conrad Stephenson, 5/28/98; George Puskar, 11/17/97; George Pea-

cock, 5/16/98; John Minikes, 12/9/98; Claude Morton, 3/7/98; Tim Welch, 6/30/98; Doug Healey, 4/21/98; Wally Antoniewicz, 5/11/98.

39. Stephenson's disappointment over the loss of the Grand Hyatt loan would lead him to develop new ways to lend money and earn him the nickname "Mr. Real Estate." Previously, a bank either handled an entire loan or, if it was too close to its loan limit, passed altogether. "We were opening the door for competitors to take a customer over," Stephenson said. "I thought that was crazy, so I developed a group of banks that shared loans, with the customer continuing to be the prime customer of the lead banks." Making large loans to developers, skimming interest off the top, and selling the rest to smaller banks eager to get in on the New York lending scene gave Chase control of the market and up to three-fourths of the loans in that era. Eventually the pattern Stephenson established would set off a spiral of lending on ever-shakier grounds, a development for which he apparently took little responsibility. After redlining Manhattan during the city's fiscal crisis, he said, other banks saw Chase's success and followed suit. "That's when the whole thing fell apart," he said, "because it got very competitive and people made loans that weren't sound."

40. Sources for this section include *New York Times*, 11/28/89; interview with Thomas Hoving, 9/9/98; Der Scutt diary, 12/13/78.

41. Sources for the following sections include *New York Times*, 3/16/80, 6/6/80, 6/7/80, 6/9/80, 6/15/80, 7/13/90, 4/27/91; *Newsday*, 1/15/84, 8/29/88, 7/8/90, 7/13/90, 4/27/91; *New York Daily News*, 8/10/80, 4/15/90, 7/20/90, 3/8/99; United Press International, 7/12/90; *New York Post*, 6/10/80; Sy Rubin and Jonathan Mandell, *Trump Tower*, 1984, passim; interviews with Tom Macari, 4/14/99; Alan Lapidus, 2/1/00, 5/10/00; Ashton Hawkins, 7/11/99; Wendy Sloan, 3/17/89.

42. Oddly, given this public claim as to the art's worthlessness, Donald apparently rescued a piece of the sculpture from under the jackhammer. During a visit to Donald's office at the time, architect Alan Lapidus saw a four-foot-tall chunk of the bas relief showing part of a stylized human form. "Donald seemed genuinely bewildered by the fuss," Lapidus said later. "When I asked him what the carving was doing there, he leaned toward me and said, 'Shut up.' "

43. In September 1979, the New York Committee for a Balanced Building Boom, a group started by an investment banker, a stockbroker, and a real estate developer, opposed rezoning for the site. Sources include *New York Times*, 9/6/79; interviews with William Hubbard, 3/4/99; Hal Negbaur, 3/2/99.

44. Der Scutt diary, 3/30/79, 4/2/79.

45. Sources for this section include press accounts at the time and interviews with Hadley Gold, 10/5/98; Jesse Masyr, 3/12/99, 6/7/99; Edith Spivack, 3/23/99; Rochelle Corson, 2/25/99, 5/12/99.

46. Sources for this section include interviews with Jesse Masyr, 3/12/99; Andrew Stein, 6/8/99.

47. Andrew Stein was head of a state assembly commission that was crit-

ical of a new program to phase out rent control in New York City, whereas Donald vigorously supported the phaseout. Although the developer himself actually had a rent-regulated apartment at that time, his family real estate business would realize enormous benefits from the end of rent control. Sources include interview with Andrew Stein, 6/8/99.

48. As quoted by Mitchell Moss in *Palace Coup: The Inside Story of Harry and Leona Helmsley*, 1989, p. 158. In helping out Stein, Donald was also evening the score with Harry Helmsley's wife, Leona. Hostility between the two dated back at least four years, to one of Leona's annual birthday parties for her husband. Donald, then busy pushing the 34th Street site for the new convention center, and Robert Tisch, a major backer of the 44th Street site, had earned her ire when they spent the party lobbying for their respective plans. Sources for this section include Dan Dorfman, "Will New York Get a New Hotel?," *New York*, 4/26/76; Donald J. Trump with Charles Leerhsen, *Trump: Surviving at the Top*, 1990, passim; Moss, *Palace Coup*, pp. 145–59.

49. According to the unpublished memoir of Milton Gould, who represented Equitable in the 412a abatement case, Equitable's general counsel told him Donald insisted that Cohn handle the appeal. The reason, Gould said, was that "Mr. Cohn had assured him [Donald] that he had the judges of the court in his pocket." Gould further said that Equitable's council would authorize hiring Cohn only if the lead lawyer was someone respectable—for example, Gould—because Equitable did not want to be involved in any "rinky-dink." Gould, "Fifth Avenue Coach Lines," p. 10. Sources include interview with Gary Schuller, 3/2/99.

50. A no-holds-barred fighter himself, Donald admired and sometimes hired those who opposed him with particular vigor. An early example occurred in 1975 when he accompanied his father to Norfolk, Virginia, in an effort to quell a rent strike at a Trump-owned property. Tempers were running high, and at a poolside meeting one tenant threatened to throw Fred into the water. At a negotiating session between the two sides, Donald told his own lawyer to sit down and shut up. Putting his arm around the tenant's representative, a local lawyer named O. L. Gilbert, who went by the nickname "Buzz," Donald said, "Buzz and I are going to settle this." Gilbert turned to him and said, "It's Mr. Gilbert, not Buzz, and I'll speak to your lawyer, not you." After the strike was settled, Donald called Gilbert and put him on retainer for a year. A dozen years later the developer tapped Tony Schwartz, who had done a critical and widely circulated article about him for *New York* ("A Different Kind of Donald Trump Story," 2/11/85), to co-author his autobiography, *The Art of the Deal* (see chapter 6). Top aides have also included Charlie Riese, former aide to Tony Gliedman and consultant to groups opposed to Trump's plans for the 60th Street yards, and Abe Wallach, vehement critic of Trump during his financial crisis in the early 1990s. Sources include interview with O. L. Gilbert, 10/23/93.

51. Sources include Philip Weiss, "The Fred," *New York Times Magazine*, 1/2/00; Plaskin, "*Playboy* Interview: Donald Trump"; Hurt, *Lost Tycoon*, p. 126.

52. Sources for this section include Wayne Barrett, *Trump*, pp. 193–201; Hurt, *Lost Tycoon*, pp. 131–32; *New York Times*, 4/25/82, 4/26/82, 7/11/82; interviews with Claude Morton, 3/7/98; Wally Antoniewicz, 5/11/98; Frank Alleva and Frank Cardile, 3/13/98; Der Scutt, 9/24/98.

53. One of the few to do so was Olympic Tower. The lower floors, which contained offices and retail space, were steel-frame, but the upper or residential section used reinforced concrete. Sources include Robert A. M. Stern et al., *New York 1960*.

54. The high price of concrete in New York was also due to bid-rigging. Sources for this section include *New York Times*, 4/25–26/82; Barrett, *Trump*, pp. 193ff.

55. Sources include Stern et al., *New York 1960*, and *New York Times*, 7/21/75.

56. Unlike Olympic Tower, where the developers used the zoning bonuses for a retail arcade but did little to develop it or invite the public inside, Donald actively pursued retailers. Charging up to $300 per square foot, he attracted European merchants for the most part, including Hermès (French scarves), Lowey's of Madrid (leather), and Fred Jouillier (French jeweler). One reason was that Europeans had the money, another was that vertical malls had a poor track record with U.S. retailers. Many of the Trump Tower boutiques were money losers and served essentially as expensive advertisements for those stores' other locations. *New York Post*, 10/10/89; *New York Times*, 8/15/89.

57. Sources include William Geist, "The Expanding Empire of Donald Trump," *New York Times Magazine*, 4/8/84; Michael Sorkin, *Village Voice*, 6/11/79; *New York Times*, 4/4/83, 11/2/83, 5/6/84; interview with Der Scutt, 9/28/98; Der Scutt diary, passim.

58. His rationale for skipping floors, he told Equitable officials, was that if the entire building were residential, the lower ceiling heights would result in more floors. To implement this creative approach, he simply used one set of elevators, accessible from Fifth Avenue, for the office floors, and another set, accessible from 56th Street and starting with a much higher number, for the residential floors. Sources include Hurt, *Lost Tycoon*, p. 136; interview with John Minikes, 12/9/98; John d'Alessio, 10/89.

59. Early in the planning stages, the developer said to Scutt he intended to use the name Trump Tower but would not do so publicly until Equitable agreed. He told Scutt to place the name on the renderings to look "natural" and to begin using the name "unobtrusively," as in "Trump Tower will be an exciting building," but to avoid suggesting a name had actually been chosen. Once the decision had been announced, Scutt incorporated the name over the entrance in discreet 18-inch-high letters. Trump quietly bypassed the architect and doubled the letter size to 36 inches.

60. Sources for this section include Leslie Marshall, "Breakfast Above Tiffany's," *In Style*, December 1995; Brenner, "Gold Rush"; interview with John d'Alessio, 10/89.

61. For the opening in February 1983, Donald planned to run a newspaper ad on behalf of Trump Tower in which he thanked a number of subcontractors and Equitable for making the new building possible. When Tim Welch, Equitable's representative on the project, reminded him that Equitable was a co-owner and thus a co-extender of thanks, Trump "was in a snit for about a day, but then he agreed." Sources include interview with Tim Welch, 6/30/98; Der Scutt's diary, 3/1/79.

62. This was principally a decision to go for immediate gain instead of long-term income. But Equitable, noting the number of retailers unable to cover their staggering overhead, was also worried about the long-term future for the retail component. Sources for this section include interview with Doug Healey, 4/21/98.

63. Interviews with Blanche Sprague, 4/13/99; Ed Murphy, 6/14/99.

64. Trump, *The Art of the Deal*, p. 54.

65. Sources for this section include Tony Schwartz, "The Show Must Go Up," *New York*, 1981; interview with Scott Mollen, 4/5/99. Trump Plaza was a $125 million project, financed by a construction loan from Manufacturers Hanover. The lawyers retained by the developer for Trump Plaza used the Trump Tower conflict to their advantage, arguing that the city could show its good faith—that it wasn't discriminating against him on Trump Tower—by granting him a tax abatement for Trump Plaza.

66. Sources include Tony Schwartz, "A Different Kind of Donald Trump Story," *New York*, 2/11/85.

67. Sources include Geist, "The Expanding Empire of Donald Trump."

68. Of the tenants in the building's 60 occupied apartments, approximately one-quarter earned $75,000 a year (in 1985 dollars), one-quarter lived on fixed incomes of less than $15,000 a year, and the rest fell in between. Schwartz, "A Different Kind of Donald Trump Story."

69. In 1998 the building finally became a condominium. By the terms of the final negotiation, tenants were able either to buy their apartments at a 33 percent discount or keep renting and remain exempt from certain rent increases for the next eight years. The tenants claimed a victory, in that 43 of the building's 80 apartments would still be occupied by rent-regulated tenants, of whom many would pay less in rent than condo owners forked over in monthly carrying charges. But as far as Donald was concerned, the victory was his. Even with a discount, the apartment prices were quite high, and he predicted that he would eventually make $50 million from the building. *New York Times*, 3/26/98.

CHAPTER FIVE: Gambling on Atlantic City

1. Donald was proud of having snagged what he obviously considered the Tiffany location of restaurant tables. When Richard Dicker, head of the reorganized Penn Central, ate lunch with him at the '21' Club in the mid-1980s and they were seated between two rooms, Dicker told Donald to get to know the maître d' better so as to get a more secluded table for private conversations. "No, no," Donald replied. "I'm just where I want to be, where I can see everybody in the place." On another occasion Donald took Robert Sturges, a former casino regulator in New Jersey, to lunch at '21.' When the developer asked him if he noticed where they were seated, Sturges said yes, at a small table. "No, Bob," the developer said. "What's important is we're between the columns. Don't ever let them sit you anywhere but between the columns, because if you're not between the columns, you're nobody." Interviews with Richard Dicker, 3/22/89; Robert Sturges, 12/22/98.

2. Sources include Marylin Bender, "The Empire and Ego of Donald Trump," *New York Times Magazine*, 8/7/83; Brenner, "Trumping the Town."

3. Geist, "The Expanding Empire of Donald Trump," *New York Times Magazine*, 4/8/84.

4. Graydon Carter, "Donald Trump Gets What He Wants," *Gentleman's Quarterly*, 5/84. A Georgian-style mansion, the house resembled Donald's childhood home in Jamaica estates but was so large that it looked more like a hotel than a private residence. As would so often be the case, Donald attempted to turn a profit by subdividing the property and selling off parcels as building lots, but he was unable to obtain the necessary variance. Sources include King, *Ivana Trump*, pp. 110–15; Tuccille, *Trump*, pp. 179–81.

5. Sources for this section include Robert H. Boyle, "The USFL's Trump Card," *Sports Illustrated*, 2/13/84; Jim Byrne, *The $1 League*, 1986; Barrett, *Trump*; *New York Times*, 10/19/84, 7/30/86; *New York Post*, 10/18/84, 10/19/84; interview with Gerald Schrager, 6/10/99.

6. Donald could not get his name on the Grand Hyatt and had to bow to Equitable's conditions to have it on Trump Tower. But in the wake of his new-found USFL notoriety, Prudential Securities, one of the largest investment companies in New York, asked him to construct and market a residential project on Madison Avenue and to name it after himself. "We went to Trump because his name had magic in it," recalled Brian Strum, Prudential vice-president at the time. Such magic, in fact, that Prudential was willing to hand over 49 percent of the project without requiring the developer to put up a cent. Soon afterward architect Philip Johnson sketched out Trump Castle, a residential apartment building with arched windows, gold-leaf turrets, spires, crenellated towers, and a miniature moat. Ultimately Prudential sold the site to another party and gave Donald a commission rather than a building with his name across the front. But although this particular deal remained unconsummated, it confirmed that Trump had indeed become a valuable label. Sources

for this section include *Los Angeles Times*, 4/7/85, *New York Times*, 4/8/84, and interview with Brian Strum, 11/17/97.

7. By 1984 Donald Trump deemed his name valuable enough to go to court to protect it. That year he filed suit against two South African brothers, Julius and Eddie Trump, who were in real estate and had offices in New York near Trump Tower. Donald lost the case. Four years later the U.S. Trademark Trial and Appeal Board ruled that although the South African Trumps could use their own surname in the ordinary course of business, Donald had the exclusive right to its use as a trademark. Sources for this section include *New York Times*, 2/7/88, 1/16/90; and interview with Charles Walker, 2/6/98.

8. In 1975 the two Hilton casino hotels in Las Vegas provided 35 percent of total Hilton Hotel Corporation revenue ($124,440,000 out of a total of $351,121,000) and 43 percent of the total HHC cash flow, then called "income contributions" ($16,683,000 out of a total of $39,153,000). Source: Hilton Hotel Corporation.

9. According to Whittier Law School professor Nelson Rose, the United States is now in what he calls the third wave of legal gambling. Lotteries helped fund early American settlements and were a regular part of colonial and post-colonial life until various scandals and Jacksonian moralism produced legislative prohibitions. After the Civil War the South turned to lotteries to rebuild its shattered economy, and gambling was a way of life on the frontier. But again scandals and a wave of moral fervor aroused anti-gambling sentiment, and by 1910 the nation was once again free of this supposed vice. It reappeared in response to the Depression, first in Nevada, which reauthorized casino gambling in 1931, and over the 1930s and '40s as other states approved pari-mutuel betting. In 1963 New Hampshire opened the first legal state lottery, and by 1997 only Utah and Hawaii had no form of legal gambling. The biggest change: Eager for increased tax revenues, state governments now support gambling through advertising and extensive promotion. Sources include Nelson Rose, "Gambling and the Law: Recent Developments, 1998," unpublished paper; interview with Nelson Rose, 6/4/99.

10. Sources for this section include Gigi Mahon, *The Company That Bought the Boardwalk*, 1980; Timothy L. O'Brien, *Bad Bet: The Inside Story of the Glamour, Glitz, and Danger of America's Gambling Industry*, 1998; David Johnston, *Temples of Chance: How America Inc. Bought Out Murder Inc. to Win Control of the Casino Business*, 1992; Ovid Demaris, *The Boardwalk Jungle*, 1986; Gwenda Blair, *Almost Golden: Jessica Savitch and the Selling of Television News*, 1989.

11. The game used names of bodies of water for avenues and omitted certain of the resort city's streets, such as Adriatic, Drexel, and Congress, because blacks lived on them.

12. In 1972 the prohibitive cost of upkeep forced the Loew's Corporation, owned by Laurence and Robert Tisch, to dynamite Atlantic City's most famous structure, the Traymore. With its four gilded domes towering over the beach,

the 600-room hotel, the first poured-concrete building in the U.S., looked like a classic sand castle and had been the centerpiece of the city's skyline since its completion in 1916. Sources include *Atlantic City Press*, 5/9/82; Vicki Gold Levi and Lee Eisenberg, *Atlantic City: 125 Years of Ocean Madness*, 1979.

13. O'Brien, *Bad Bet*, p. 72.

14. Approximately the northern half of Absecon Island, Atlantic City comprises 6.7 square miles, two-thirds of which consists of federally protected wetlands. By way of comparison, Atlantic City is just over five times as large as Central Park (840 acres, or 1.3 square miles) and less than one-third the size of the island of Manhattan (22.6 square miles). With the legalization of casino gambling, job opportunities and, in turn, the population, increased. But the amount of housing, especially at low rents, plummeted as speculators rushed to tear down marginal properties. Citywide, vacant land, which was only 4 percent of the city's real property in 1977, jumped to 17.6 percent in 1980. Nonetheless, the area zoned specifically for casinos remained small, and property within those borders became phenomenally valuable. Sources include the *Philadelphia Inquirer*, 6/16/85; George Sternlieb and James W. Hughes, *The Atlantic City Gamble*, 1983, pp. 100–101.

15. A standing joke at the time was that the Chalfonte-Haddon used to be a shithouse, and now it was a shithouse with carpeting. Because retrofitting an old hotel was the cheapest and fastest way to get up and running, other casinos followed Resorts' lead, snapping up shabby old facilities with an eye to slapping on additions. But after a Resorts-friendly amendment to the Casino Control Act upped the minimum number of rooms to 500, leaving Resorts the only facility large enough to qualify, newer casinos simply tore down existing structures and erected impersonal modern buildings unconnected architecturally, historically, or culturally to the city in which they were located.

In the years that followed, the two largest gambling markets in the nation, Atlantic City and Las Vegas, would diverge sharply. Because Atlantic City lacked a commercial airport or direct rail connections to anyplace but Philadelphia, affluent jet-setters were more likely to go to Vegas. By contrast, Atlantic City attracted bus travelers, who were less affluent and headed straight for casinos, bringing little business to the rest of the town. Being within easy driving distance from large cities did bring Atlantic City more customers than Vegas, but most came only for the day and spent less than Vegas customers, who stayed at least one night. Nor was this likely to change; by 1999, Las Vegas had 120,205 hotel rooms, whereas Atlantic City had fewer than 12,000. This, too, was in large part the result of geography: Las Vegas casinos could expand into the desert, but Atlantic City was a small island with little available land. As a result of these and other factors, two decades after the opening of Resorts, Atlantic City was number one in casino revenues, but Las Vegas, which took in more from noncasino sources than the actual casinos themselves, came in number one overall.

16. Bill Cosby, who opened a show at Resorts within a few weeks of the

casino's debut, joked that people used to come to Atlantic City for the beach, but now they were lined up around the block to get away from it.

17. Rose, "Gambling and the Law," p. 17.

18. For the next two years other investors went through all manner of intricate maneuvers over the same site. Howard Weingrow, a former hotel chain owner and national treasurer of the Democratic Party, was one of the most dogged. He struck a deal for one parcel with Robert Maheu, chief of staff for the legendary Howard Hughes, tracked down the dozen or so heirs to an adjacent motel and cocktail lounge and convinced them to put aside their squabbles long enough to sell their property to him, negotiated with the owners of half a dozen individual houses, and promised the owner of yet another lot that he would send a car to take her to church every Sunday for five years. But despite relentless effort, control of the site continued to elude Weingrow's grasp. Interview with Howard Weingrow, 11/18/98.

19. Interview with G. Michael Brown, 12/17/98.

20. With the Trumps was a real estate broker named Richard Levy who had done business in New York and Atlantic City and was a close friend of Robert Trump. According to Levy, Donald drove his own limousine, Ivana sat next to him in the front, and Levy was in the back. When they arrived in Atlantic City, a man stuck his hand into the rear window and said to Levy that he had always wanted to meet him. Surprised, Levy asked why. "I wanted to meet the guy Donald Trump chauffeured," the man replied and introduced himself as Mickey Rudin, Frank Sinatra's attorney. Rudin ushered the party into Resorts, where they sat at a table with Faye Dunaway and watched Sinatra perform. Sources for this section include interviews with Paul Longo, 11/23/98; Richard Levy, 11/17/98.

21. Interview with Alan Lapidus, 4/18/90.

22. Interview with Jeff Walker, 10/98.

23. The Trump presence in New Jersey would be enhanced still further in 1983, when Maryanne Trump Barry, then an assistant U.S. attorney in Newark, was appointed to the federal bench. Married to John Barry, an ex-prosecutor who represented Donald as well as major corporate clients, Maryanne had been a lawyer only nine years and could not leapfrog over senior colleagues by herself. "There's no question Donald helped me get on the bench," she said. "I was good, but not that good." For this coup, which needed support from the governor, nomination by the president, and approval by the U.S. Senate, Donald got help from Roy Cohn and Cohn's old pal Roger Stone, a Republican political analyst and Washington insider who included Richard Nixon among his clients. Stone had run Ronald Reagan's 1980 New York campaign out of Cohn's town house, and in 1981 he had produced a squeaky 1,797-vote margin in the New Jersey gubernatorial race for Thomas Kean, a liberal Republican millionaire with a gap-toothed smile, a nice-guy persona, and razor-sharp political instincts. Ultimately Donald, Cohn, Stone, and Kean all played a part in the effort to put Maryanne in judicial robes. "Roy can do the

impossible," Donald declared after the appointment came through, and the new judge called Cohn personally to say thank you. Sources include *New York Times*, 10/9/86; *Bergen Record*, 10/27/91; Barrett, *Trump*, pp. 248–49; interview with Maryanne Trump Barry, 2/9/98.

24. Building such a large passageway was an engineering challenge. Because the building was within 100 feet of the beach, supporting the street overhang on columns meant sinking piles into the sand, a method requiring a lengthy federal review. The other obvious approach would be to attach the overhang to an adjacent building, but this would require the owner's permission and, presumably, significant financial compensation. Instead, Lapidus cantilevered the passage from Trump's structure so that it literally hangs out over Mississippi Avenue without touching any other surface or requiring support from columns. Interview with Alan Lapidus, 4/18/90.

25. A nearby condominium, the Ocean Club, was a few feet taller.

26. Regulators might have had problems with certain details, such as having Roy Cohn as his lawyer. But the developer apparently did not mention his ties to Cohn, and officials later said that Cohn, who was not working directly on the developer's Atlantic City deals, seemed basically a figure out of the nation's political past and thus irrelevant—despite having been charged with bribery, conspiracy, and bank fraud. Nick Ribis, the local lawyer who would be Donald's major representative in Atlantic City, had worked for a firm linked to Cohn, but that, too, seemed to be of little interest. Sources for this section include interviews with Ben Borowski, 12/2/98; Bob Sturges, 12/22/98.

27. Sources for this section include Gwenda Blair, "Citizen Guccione," *Attenzione*, 6/81; *Los Angeles Times*, 4/7/85.

28. Sources for this section include O'Brien, *Bad Bet*, pp. 47ff.; John L. Smith, *Running Scared: The Life and Treacherous Times of Las Vegas Casino King Steve Wynn*, 1995, pp. 35ff.; Connie Bruck, *The Predators' Ball: The Junk Bond Raiders and the Man Who Stalked Them*, 1985, pp. 58ff; *New York Times*, 7/6/97.

29. For this section I am particularly indebted to David Johnston's *Temples of Chance*. Sources also include interviews with George Rinaldi, 5/28/99; Jeff Walker, 10/20/98; Bob Sturges, 12/22/98; Richard Goeglein, 12/18/98; Darrell Luery, 1/6/99.

30. In February 1980 Holiday bought Harrah's and used that name for its first Atlantic City casino, already under construction at a marina across town from the Boardwalk. The location was risky, for Harrah's Marina Hotel and Casino was the only operation so far away from the historic tourist magnet, the beach. But the bet paid off, for the Queen of Resorts was no longer about the beach. Instead it was about gambling in the most appealing possible surroundings. Indeed, middle-class, middle-aged patrons who drove their own cars preferred to keep some distance from the legendary but seedy Boardwalk. They also favored Harrah's relatively low-key, restrained decor, which featured the usual mirrors and marble but was less flashy than the competition. Most of all they liked the fact that Harrah's, unlike every other casino hotel in town, had

its own garage. Within a year after its November 1980 opening, Harrah's was well on its way to becoming the most profitable casino in town. By 1983 Harrah's four casinos, including three in Nevada and Harrah's Marina in Atlantic City, provided 40 percent of Holiday Inn's net profit of $124.4 million. Sources include *Nation's Restaurant News*, 8/27/84.

31. Sources for this section include Johnston, *Temples of Chance*; O'Brien, *Bad Bet*; interview with Richard Goeglein, 12/18/98.

32. So declared Daniel Lee, casino analyst for Drexel. Although Lee did not work for Donald Trump in a paid capacity, he advised him on several key moves against other casino corporations and then earned large fees for advising those targets on how to counter Donald's offensives. Sources include Barrett, *Trump*, passim.

33. Sources for this section include Trump, *The Art of the Deal*, chapter 9; Johnston, *Temples of Chance*, chapter 10; interviews with Frank Bryant, 3/2/98, 9/10/99; Ben Lambert, 8/5/98; John Torrell, 6/10/98; *San Diego Union-Tribune*, 12/12/93.

34. Regardless of whether blame belongs to Harrah's for poor management or to Donald for not making necessary changes, there were major problems with Trump Plaza at the opening and afterward. Perhaps the biggest was the unexpectedly large crowds, which put a strain on the already inadequate elevator system. The fire alarms rang constantly, each time necessitating evacuation of the entire facility, and malfunctions in the accounting systems required closing slot machines and, in turn, losing potential revenue. To have such problems at the opening of a large facility is not unusual, as the Trump Organization learned later at the opening of the Taj, but at the time Trump executives assumed the cause was Harrah's ineptness.

35. In one four-page single-spaced letter from Donald to Philip G. Satre, president and chief executive officer of Harrah's, the developer claimed, among other things, that Harrah's operated in a "purposefully negative way," was in "a disgraceful situation for which you should be ashamed," that employees at the joint facility were "unhappy working for Harrah's [and] who can blame them," and that matters were now in a "deplorable" state.

36. In March 1986, when the developer bought Harrah's half of Trump Plaza for $223 million, he followed his earlier game plan: an initial Manufacturers Hanover bridge loan followed by a $250 million bond issue from Bear, Stearns. Again the developer had complete financing, plus, in this case, a $20.7 million payment made directly to him. Sources include John Connolly, "All of the People, All of the Time," *Spy*, 4/5/91.

37. A U.S. football field, including the end zones, is 360 feet long and 160 feet wide, a total of 57,600 square feet; Resorts had a 59,857-square-foot casino. Sources for this section include *New York Times*, 3/16/86; *Atlantic City Press*, 3/15/86, 3/18/86; and *Variety*, 3/26/86.

38. Caesars World Inc. defended its right to the word *palace* by emphasizing the motif of Greco-Roman splendor in its three casinos, including Caesars

Atlantic City Hotel Casino. Caesar's creative lawyers found evidence of this motif in the faux Roman-style lettering used in Caesars signage; the reproductions of sculptures with what might be loosely termed "antique" themes (thus Michelangelo's *David*, a sixteenth-century rendering of a biblical subject, is included); a Chinese restaurant, inaccurately linked to the Roman Empire through reference to Marco Polo; and advertisements showing comedian Buddy Hackett as Caesar in a palace. Perhaps the most startling citation is the use of pig Latin in radio ads for Caesars. U.S. Court of Appeals Judge Dickinson R. Debevoise dismissed these arguments but seemed impressed by polls that showed that the public associated the word *palace* with Caesars' operations. On May 14, 1987, he held that although Donald Trump didn't intend to steal any of Caesars' goodwill because he had plenty through the use of the name Trump alone, he would not allow the developer to use the word *palace* because it would inevitably infringe on Caesars' turf and cause confusion. Sources include 1987 U.S.App.LEXIS 6988; 1 U.S.P.Q.2D (BNA) 1806. I am indebted to Leon Friedman for pointing out this material to me.

39. The original idea had been to tap New Jersey casino reinvestment taxes—a 2 percent levy on each casino's gross win—to pay for the reconstruction project. Now, though, the developer offered one reason after another why he should not have to pick up the tab, including his claim that there was no traffic problem and the project was overkill ("a howitzer to kill a fly," as Robert Trump put it). Interview with David Sciarra, 8/16/99.

40. There were a few disappointments, including the reinvestment authority's refusal let Donald write off the $30 million cost of his gleaming new parking garage as a civic improvement, even though he had a horse and carriage specially painted along one wall. But he could console himself with the increase in revenues the garage brought, just as Harrah's had predicted.

41. Sources for this section include John Connolly, "All of the People"; Harry Hurt, *Lost Tycoon*, pp. 179–81.

42. In addition, the deal neatly removed Steve Wynn, the only figure who offered real competition to Donald as Mr. Atlantic City. Long before the developer's arrival there, Wynn had promoted himself along with his casino. He played opposite Frank Sinatra in television ads, mixed with the crowds on the casino floor, and successfully targeted the same upscale, high-roller market Donald wanted for Trump Plaza. But Wynn found the Casino Control Commission's constant micromanagement onerous and happily took himself and the $250 million he made on the Golden Nugget sale back to Las Vegas, leaving the field wide open for Donald.

43. Sources include application of Trump Plaza Associates and Trump's Castle Associates for casino license renewal, 4/4/88.

44. Sources include Lenny Glynn, "Blowout on the Boardwalk," *Institutional Investor*, December 1989. Parrillo was also director of the Division of Gaming Enforcement.

45. Trump, *Trump: Surviving at the Top*, 1990, p. 6.

46. In the early 1980s an old friend of Sprague's family, prominent hotelier Robert Tisch, arranged a job for her with Donald. Although the two men had tangled about the convention center site, Tisch told her that Donald was the only game in town, the only high-profile developer, and the only one doing anything interesting. Interview with Blanche Sprague, 4/13/99.

47. Sources for this section include Brenner, "Gold Rush."

48. Sources for this section include Hurt, *Lost Tycoon*, passim; interviews with Ana Zanova Steindler, 3/18/99; Mai Hallingby, 3/17/99; Nikki Haskell, 2/28/98; Vivian Serota, 12/15/98; Sugar Rautbord, 1/14/99, 2/14/00; Fran Freedman, 2/9/98.

49. Interview with Nikki Haskell, 2/28/98.

50. *Primetime Thursday*, 9/16/04; interview with Donald Trump, 12/12/97.

CHAPTER SIX: The Tallest Building in the World

1. United Press International, 1/7/87.

2. For some years Rockefeller gave money away on an ad hoc basis and attempted to diversify through friends' business propositions, including Monte Cristo, the ill-fated mining venture in the Pacific Northwest where Friedrich Trump sought his fortune. Eventually the oil tycoon resolved the issue of how to spend what he had made by pouring vast sums into large-scale philanthropy, bankrolling the University of Chicago and the largest nonprofit organization in history, the Rockefeller Foundation. His other two major philanthropic projects were Spelman Seminary, a black institution now known as Spelman College, in Atlanta, and the Rockefeller Institute for the Study of Medicine, a large research facility in Manhattan.

3. Flagler was the bold innovator behind the system of illegal rebates from northeastern railroads that established the mighty Standard Oil monopoly. He used the same force of will to develop the east coast of Florida and to build resorts at St. Augustine, Daytona, Miami, and Palm Beach. In 1901, at the age of 71, he made his final lavish gesture. On the occasion of his third marriage, he presented his 33-year-old bride with an enormous Neoclassical mansion in Palm Beach called Whitehall. Immediately dubbed "the Taj Mahal of North America," the huge white mansion contained 55 rooms stuffed with art and antiques and set a standard of ultimate personal luxury that would last for a quarter century. The architects, John M. Carriere and Thomas Hastings, had built Flagler's first grand hotel in St. Augustine and would later design the New York Public Library, the Henry Clay Frick mansion, the U.S. House and Senate office buildings, and the Memorial Amphitheater in Arlington National Cemetery. Sources for this section include "Whitehall: The Henry Morrison Flagler Museum," published by the museum in 1988; Ron Chernow, *Titan: The Life of John D. Rockefeller, Sr.*, 1998; Edward N. Akin, *Flagler: Rockefeller Partner & Florida Baron*, 1992; and James R. Knott, *The Mansion Builders*, 1990.

4. Marjorie Merriweather Post, born in 1887, was already rich when she married her second husband, Edward F. Hutton, founder of the first wire bro-

kerage service in history, in 1920. Together they went on an extraordinary shopping spree, buying Jell-O, Baker's chocolate, Hellmann's mayonnaise, Log Cabin syrup, Maxwell House coffee, and Birds Eye, maker of the world's first frozen foods. Post's original legacy, the Postum Company, became the food conglomerate General Foods, and she became even richer. Her only child, Nedenia, an actress known as Dina Merrill, was born during this marriage; her other husbands included Edward Bennett Close, whose descendant is the film star and actress Glenn Close; Joseph Davies, ambassador to the Soviet Union; and Herbert May, a prominent industrialist.

5. Noted Palm Beach architect Marion Sims Wyeth designed Mar-a-Lago. Joseph Urban, who had helped stage Florenz Ziegfeld's Follies and went on to be art director of the Boston Opera and a set designer for Covent Garden and the Paris Opera, did the interior detailing, and his theatricality and extravagance are everywhere apparent. Occupying a 17-acre site, the estate is a gold mine of statistics. They include boatloads of Dorian stone imported from Genoa and used on the exterior (3); total room count (118); Spanish tiles dating back to the fifteenth century (36,000); fireplaces (12); flower pots on outside terraces (700); solid marble dining table's full length (29 feet), weight (2 tons), and number of place settings (50); separate staff residences (5); greenhouses (4); bomb shelters (3); and cloisters (2). The quarters designed for Post's daughter include a silver-plated, elaborately carved canopy bed, silver-squirrel doorknobs, and hand-loomed carpets with fairy-tale themes. The living room's 30-foot-tall ceiling is covered in gold leaf in imitation of the "Thousand Wing Ceiling" of the Accademia of Venice, and the loggia features a copy of the Benozzo Gozzoli frescoes from the Medici Palace in Florence. Every room in the house contains wood carvings and stone sculptures and the dance pavilion doubles as a movie theater. The dining room is a copy of the dining salon at the Chigi Palace in Rome, and the massive marble table is inlaid with more marble and semiprecious stones arranged in a complex floral pattern. Outside, the pavement of the patio contains thousands of glacially polished stones shipped from Mrs. Post's Long Island hunting preserve. In addition, the estate includes a 75-foot tower, a small "pitch and putt" golf course, citrus groves, cutting gardens, guest houses, and a tunnel underneath the main road that gives access to a private beach. The only thing missing when Donald bought Mar-a-Lago in late 1985 was a swimming pool, which he added soon afterward.

6. Sources for this section include *Palm Beach Life*, July 1986; and Brenner, "Gold Rush."

7. *Town & Country*, 3/86.

8. *Playboy*, 5/87.

9. It had been public knowledge for years that Mar-a-Lago was squarely in the airport's flight path. What is curious is that deal-making legend Donald Trump apparently did not know this, chose to ignore it, or thought that he would somehow be able to change it.

10. The complex's 32-story twin towers, gleaming white and the tallest

buildings in the area, looked like a slice of Manhattan transplanted to south Florida. Poor construction, lack of maintenance, and the fact that only six out of 221 units had sold had discouraged other potential buyers. Sources for this section include *Wall Street Journal*, 11/7/76; interview with Charles Kimball, 12/18/90.

11. As with Bonwit Teller, the jewel of the 68-year-old, 16-store Alexander's chain was the flagship, located in New York directly across from Bloomingdale's at the corner of 59th Street and Lexington Avenue. For years brokers and developers had been vying to pull off the ultimate Alexander's deal. "It was one of those classic undoable deals everybody took a shot at," recalled investment banker Peter Solomon, who made his own unsuccessful effort after leaving the Koch administration. "It always looked like somebody should be able to do it, like it should happen." Rising to the challenge, Donald paid more than $40 million to the bookish Texas investor and oil heir Robert Bass for about 20 percent of the outstanding stock. But the other major shareholder, a tough-talking New Jersey strip-mall czar named Steven Roth, was just as determined as Donald and just as competitive. A friend reportedly once said that Roth, a compact figure with a blunt manner, was only half kidding when he told his golf teacher he would give him a small shopping mall if he could lower Roth's handicap. Sources for this section include *New York Post*, 12/9/86; *Aspen Times*, 2/6/86; and interview with Peter Solomon, 11/24/99.

12. Interview with Jerry Schrager, 5/7/99.

13. Sources for this section include Barrett, *Trump*; Hurt, *Lost Tycoon*; Francisco Macri, "Lincoln West or Who Trumped Whom," from an unpublished autobiography written with Judith Murphy; interviews with Conrad Stephenson, 5/28/98, 6/12/98.

14. They included a 26-acre park, low-income housing, a new smoke-stack for an adjacent power plant, funds for redoing nearby subway stops, and a new rail freight depot in the Bronx.

15. Community activists discerned the heavy hand of Donald Trump in the complicated scenario that followed. After he surrendered his $400,000 option, the Palmieri Company, hired to sell off Penn Central properties at the highest possible prices, made no effort to solicit interest among other developers. Instead Palmieri official Larry Schafran sold the option for the same price to Abraham Hirschfeld, a parking-garage czar, Lindenbaum client, and Fred Trump associate known for bizarre antics in his many runs for public office. Hirschfeld then sold 65 percent of his interest to Francisco Macri, who managed to obtain the necessary rezoning for the site—at which point Donald resurfaced and eventually bought the property from the financially pressed Macri. Hirschfeld retained a 20 percent interest, but sold it to Donald some years later. According to one anti-Trump line of thought, Hirschfeld, with the cooperation of the Palmieri Company, was a stalking horse for a Chase-backed attempt to retain the yards for Donald, and Macri, perhaps unwittingly, became part of that effort. Schafran said that the sole reason Hirschfeld got the option

was that Palmieri was facing a tight deadline and Hirschfeld was ready to deal. Hirschfeld insisted that although he was a longtime friend of Fred's, he had pursued the yards on his own. Macri later wrote that he, too, had launched the project on his own, that community suspicion had contributed to his difficulties, and that the constant collusion between Stephenson and Donald had made his situation impossible. Stephenson said that he simply acted appropriately in the face of mounting uncertainty that Macri could handle the project. Whatever the merits of these various claims and counterclaims, it is at the very least a measure of Donald's stature that everyone involved seemed to consider him the critical figure. Sources include Barrett, *Trump*; Macri, "Lincoln West"; and interviews with Larry Schafran, 9/2/98; Abraham Hirschfeld, 12/90; Conrad Stephenson, 5/28/98, 6/12/98.

16. *New York Daily News*, 11/24/85; *New York Times*, 12/23/86; *Newsday*, 5/15/86.

17. Sources for this section include Jonathan Greenberg, "Clash of the Titans," *Manhattan, inc.*, 1/86.

18. Donald announced proposals to build the world's tallest buildings on lower Manhattan sites in 1983 and 1984. When *Chicago Tribune* architecture critic Paul Gatt panned the second announcement, the developer sued him for defamation and asked $500 million in damages. David Berger, the developer's last-minute ally back in 1974 when he was maneuvering to land the rail yard option, served as his attorney. The claim was that Gapp's critique subjected the developer "to ridicule, contempt, embarrassment and financial harm" and "had a devastating effect" on the project. In September 1985 U.S. District Court Judge Edward Weinfeld, citing the Latin proverb *De gustibus non est disputandum* ("There is no disputing about taste"), dismissed the developer's complaint. I am grateful to Leon Friedman for bringing this material to my attention.

19. Sources for this section include Joshua Hammer, "He Wants to Take You Higher," *Manhattan, inc.*, 1/86.

20. Donald's first assignment for Jahn was to create a version of the world's tallest building for a competition to develop the old New York Coliseum site on Columbus Circle. The city and the Metropolitan Transit Authority, joint owners of the site, had requested bids on the site in February 1985. Donald Trump and Peter Kalikow—like Donald, a successful New York developer, member of an old real estate family, and client of Jerry Schrager—teamed up and presented two entries, Jahn's design for a 121-story building and another, by architect Eli Attia, for a 137-story structure. The winner was Mort Zuckerman, in large part because he had a commitment from Salomon Brothers to be a primary tenant. Donald later told a reporter that he was the "biggest winner" of the process and had entered it only to ensure that something good would be built near his rail yard site.

21. Sources for for this section include Frank Rose, "Celebrity Zoning," *Manhattan, inc.*, 11/89.

22. Sources for this section include *New York Daily News*, 11/19/85,

11/21/85 (Bob Herbert column); *New York Post*, 11/19/85; *New York Times*, 11/19/85.

23. Sources include *Time*, 12/2/85; *New York Times*, 11/19/85, 12/22/85; *New York Post*, 12/31/85; interview with Paul Goldberger, 2/26/99.

24. Sources for this section include *New York Post*, 6/25/86; Karen Cook, "Trumping Trump," *Manhattan, inc.*, 11/86; Rose, "Celebrity Zoning."

25. Interview with Dan Gutman, 4/91.

26. Sources for this section include interviews with Henry Kanegsberg, 7/30/99; Bill Maloney, 8/20/99.

27. Interview with Matthew Lifflander, 10/20/97.

28. Sources for this section include *Time*, 11/10/86; *New York Times*, 11/15/86; interviews with Henry Stern, 11/24/98, 12/1/99; Kent Barwick, 8/24/99, 11/24/99; Bronson Binger, 11/30/99; Gordon Davis, 11/26/99.

29. In a meeting of USFL owners in 1984, Donald said, "When I build something for somebody, I always add $50 million or $60 million onto the price. My guys come in, they say it's going to cost $75 million. I say it's going to cost $125 million, and I build it for $100 million. Basically I did a lousy job. But they think I did a great job." During the Wollman reconstruction, he said that the job was simple so he would not need to add contingency money; if he actually refrained, it was apparently an unusual and possibly unique move. *New York Times*, 7/1/86.

30. He was referring to the famously disaster-plagued Francis Ford Coppola film, which was finally completed in 1979. Scheduled to take six weeks, it ended up requiring 16 months, and the budget, originally projected at $12 million to $14 million, more than doubled to $30 million, a colossal sum at the time.

31. Instead of becoming a reflecting pond in warm months, Wollman returned to being a roller rink. Three summers later it became a miniature golf course adorned with models of Manhattan landmarks—including, of course, everything that bore the name Trump.

32. Soon after Ed Koch was reelected for a third term in November 1985, his administration became engulfed in a series of corruption scandals that included former deputy mayor Stanley Friedman (who went to jail) and Queens borough president Donald Manes (who committed suicide). Although Koch himself was not tied to the scandal, his leadership came under heavy fire.

33. This was a rewarding victory for Mike Bailkin, the former Beame administration lawyer who had authored the Grand Hyatt tax abatement. Although he was proud of his Grand Hyatt work and remained friendly with Donald, Bailkin had been annoyed that after he left city government Donald had slipped in a more favorable profit-sharing arrangement. In late 1986 Rockefeller Center retained Bailkin for what both center and lawyer considered a long-shot effort to hold on to the network. "Trump had a lock on NBC," Bailkin later told the *New York Post*. "He could have pulled that one off." But having worked with the developer, Bailkin told the center that Donald was

likely to overreach himself. "I told my client we should wait this one out," he said later. "A problem might arise, and we might get some reconsideration." When Donald and Koch began feuding publicly over the matter, Bailkin knew he was right. As the Television City deal fell apart, he sprang into action and retained the network for Rockefeller Center. Sources include *New York Post*, 5/5/96; Barrett, *Trump*; interview with Mike Bailkin, 4/12/00.

34. *New York Daily News*, 11/8/87.

35. In December 1987 Donald offered to complete the renovation of the Central Park Zoo, saying that otherwise his children would outgrow the zoo before they could see it. Declining the offer, parks commissioner Henry Stern said that the developer's help was unnecessary because the long-delayed project was nearly finished. The next April, inspectors found hazardous conditions at the Williamsburg Bridge, which links lower Manhattan to Brooklyn, and the 85-year-old suspension bridge was abruptly closed. Alfred Delli Bovi, head of the Federal Urban Mass Transit Administration and a former Republican state legislator from Queens, asked Donald for help. Seizing the opportunity, the developer invited the news media to accompany him on a visit to the bridge and then offered to carry out—but not pay for—the job himself. Again the city declined the offer and handled the repair itself. A year later, after a gang of young men raped and critically injured a jogger in Central Park, Donald ran full-page ads in all four New York dailies denouncing the crime, disagreeing with Koch's stance, and saying that he wanted not to understand criminals but to hate, frighten, and punish them. *New York Times*, 5/1/89.

36. Since time immemorial, boxing and gambling have gone together, presumably because both involve risk-taking behavior. For most of this century Las Vegas had a hammerlock on both pursuits. Casinos put up the purses for bouts, originally to entice high rollers who would then gamble, but later because the fights themselves generated profits. On June 15, 1987, Donald Trump backed a Michael Spinks–Gerry Cooney bout at Atlantic City Convention Hall and recouped his $3.5 million investment from the gate receipts. On fight night he reaped a $7.2 million spike in gaming revenues at Trump Plaza, which he had linked to Convention Hall by an overpass in order to maximize the casino's floor space. Over the entire four-day fight weekend, the total increase in Trump Plaza revenues was about $10 million. The following October the developer staged his second lucrative match, between Mike Tyson and Tyrell Biggs, then a third four months later between Tyson and Larry Holmes. He subsequently went on to promote a number of other matches and to become a major player in the boxing industry. Sources for this section include *New York Times*, 1/18/88; *Wall Street Journal*, 10/8/87.

37. His account of the profits he made on the Golden Nugget was $2 million, but the actual amount was $100,000; on Gillette, he claimed to have netted $2 million, but the real number was $1.1 million; on Federated, he asserted that he made $22 million, as opposed to his actual profit of $14.7 million.

38. Interview with Edward S. Gordon, 2/5/98.

39. *BusinessWeek*, 7/20/87.

40. *Newsweek*, 9/28/87.

41. *New York Post*, 10/20/87; *Newsday*, 10/27/87.

42. *People*, 12/7/87.

43. Interview with Charles Walker, 2/6/98.

44. Sources for this section include *Wall Street Journal*, 9/5/90, 11/30/87; Der Scutt diary, 12/12/87.

45. In an open letter published on September 2, 1987, and addressed "To the American People," Donald charged that "Japan and other nations have been taking advantage of the United States" and called on the nation to stop "protect[ing] ships we don't own, carrying oil we don't need, destined for allies who won't help." Sources include *New York Times*, 9/2/87; Hurt, *Lost Tycoon*, p. 190.

46. "Report to Donald Trump on Public Opinion in America," Penn & Schoen Associates Inc., 10/88; interviews with Doug Schoen, 8/20/99, 11/5/99.

47. In 1988 the city's largest private landlord was Samuel LeFrak, who housed one out of every 16 New Yorkers. In four generations, the LeFrak family constructed more than 200,000 apartments. United Press International, 7/24/88. Reliable numbers for the Trump Organization are hard to obtain. The usual figure is 25,000, which is almost certainly inflated; an educated guess is in the neighborhood of 15,000.

48. *New York Post*, 7/1/88.

49. Sources for this section include interviews with Blanche Sprague, 4/13/99; Gerald Schrager, 5/7/99.

CHAPTER SEVEN: Spinning out of Control

1. Sources for this section include Brenner, "Gold Rush"; Trump, *Surviving*; Hurt, *Lost Tycoon*; interviews with Jack Schaffer, 7/30/99; Edward S. Gordon, 2/5/98.

2. Sources include John Connolly, "Just Say 'Please,' " *Spy*, 2/92; Hurt, *Lost Tycoon*, pp. 136–37.

3. Hurt, *Lost Tycoon*, pp. 52ff.

4. Mary Billard, "The Art of the Steal," *Manhattan, inc.*, 4/88.

5. The *Nabila* came in behind King Fahd's *Abdul Aziz* (482 feet) and Queen Elizabeth's *Britannia* (412 feet). Sources for this section include John Taylor, "Trump's Newest Toy," *New York*, 7/11/88; *Newsday*, 5/16/90; *Newsweek*, 7/18/88; interview with Jeff Walker, 3/17/98.

6. Interview with Edward S. Gordon, 2/5/98.

7. It would also provide still more bragging rights. Soon after the developer acquired the yacht, he met with Tom Messer, director of the Guggenheim Museum, to discuss underwriting an exhibit of the museum's paintings in Czechoslovakia. When Messer, an erudite art historian, began to describe the works in the show, the developer interrupted and said, "I'd like to show you

something." Then he pulled out a package of photographs of the *Trump Princess* and began passing them around, pointing out the lines of the boat, the distance between bow and stern, and other particularly fine details. Interview with Stephen Swid, 9/99.

8. Sources for this section include William H. Meyers, "Stalking the Plaza," *New York Times Magazine*, 9/25/88; Connolly, "All of the People"; interviews with Alan Lapidus, 11/6/98; Blanche Sprague, 4/13/99.

9. At one point, society notables, including the Vanderbilts, had permanent apartments. Frank Lloyd Wright lived there while designing the Guggenheim Museum, the Duke and Duchess of Windsor made it their New York base, and Elizabeth Taylor and Richard Burton used it to hold court.

10. His purchase of stock in United Airlines' parent corporation in March 1987 was an early attempt to purchase the Plaza, then owned by a UAL Inc. subsidiary, the Westin chain, but instead of pursuing this effort, he sold the stock for a profit pegged by the *New York Times* at $80 million. *New York Times*, 6/11/87.

11. See Chapter 5 for Donald's purchase of the Hilton casino in 1985.

12. *New York Times*, 9/14/88.

13. Sources include Michael Schnayerson, "Power Blonde," *Vanity Fair*, 1/88; Hurt, *Lost Tycoon*, passim; Barrett, *Trump*, passim.

14. Sources for this section include Billard, "The Art of the Steal"; Maggie Mahar, "The Merv and Donald Show," *Barron's*, 5/23/88; Mary Billard, "Revenge of the Merv," *Manhattan, inc.*, 6/88; Evan Simonoff, "Deal of Misfortune," *Investment Dealers' Digest*, July 3, 1989; Glynn, "Blowout on the Boardwalk"; Connolly, "All of the People"; *Time*, 9/25/89; *Atlantic City Press*, 12/8/86; Johnston, *Temples of Chance*, chapter 21; Barrett, *Trump*, chapter 13; and interviews with Ace Greenberg, 8/18/99; Jonathan Arneson, 1/6/99; Tom Gallegher, 5/4/99; Kevin DeSanctis, 6/23/99; Marvin Roffman, 4/16/99; Ken Platt, 3/30/99; Mitchell Etess, 1/11/99; Jack O'Donnell, 7/29/88.

15. Donald would also receive an adjacent retail and entertainment complex known as the Steel Pier and the estate's helicopters, on which he had already painted his name.

16. Griffin would have to make $133 million in debt-service payments in 1989, his first year out. Because he could expect a cash flow of only about $55 million, he would face a shortfall of $148 per minute, or $214,000 each day. To stay afloat he would need a major miracle; instead he encountered an epic disaster. In a replay of the faked construction activity once used to impress Harrah's executives, Donald had persuaded Griffin of Resorts' potential through a carefully orchestrated tour of a small area that had been repainted and fixed up for the occasion. In fact, the facility was so dilapidated that it required immediate and costly first aid to remain even moderately competitive. Worse, because the market for both the Bahamas casino and the Atlantic City real estate was poor, these assets could not bail Griffin out. In August 1989, just months after the deal with Donald finally closed, Griffin suspended interest

payments. Soon afterward he asked bondholders for a pared-down rate—a "haircut," in Wall Street parlance.

17. To fend off their possible purchase by Steve Wynn, Donald put out another $115 million to buy two more properties for use as noncasino hotels: the never-finished Penthouse casino (plus an associated parking lot) and the Atlantis, a bankrupt casino once owned by Playboy and renamed the Trump Regency. Donald also continued a $90 million remodeling of the Castle. Reportedly, the Penthouse purchases were in part a response to implications that the magazine planned an exposé of the developer's extramarital life. Sources include Barrett, *Trump*, pp. 446–67; Hurt, *Lost Tycoon*, p. 246. In 1996, when it became legal to own four casinos in Atlantic City, Trump Hotels and Casino Resorts, the public company that owns the Trump casinos, renovated the Regency and reopened it as the Trump World's Fair Casino. It flopped and was demolished in 1999. Although THCR announced plans for a new megaresort, the 12-acre property, the largest casino site on the Boardwalk, is now a vacant lot. Sources include THCR press release, 7/9/99; *Las Vegas Review-Journal*, 7/10/99.

18. Sources for this section include interviews with Glen Ingalls, 11/17/99; Michael Conway, 1/17/99; Bruce Nobles, 11/19/99.

19. Hotel experts were surprised at the price Bond paid, although he had already made jaws drop with a winning $53.9 million bid for Vincent van Gogh's *Irises* at a Sotheby's auction. Bond made jaws drop again when word leaked out that a secret Sotheby's loan had figured in the astronomical bid, which had an inflationary effect on art prices in general. Because Bond was unable to pay for the masterpiece, it remained at Sotheby's, which eventually repossessed it.

20. Sources for this section include interviews with David Lefever, 11/22/99; David Saltzman, 10/19/99; Scott Carlin, 11/18/99.

21. Hurt, *Lost Tycoon*, p. 45.

22. Hurt, *Lost Tycoon*, chapter 8; *Primetime Thursday*, 9/16/04.

23. Among its other distinguishing characteristics, the New York real estate community is known for its generosity to charity. Fred regularly donated space, services, and, often, funds to a number of causes, and his youngest son, Robert, and his wife, Blaine, have long been heavily involved in organizing efforts to assist the sick and the homeless. By contrast, Donald has avoided major charity commitments and instead tended toward occasional and usually highly publicized gestures, such as providing a plane ride to a hospital for a sick child, donating book and product royalties to charity, helping pay off a farm mortgage for a Georgia widow whose husband killed himself to fend off bank foreclosure, and contributing to a Big Apple Circus tent provided it bore his name.

24. It was not an exaggeration. When Roffman, a faithful reader of *Consumer Reports*, wanted to buy a car, he would test-drive dozens; when he needed a new coat, he went to 10 stores and tried on every style; and when he wrote up a casino, he scrutinized the numbers closely.

25. For Roffman, who could not find another job, the episode seemed a disaster. As it turned out, however, he collected a $750,000 arbitrator's award from his former employer. After suing Donald and receiving a handsome out-of-court settlement, Roffman opened his own highly successful money-management company and wrote a popular investment guide. He recalled his dismissal when he watched Donald's popular reality TV show *The Apprentice*. Each episode ends with a musical-chairs-style boardroom showdown in which Donald fires yet another of the contestants vying for a job with the Trump Organization. "I've survived the firing," Roffman said. "All those kids sitting around the boardroom each week—my advice is five years from now, you'll laugh and see there is life after Trump." Interviews with Marvin Roffman, 2/28/04, 10/27/04.

26. *Wall Street Journal*, 4/27/90; interview with Neil Barsky, 5/1/90.

27. *Forbes*, 5/14/90.

28. He had $320 million in personally guaranteed loans from Citicorp, including $135 million for the Trump Shuttle, $125 million for the Plaza Hotel, and $60 million as part of a $220 million construction loan for the Trump Palace condominiums in New York. He also had an unsecured loan of $104 million from Bankers Trust and $47 million from Boston Safe Deposit & Trust Co. for Mar-a-Lago, the *Trump Princess*, and "personal use." *Wall Street Journal*, 6/4/90, 6/18/90, 8/16/90.

29. Sources include *New York Post*, 9/14/90; interview with Harry Blair, 2/9/00.

30. *Philadelphia Inquirer*, 7/1/90.

31. Interview with Sandy Moorehouse, 3/9/99.

32. Interview with Jerry Jagendorf, then head of real estate for the Bank of Tokyo, 3/17/99.

CHAPTER EIGHT: Pulling Back from the Brink

1. Sources for this section include newspaper clippings of the period and Casino Control Commission hearings, August 16, 17, and 21, 1990, Lawrenceville and Atlantic City, N.J.

2. Sources for this section include *New York Times*, 4/28/91; *Wall Street Journal*, 8/13/90 and 8/15/90; interview with Steve Bollenbach, 8/12/99.

3. Sources for this section include Brenner, "Gold Rush"; *Forbes*, 10/90; interviews with Steve Bollenbach, 8/12/99; Wilbur Ross, 8/2/99; Ken Moelis, 8/27/99, 9/19/99, 12/1/99.

4. *Bergen Record*, 8/5/91; *New York Post*, 8/8/91.

5. *Wall Street Journal*, 11/19/90.

6. Unfortunately for Donald, there was no simulcast auction in New York City, presumably an important market, because of complications related to his newest Manhattan project, the 283-unit Trump Palace. Usually buildings of this size were sponsored by a partnership or a corporation with a number of partners, but in this case Donald was the only sponsor. This fact was disclosed

in Trump Palace's 1½-inch-thick offering plan and had apparently been of little concern to buyers, almost all of whom were Asians purchasing the condominiums as investments. But now Donald was facing severe financial problems and he was the defendant in more than 100 court actions, including suits by Taj contractors, Resorts bondholders, Merv Griffin, Ivana Trump, and Blanche Sprague, that sought awards totaling hundreds of millions of dollars. Although Donald was current with all Trump Palace obligations, buyers were concerned that the building, which was less than one-third sold, would go into default. Accordingly, they had asked state attorney general Robert Abrams, whose office oversaw all condominium sales within the state, to be released from their contracts. As a matter of course, before approving a simulcast auction of condominium units, Abrams' office required disclosure of Donald's liabilities, an undertaking so complex that the auction house handling the sale instead cancelled the New York simulcast. Sources include interview with Frederick K. Mehlman, assistant attorney general, Real Estate Financing Bureau, office of the New York State attorney general, 4/17/91.

7. Interview with Susan Stevens, 4/3/91.

8. I am indebted to Charles Mann for coverage of this event.

9. The second auction occurred at the PGA National Resort, which was not in Palm Beach itself but rather in the nearby resort town of Palm Beach Gardens. By holding the first auction at the Breakers, Donald had tried to blur over the fact that Trump Plaza was not actually in Palm Beach; this time the auctioneers took a more positive approach and positioned the complex as a way for people to have access to Palm Beach and its fabled lifestyle without paying Palm Beach prices. Sources for this section include *Newsday*, 4/29/91; *Palm Beach Daily News*, 4/29/91; interviews with Edward J. Meylor, vice president, Real Estate Industries Division, Marine Midland Bank, 5/91; Rick Edmonds, 4/91.

10. Meanwhile Donald had to dodge his other financial obligations. One of the more pressing was the $11 million he had agreed to pay for a heavyweight title fight between Evander Holyfield and George Foreman, scheduled for the Atlantic City Convention Center in April 1991. Usually such big-name bouts drew business to Trump Plaza, which was next door, but because of the dampening effect of the Gulf War on the casino business, it seemed possible that this deal might lose money. At a meeting of parties to the fight, Donald announced that he was going to invoke his contractual right to cancel in wartime. "Those guys just freaked, called him every name in the book," said Kevin DeSanctis, a Trump Plaza executive at the time. "We walked back into Donald's office, and he said, 'They want to do it, they want the fight.' Sure enough, they called us back and let us off the hook. Anybody else would have had an $11 million problem, but he made it go away." Sources include *New York Times*, 2/7/91; interview with Kevin DeSanctis, 6/23/99.

11. *Wall Street Journal*, 1/21/91. Barsky received the prestigious Gerald Loeb Award for Distinguished Business and Financial Journalism for his report-

ing on the developer's financial meltdown. But Donald struck back: Three months later he offered the reporter a $1,000 ticket to the Holyfield-Foreman fight (see previous note) and then, when Barsky asked to buy another ticket, offered him two more for free. Having received permission from his editor to accept the first one, Barsky assumed there would be no problem taking the others for his father and brother. Big mistake: The developer complained publicly that Barsky had squeezed him for the tickets. Both Barsky and his paper were in an awkward position, for editor in chief Norman Perlstein had accepted a ticket and a helicopter flight for the same fight. Ultimately the *Journal* defended Barsky but reassigned him to another beat. Eventually he left the profession altogether and became a financial analyst. Sources for this section include Hurt, *Lost Tycoon*, chapter 12.

12. United Press International, 6/26/91.

13. Sources for this section include *Washington Post*, 11/29/92; interview with Charlie Reiss, 3/12/98.

14. Sources for this section include *Wall Street Journal*, 12/24/86, 12/12/88; *New York Daily News*, 11/8/88; interviews with Jack Shaffer, 7/30/99; William Stern, 1/15/99.

15. Sources for this section include *New York Times*, 2/13/88; *Wall Street Journal*, 3/23/88.

16. The hush was also a reflection of a widespread unwillingness to tangle wth someone who did not hesitate to take on adversaries in print. He had launched dozens of lawsuits over alleged offenses to his well-being, zapped the mayor whenever possible, and taken potshots at any number of other opponents in his books. Recently the *Village Voice* and *7 Days*, both of which were owned by pet food billionaire and New Jersey real estate developer Leonard Stern, had published scathing attacks on Donald, and Stern was also financing an anti-Trump television documentary. In February 1989 Donald told the *New York Daily News* that Stern's second wife, a filmmaker who was at least 20 years his junior, had phoned Donald for a date. The ensuing news coverage humiliated and infuriated Stern—but perhaps also contributed to his eventual decision to end his support for the film. Sources include *New York Daily News*, 2/26/89, 2/28/89; *New York Post*, 2/28/89; *Newsday*, 3/1/89.

17. Sources for this section include Frank Rose, "Celebrity Zoning"; *Wall Street Journal*, 3/23/88; interviews with Charlie Reiss, 3/12/98; Marla Simpson, 8/8/99; Madeleine Polayes, 4/12/00; Jerrold Nadler, 4/4/00; Ronnie Eldridge, 4/8/00; Roberta Brandes Gratz, 8/23/99; Anne Sperry, 12/6/99; Stephen Swid, 9/7/99, 4/10/00; Linda Davidoff, 8/30/99; Richard Kahan, 9/29/88, 9/8/99; Kent Barwick, 8/24/99; Dick Anderson, 8/4/99; Claude Shostal, 7/29/99; Philip Howard, 8/3/99, 8/17/99; Mary Frances Shaughnessy, 8/4/99; Catherine Cary, 11/27/99; Ruth Messinger, 8/11/99; Richard Bass, 1/2/00; Steve Robinson, 7/7/91; Dan Gutman and Ethel Scheffer, numerous interviews beginning in 1990.

18. The protest occurred on October 18, 1987. Speakers at a rally before-

hand included Bill Moyers and David Dinkins, then Manhattan borough president. *New York Times,* 10/19/87.

19. Estimates of the hole Donald was in continued to grow, reaching a negative $1.4 billion in March 1992. *BusinessWeek,* 3/23/92.

20. Although the developer was the one in fiscal hot water, he seemed to have less difficulty with the situation than the bankers who were questioning him. "If Donald didn't have an answer," Charlie Reiss said later, "it didn't matter. He just put more words on the table, made a joke, said something diversionary. He understood that no one really understood anything." In fact, it seemed to Reiss that he and the developer knew far more about the bankers' business than they did. "They really weren't very prepared for those meetings," Reiss said. He recalled being surprised "at how little they knew about their own quarter-of-a-billion-dollar loan. It became sort of a joke for me, and I think for Donald, too." Interviews with Charlie Reiss, 3/12/98; Richard Kahan, 9/8/99.

21. Just five days earlier such an event had seemed out of the question. When West Side elected officials and community groups had a breakfast meeting with Mayor David Dinkins to discuss the issue, the most low-key mayor in city history, dressed in his usual blue satin baseball warm-up jacket, blew up. To him the paramount issue was not the future potential for a smaller project and a park, but the immediate potential for the elevated highway to give way and cause a tragedy from which the city and its mayor might never recover. But the next day Kahan and Donald reached an agreement. When told that there would be a press conference at the governor's office to announce a historic agreement within his own city, Dinkins had no choice but to climb aboard and host it himself.

22. Sources for this section include *New York Times,* 3/6/91, 8/11/91; *Newsday,* 3/5/91, 3/6/91.

23. The final version of Riverside South would be 7.9 million square feet, down from Television City's 14.5 million square feet; the estimated cost would be $2.4 billion; and the commitment to subway renovation would be $12 million, down from Macri's promise of $30 million. In exchange, the city had extended the usual three-year deadline for commencement of construction to seven and a half years, a change that could make a big difference if the real estate market's recovery was slow.

24. The 323-acre Riverside Park was originally designed by Frederick Law Olmsted in the late 1870s, nearly 20 years after his masterwork, Central Park, and reconstructed in the late 1930s by park commissioner Robert Moses.

25. In fact, the most recent restructuring plan for the Castle, which subsequently underwent numerous revisions, called for a reduction of interest rates from 13.75 percent to 9.5 percent and required the casino to file for Chapter 11 reorganization in U.S. Bankruptcy Court. United Press International, 6/26/91. In their final report, the planners deemed the Riverside South proposal a good one but suggested that it be cut 16 percent to fit into the "spatial character" of the West Side. Sources include *Newsday,* 7/1/91.

26. Because property valuation is a highly subjective enterprise, estimates of just how much the developer owed at any particular moment vary widely. These numbers, cited in the *Washington Post*, 11/29/92, appear to be consensus figures adopted by most of the press.

27. $447,145, according to *Newsday*, 8/22/93.

28. The constituent members of Riverside South Inc., the not-for-profit corporation formed to guide the development process, were the Trump Organization, Westpride, the Municipal Art Society, the Parks Council, the Riverside Park Fund, the Natural Resources Defense Council, and the Regional Plan Association.

29. Interview with Paul Willen, 12/92.

30. *New York Times*, 12/16/92.

31. Attracted by the Trump name, wealthy Asians had purchased many luxury condominiums in the developer's earlier buildings. But apparently it was the low price and the opportunity to diversify their portfolio that attracted the father-and-son team who headed New World to the rail yards, not the name of its owner. Henry Cheng and his father, Cheng Yu-tong, whose first job was as an apprentice jewelry maker, ran a publicly traded company whose holdings included the Hong Kong Grand Hyatt and the Ramada and Stouffer hotel chains in the United States. Sources include *New York Times*, 7/15/94; interview with Sin-ming Shaw, 7/19/94.

32. Because the project was on underutilized land, it received the same 421a city tax abatement that Donald got for Trump Tower and the East Side co-op Trump Plaza. However, at least in part due to Jerrold Nadler's vigorous opposition, Riverside South failed to obtain HUD mortgage insurance—the current version of the same FHA mortgage insurance that Fred Trump had used decades earlier in Brooklyn. *New York Times*, 7/24/98; interview with Jerrold Nadler, 4/4/00.

33. Johnson himself was not thrilled with the finished product. "Donald says these buildings are great architecture, but I don't agree," he said. "There were too many rules and too many previous architects—too many cooks in the broth, including the investors, [and] the West Siders also had a lot to say." Interview with Philip Johnson, 3/99.

34. Westpride was the only West Side organization in Riverside South Inc.

35. Sources include *New York Times*, 7/31/98, 6/25/99.

CHAPTER NINE: Trump™

1. Sources for this chapter include Jerry Useem, "What Does Donald Trump Really Want," *Fortune*, 4/3/00.

2. Sources for this section include interviews with Peter Ricker, 2/19/99; Dave Wiederecht, 5/11/99; Mike Simmons, 2/16/99; John Meyers, 2/12/99; Sandy Moorehouse, 3/9/99; Scott Coopchick, 4/30/99; Dale Frey, 3/8/99; Charlie Reiss, 3/12/98; Abe Wallach, 1/98; Donald Trump, 12/12/97.

3. Soon after Donald Trump met with Frey, the chairman called him and said it was time to start working on the building. "Then I said we would be pleased to accept a bid from him and incidentally there were seven other people asking," Frey said. "That really set him back—he thought he should just win." Although the developer was offended by being asked to compete for the job, he still wanted the deal. Accordingly, he too, did some homework. What he found was that the Galbreath Company, a mainline development concern that had an inside track because it had already been consulting with Frey's office on the project, was interested in doing the job itself but lacked actual experience producing luxury condominiums in New York City. Recognizing the potential fit between them, Galbreath and Trump then teamed up and submitted what turned out to be the winning proposal.

4. In this and subsequent projects, Donald proved adept at a peculiar New York art known as "remeasuring"—increasing the square footage in rentable areas by charging tenants for what in other cities would be considered common space and also measuring space from the outside walls of a building. Then, to justify far higher prices for Trump International Hotel and Tower than anyone else had thought possible, the building's old low-cachet One Columbus Circle address became higher-cachet One Central Park West, subsequently touted in ad copy as "the most important address in the world," and Philip Johnson became the architect. After Johnson updated the exterior with bronze columns and a curtain wall of champagne-colored glass, the developer slashed the expected price of the curtain wall by waiting until three days before Christmas to let the contract. "He called the contractor and said, 'I know it's your year's end, you want to wind things up, I'll book it at this price,'" recounted Abe Wallach, Donald's chief of staff. "The guy was so desperate to land the job, he took it. Where did Donald learn this? From his dad—he instilled these ideas in Donald."

5. Sources include James Traub, "Trumpologies," *New York Times Magazine*, 9/12/04; *New York Times*, 3/19/02.

6. A 72-story office building, 40 Wall Street had a distinctive pyramid top and a brief reign as the world's tallest structure before being eclipsed in 1929 by the Chrysler Building and, soon afterward, the Empire State Building. When Donald bought what would become The Trump Building, it was, as he liked to point out, "the tallest building in downtown Manhattan after the World Trade Center." After the destruction of the World Trade Center on September 11, 2001, 40 Wall Street was once again the tallest structure in

lower Manhattan, but such a distinction was no longer something to boast about.

7. To obtain air rights over an adjacent Roman Catholic church, the developer promised that Trump World Tower would ban discussion of condoms or birth control pills in public areas.

8. Sources include *Los Angeles Times*, 2/14/99; interview with Charlie Miesmer, 7/8/99.

9. After the debt was paid off, the partners would share any subsequent profits 50/50. To outsiders, the financial arrangement looked decidedly lopsided, but to Steve Hilbert, founder and president of Conseco, it seemed eminently fair. Not because he didn't know about the importance of branding—he had recently forked over $40 million just to put his company's name on a new field house in Indianapolis. But here, he said, it made more sense to ride on someone else's coattails. "This isn't part of our branding," he explained. "It's about making money." Using the Trump name would allow the partners to bring in premium rents; better yet, the developer's innovative plan to sell office space on a condominium basis could have the entire building paid off in record time. Interview with Steve Hilbert, 11/18/99.

10. The Trump name also appeared on the corners of the building in shiny letters about two feet high. A few of the tenants, a high-profile list that included Estée Lauder and the toy store FAO Schwarz, complained, but to no apparent avail. Then CBS weighed in. CBS Chairman Mel Karmazin gave the developer a call and said that a corner Trump would be visible in any external camera shots. Karmazin said that this would be a problem for CBS, and he asked the developer to take care of it. Sources include *New York Times*, 10/18/99, 8/30/03; *New York Daily News*, 2/9/02, 6/14/03, 6/25/03; 8/30/03.

11. Mark Singer, "Trump Solo," *New Yorker*, 5/19/97.

12. By 1997, *Forbes* listed Donald as the 105th richest American, with $1.4 billion (Trump's figure: $3.7 billion); in 1998, *Forbes* put him at 110th richest, with $1.5 billion (Trump's figure: $5 billion); and in 1999, although *Forbes* upped its estimate of his assets to $1.6 billion, his rank had slipped to 145th richest (Trump's figure: $4.5 billion). Source: *Forbes*.

13. Interview with Kevin DeSanctis, former president of Trump Plaza, 6/23/99.

14. *New York Post*, 4/27/96, 4/28/96.

15. Interview with Jack Shaffer, 7/30/99.

16. Sources include interviews with Sugar Rautbord, 1/14/99, 2/27/99, 2/14/00. I am particularly grateful to Ms. Rautbord for her keen observations of high society in New York and Palm Beach.

CHAPTER TEN: The Legacy

1. Sources for this section include interviews with Edward S. Gordon, 2/5/98; Barbara Corcoran, 2/27/04. Sources for the chapter include newspaper clippings for the time periods; Daniel Ruth, "The Trophy Life," *Time*, 4/19/04;

Traub, "Trumpologies," *New York Times Magazine*. I am grateful for permission to use material which first appeared in my article, "Donald Trump," published in *Razor*, 3/04.

2. They included The Trump Building, Trump International Hotel and Tower, Trump Palace, Trump Parc, Trump Park Avenue, Trump Plaza, Trump Tower, Trump World Tower, and three of the five completed buildings in the Trump Place complex. When finished, Trump Place was scheduled to include the 16 buildings already planned plus an undetermined number on the southernmost and largest parcel. Sources include interview with Michael Bradley, 12/7/04.

3. Traub, "Trumpologies."

4. Interviews with Donald Trump, 2/28/04, 11/3/04.

5. Sources for this section include interviews with Marvin Roffman, 2/28/04, 10/27/04; Jacques Comet, 2/25/04, 11/2/04; Michael Scerbo, 10/27/04.

6. Sources include *New York Times*, 10/21/04; interview with Donald Trump, 11/3/04.

7. *Newsday*, 10/22/04.

8. Interview with Bernd Schmitt, 3/3/04.

9. *Forbes*, 9/24/04.

10. Interview with Donald Trump, 11/3/04.

11. Traub, "Trumpologies."

12. Sources for this section include David Grainger, "Hollywood Hitman," *Time*, 8/23/04; *Newsweek*, 3/1/04; *New York Times*, 10/19/03; interviews with Donald Trump on 2/28/04, 11/3/04; Jim Dowd, 2/27/04, 10/27/04; Jarle Nakken, 10/25/04; Ken Austin, 11/5/04; Michele Greppi, 2/27/04, 10/15/05, 10/22/04, 11/2/04, 11/5/04; Nick Warnock, 11/11/04; Victor Btesh, 11/11/04; Rob Flanagan, 11/11/04; Pam Day, 11/15/04; Jennifer Crisafulli, 11/16/04; Wesley Moss, 12/21/04.

13. Btesh didn't make it onto the show, but he had his own personal brush with fame when Donald walked over, shook his hand, and asked his name. "Afterward, everyone came over to me," Btesh said. "It was like suddenly I had become a celebrity." After his audition, Btesh, who had already learned that the Trump Organization executive in charge of licensing the name was Bernie Diamond, went over to Donald and told him that he had a great idea. When Donald said he didn't have a minute to listen, or even 20 seconds, Btesh asked for two seconds, then blurted out that he wanted to make a Donald Trump doll that says, "You're fired," he had a company that could do it, and he was supposed to talk to Mr. Diamond. "Call Bernie," Donald said. Btesh did so; eight months later, Donald sat in Toys R Us autographing the result.

14. One contestant who actually wanted the job learned the hard way the potential downside of being featured on a hit television show. Before she got the axe, Jennifer Crisafulli, a Manhattan real estate broker from a real estate family, had been featured in ads by her proud employer, the Douglas Elli-

man brokerage house. But on the fourth episode, which involved the opening of a new restaurant, her team made less money and got lower Zagat ratings, and team leader Crisafulli was fired. As usual, editors then raced through hundreds of hours of videotape (on every Burnett show, a separate camera follows each contestant at all times) and came up with a story line that would support this denouement. Included in the broadcast version was a conversation during which Crisafulli made offhand reference to two customers at her team's restaurant as "old Jewish fat ladies." The aside brought her scathing reviews and a pink slip from Elliman, although Crisafulli said the remark was taken out of context and that her own family is half Jewish. "My life is a train wreck," she said afterward. Sources include *New York Post*, 10/4/04; interview with Jennifer Crisafulli, 11/16/04.

15. The network still pursued traditional advertising. At the opening of the second season, a 30-second spot on *The Apprentice* cost an average of $409,877, making it the fifth-most expensive network series for advertisers. *New York Times*, 9/28/04.

16. Procter & Gamble press release, PR Newswire, 9/28/04.

17. About 10 percent of the buyers were Trump collectors—that is, people who owned units in other Trump buildings. Interview with Charlie Reiss, 10/29/04.

18. Interview with Bob Horowitz, 11/1/04.

19. Sources for this section include interviews with Michael Romano, 11/3/04; Jim Silver, 11/3/04; Bernd Schmitt, 11/3/04; Randall Rothenberg, 11/1/04; Peter Arnell, 11/9/04.

20. *New York Times*, 8/30/04; *Washington Post*, 8/30/04; *New York Observer*, 1/25/99.

21. *New York Times*, 9/9/04.

22. Interviews with Donald Trump, 5/31/01, 11/3/04.

23. Sources for this section include Steve Rhodes, "Ode to an Eyesore," *Chicago*, 1/04; *New York Times*, 1/18/05; interviews with Albert Hanna, 10/21/04; Alicia Berg, 10/21/04; Allison Davis, 10/15/04; Blair Kamin, 10/15/04; Burton Natarus, 10/31/04; David Roeder, 10/18/04; Jack Swenson, 10/21/04; John Vinci, 10/15/04; Billy Marovitz, 10/18/04; Tim Samuelson, 10/15/04; Don Trump Jr., 10/28/04, 11/3/04, 11/5/04; Adrian Smith, 10/28/04; Richard Tomlinson, 10/28/04; Robert Shearer, 10/17/04; Jane Field, 10/17/04; Michael McKewin, 10/28/04; Charlie Reiss, 2/27/04, 10/29/04.

24. Smith was no stranger to architectural behemoths. He had designed the nearby NBC Tower, had been the lead architect on a recent unsuccessful effort to recapture for Chicago the world's tallest building title, and was now working on the newest candidate, a structure in Dubai that would break the 2,000-foot barrier by several hundred feet.

25. Unlike many Trump projects in New York City, this one in Chicago was welcomed by its neighbors. The *Sun-Times* building, an inelegant industrial holdout next to architectural superstars, including the 80-year-old

Wrigley Building, Mies van der Rohe's IBM building, and Bernard Goldberg's Marina City, had few defenders. In contrast to Manhattanites, often ambivalent about adding yet another tower to their concrete canyons, Chicagoans like skyscrapers and are eager to develop the north side of the riverfront, historically a warehouse area known as "The Shadows" because after the working day was over, its streets were dark and deserted.

Bibliography

BOOKS

Akin, Edward N. *Flagler: Rockefeller Partner and Florida Baron*. Gainesville: University Press of Florida, 1992.

Auletta, Ken. *The Streets Were Paved with Gold*. New York: Random House, 1975.

Baida, Peter. *Poor Richard's Legacy: American Business Values from Benjamin Franklin to Michael Milken*. New York: Quill/William Morrow, 1990.

Barlett, Donald L., and James B. Steele. *Empire: The Life, Legend, and Madness of Howard Hughes*. New York: W. W. Norton and Company, 1979.

Barrett, Wayne. *Trump: The Deals and the Downfall*. New York: HarperCollins, 1992.

Bruck, Connie. *The Predators' Ball: The Junk Bond Raiders and the Man Who Stalked Them*. New York: American Lawyer/Simon & Schuster, 1988.

Burrows, Edwin G., and Mike Wallace. *Gotham*. New York: Oxford University Press, 1999.

Buttenweiser, Ann L. *Manhattan Water-Bound*. New York: New York University Press, 1987.

Byrne, Jim. *The $1 League: The Rise and Fall of the USFL*. New York: Prentice-Hall Press, 1986.

Caro, Robert. *The Power Broker*. New York: Vintage Books, 1975.

Chalmers, David. *Neither Socialism nor Monopoly*. Philadelphia: Lippincott, 1976.

Chamberlain, John. *The Enterprising Americans: A Business History of the United States*. New York: Harper & Row, 1974.

Chernow, Ron. *Titan: The Life of John D. Rockefeller, Sr.* New York: Random House, 1998.

Clark, Norman H. *Milltown*. Seattle: University of Washington Press, 1970.

Colean, Miles. *A Backward Glance: The Growth of Government Housing Policy in the United States, 1934–1975*. Washington: Research and Educational Trust Fund of the Mortgage Bankers Association of America, 1975.

Connery, Robert H., and Gerald Benjamin. *Rockefeller of New York*. Ithaca: Cornell University Press, 1979.

Daughen, Joseph R., and Peter Binzen. *The Wreck of the Penn Central*. Boston: Little, Brown, 1971.

Davies, John. *Housing Reform During the Truman Administration*. Columbia: University of Missouri Press, 1966.

Demaris, Ovid. *The Boardwalk Jungle*. New York: Bantam Books, 1986.

Eccles, Marriner. *Beckoning Frontiers*. New York, Alfred A. Knopf, 1951.

Fischler, Stan. *Uptown, Downtown: A Trip Through Time on New York's Subways*. New York: Hawthorn Books, 1976.

Freund, Christian. *Kallstadt in alten Ansichten*. Kallstadt, 1985.

Friedman, Milton, and Anna Jacobson Schwartz. *Monetary History of the United States*. Princeton: Princeton University Press, 1963.

Gancarz, Jack Andrzej. *Palm Beach: Florida's Riviera*. Lake Worth, Fla.: Downtown Photo Service Press, 1989.

George, Carol V. R. *God's Salesman*. New York: Oxford University Press, 1993.

Henry, John Robertson. *Fifty Years on the Lower East Side of New York*. Privately printed, 1966.

Hood, Clifton. *722 Miles: The Building of the Subways and How They Transformed New York*. New York: Simon & Schuster, 1993.

Hurt, Harry. *Lost Tycoon*. New York: W. W. Norton, 1993.

Institute for Policy Studies. *America's Housing Crisis*. Edited by Chester Hartman. Boston: Routledge & Kegan Paul, 1983.

Jackson, Anthony. *A Place Called Home*. Cambridge, Mass.: MIT Press, 1976.

Jacobs, Jane. *The Death and Life of Great American Cities*. New York: Vintage Books, 1961.

Johnston, Alva. *The Legendary Mizners*. New York: Farrar, Straus & Giroux, 1953.

Johnston, David. *Temples of Chance: How America Inc. Bought Out Murder Inc. to Win Control of the Casino Business*. New York: Doubleday, 1992.

Kepcher, Carolyn. *Carolyn 101*. New York: Fireside, 2004.

King, Norma. *Ivana Trump: A Very Unauthorized Biography*. New York: Carroll and Graf, 1990.

Knott, James R. *The Mansion Builders Palm Beach Revisited III*. Palm Beach: Best of the Brown Wrappers, 1990.

Koch, Edward I. *Mayor*. New York: Simon & Schuster, 1984.

———. *Politics*. New York: Simon & Schuster, 1985.

Kramer, Michael, and Sam Roberts. *"I Never Wanted to Be Vice President of Anything!"* New York: Basic Books, 1976.

Levi, Vicki Gold. *Atlantic City: 125 Years of Ocean Madness*. New York: C. N. Potter, 1979.

Lovely, Thomas J. *The History of the Jamaica Estates, 1929–1969*. Jamaica, N.Y.: Jamaica Estates Association, 1969.

Mahon, Gigi. *The Company That Bought the Boardwalk*. New York: Random House, 1980.

McFarland, M. Carter. *Federal Government and Urban Problems: HUD: Successes, Failures, and the Fate of Our Cities*. Boulder, Colo.: Westview Press, 1978.

Moscow, Warren. *Last of the Big-Time Bosses*. New York: Stein and Day, 1971.

———. *Politics in the Empire State*. New York: Alfred A. Knopf, 1948.

Moss, Mitchell. *Palace Coup: The Inside Story of Harry and Leona Helmsley*. New York: Doubleday, 1989.

Nevins, Allan. *John D. Rockefeller: The Heroic Age of American Enterprise*. New York: Charles Scribner's Sons, 1940.

Newfield, Jack, and Wayne Barrett. *City for Sale: Ed Koch and the Betrayal of New York*. New York: Harper & Row, 1988.

Newfield, Jack, and Paul DuBrul. *The Permanent Government: Who Really Runs New York?* New York: Pilgrim Press, 1981.

Norman, Elof. *The Coffee Chased Us Up: Monte Cristo Memories*. Seattle: Mountaineers, 1977.

O'Brien, Timothy L. *Bad Bet: The Inside Story of the Glamour, Glitz, and Danger of America's Gambling Industry*. New York: Times Business, 1998.

O'Donnell, John R., with James Rutherford. *Trumped! The Inside Story of the Real Donald Trump—His Cunning Rise and Spectacular Fall*. New York: Simon & Schuster, 1991.

Onorato, Michael P. *Another Time, Another World: Coney Island Memories*. Fullerton: California State University Oral History Program, 1988.

———. *Steeplechase Park: Sale and Closure. 1965–1966: Diary and Papers of James J. Onorato*. Bellingham, Wash.: Pacific Rim Books, 1998.

Persico, Joseph E. *Rockefeller: A Biography of Nelson A. Rockefeller*. New York: Simon & Schuster, 1982.

Rancic, Bill. *You're Hired*. New York: HarperBusiness, 2004.

Rubin, Sy, and Jonathan Mandell. *Trump Tower*. Secaucus, N.J.: Lyle Stuart Inc., 1984.

Sale, Roger. *Seattle: Past to Present*. Seattle: University of Washington Press, 1976.

Schwartz, Joel. *The New York Approach: Robert Moses, Urban Liberals, and Redevelopment of the Inner City*. Columbus: Ohio University Press, 1993.

Seligman, Ben B. *The Potentates*. New York: Dial Press, 1971.

Seyfried, Vincent. *Queens: A Pictorial History*. Norfolk, Va.: Donning Co., 1982.

Shachtman, Tom. *Skyscraper Dreams*. Boston: Little, Brown, 1991.

Sinkevitch, Alice. *AIA Guide to Chicago*. Orlando: Harcourt, 2004.

Smith, John L. *Running Scared: The Life and Treacherous Times of Las Vegas Casino King Steve Wynn*. New York: Barricade Books. 1995.

Stern, Robert A. M., et al. *New York 1960*. New York: Monacelli Press, 1995.

Stemlieb, George, and James W. Hughes. *The Atlantic City Gamble*. Cambridge, Mass.: Harvard University Press, 1983.

Stover, John F. *The Life and Decline of the American Railroad*. New York: Oxford University Press, 1970.

Sulloway, Frank. *Born to Rebel: Birth Order, Family Dynamics and Creative Lives*. New York: Pantheon Books, 1996.

Trump, Donald, and Kate Bohner. *The Art of the Comeback*. New York: Times Books, 1997.

Trump, Donald, and Charles Leerhsen. *Trump: Surviving at the Top*. New York: Random House, 1990.

Trump, Donald, and Meredith McIver. *Trump: How to Get Rich*. New York, Random House, 2004.

———. *Think Like a Billionaire*. New York: Random House, 2004.

Trump, Donald, and Tony Schwartz. *The Art of the Deal*. New York: Random House, 1987.

Trump, Donald, and Dave Shiflett. *The America We Deserve*. Los Angeles: Renaissance Books, 2000.

Tucille, Jerome. *Trump*. New York: Jove, 1987.

von Hoffman, Nicholas. *Citizen Cohn*. New York: Doubleday, 1988.

Welfeld, Irving. *HUD Scandals: Howling Headlines and Silent Fiascoes*. New Brunswick, N.J.: Transaction Publishers, 1992.

Wilensky, Elliot, and Norval White. *AIA Guide to New York City*. San Diego: Harcourt Brace Jovanovich, 1988.

Woodhouse, Philip R. *Monte Cristo*. Seattle: Mountaineers, 1979.

Zeckendorf, William, and Edward McCreary. *The Autobiography of William Zeckendorf*. New York: Holt, Rinehart and Winston, 1970.

ARTICLES

Architectural Forum. Coverage of FHA, January to December, 1949.

Armtrong, Jennifer. "Full Greed Ahead!" *Time*, September 3, 2004.

Barrett, Wayne. "Donald Trump Cuts the Cards." *Village Voice*, January 22, 1979.

———. "Like Father, Like Son." *Village Voice*, January 15, 1979.

Barry, Andrew. "Still Rolling the Dice." *Barron's*, September 27, 2004.

Bender, Marylin. "The Empire and Ego of Donald Trump." *New York Times*, August 7, 1983.

Billard, Mary. "The Art of the Steal." *Manhattan, inc.*, April 1988.

———. "Revenge of the Merv." *Manhattan, inc.*, June 1988.

Blair, Gwenda. "Donald Trump." *Razor*, May 2004.

———. "How I Did a Great Job." *Forbes*, December 3, 2004.

Bouvier, Leon F., and Carol J. De Vita. "The Baby Boom—Entering Midlife." *Population Bulletin*, November 1991.

Bowden, Mark. "The Trumpster Stages the Comeback of a Lifetime." *Playboy*, May 1997.

Boyle, Robert H. "The USFL's Trump Card." *Sports Illustrated*, February 13, 1984.

Brenner, Marie. "After the Gold Rush." *Vanity Fair*, September 1990.

———. "Trumping the Town." *New York*, November 17, 1980.

Byron, Christopher. "Other People's Money." *New York*, September 17, 1990.

Cameron, David A. "The Everett and Monte Cristo Railway: A Lifeline to the Mines of Eastern Snohomish County." *Journal of Everett & Snohomish County History*, Winter 1988–89.

Carter, Graydon. "Donald Trump Gets What He Wants." *Gentleman's Quarterly*, May 1984.

Connolly, John. "All of the People, All of the Time." *Spy*, April 1991.

Cook, Karen. "Street Smart." *Manhattan, inc.*, December 1986.

———. "Trumping Trump." *Manhattan, inc.*, November 1986.

Cox, Hank. "Greed Is Good." *Regardie's*, July 1989.

David, Paul A., and Peter M. Solar. "A Bicentennial Contribution to the History of the Cost of Living in America." In *Research in Economic History*, edited by Robert E. Gallman. Greenwich, Conn.: JAI Press, 1977.

De Vita, Carol J. "The United States at Mid-Decade." *Population Bulletin*, March 1996.

Dorfman, Dan. "The Bottom Line." *New York*, November 13, 1975.

———. "Will New York Get a New Hotel?" *New York*, April 26, 1976.

Edwards, Owen. "All the King's Women." *Savvy Woman*, November 1989.

Friedrich, Otto. "Flashy Symbol of an Acquisitive Age." *Time*, January 16, 1989.

Gardiner, Nancy Tuck. "Mistress of Mar-A-Lago." *Town & Country*, March 1986.

Geist, William. "The Expanding Empire of Donald Trump." *New York Times Magazine*, April 8, 1984.

Gerard, Jeremy. "Trumped Up." *Fame*, Summer 1989.

Glynn, Lenny. "Blowout on the Boardwalk." *Institutional Investor*, December 1989.

Goldberger, Paul. "Zone Defense." *The New Yorker*, February 22 & March 1, 1999.

Grainger, David. "Hollywood Hitman." *Fortune*, August 23, 2004.

Greenberg, Jonathan. "Clash of the Titans." *Manhattan, inc.*, January 1986.

Hammer, Joshua. "He Wants to Take You Higher." *Manhattan, inc.*, January 1986.

Horowitz, Craig. "Trump's Near-Death Experience." *New York*, August 15, 1994.

Klein, Edward. "Trump Family Values." *Vanity Fair*, March 1994.

Koroscil, Paul M. "The Historical Development of Whitehorse." *American Review of Canadian Studies*, Vol. 18.

Kunen, James S. "Pop Goes the Donald." *People*, July 9, 1990.

Leibovich, Audrey, Magali Rheault, and Dan Wilchins. "An Amazing Half Century of Progress." *Kiplinger's*, January 1997.

Lieblich, Julia. "The Billionaires." *Fortune*, September 12, 1988.

Mahar, Maggie. "The Merv and Donald Show." *Barron's*, May 23, 1988.

Marshall, Leslie. "Breakfast Above Tiffany's." *In Style*, December 1995.

Meyers, William H. "Stalking the Plaza." *New York Times Magazine*, September 25, 1988.

Naughton, Keith, and Mark Peyser. "The World According to Trump." *Newsweek*, March 1, 2004.

"Now is the Time to Speak Up for FHA." *House and Home*, May 1954.

O'Keefe, Eric. "The Peter Principle." *Polo*, March/April 1998.

Pileggi, Nicholas. "How to Get Things Done in New York: A Case History." *New York*, November 1973.

Plaskin, Glenn. *"Playboy* Interview: Donald Trump." *Playboy*, March 1990.

———. "Queen Ivana Approximately." *New York Daily News Magazine*, December 17, 1989.

———. "The People's Billionaire." *New York Daily News Magazine*, February 26, 1989.

Posner, Eric. "The Political Economy of the Bankruptcy Reform Act of 1978." *Michigan Law Review*, October 1997.

Powell, Bill, and Peter McKillop. "Citizen Trump." *Newsweek*, September 28, 1987.

"Private Enterprise Breathes New Life into Old Cities." *Dun & Bradstreet Reports*, November/December 1978.

Rhodes, Steve. "Ode to an Eyesore." *Chicago*, January 2004.

Rose, Frank. "Celebrity Zoning." *Manhattan, inc.*, November 1989.

Roth, Daniel. "The Trophy Life." *Fortune*, April 19, 2004.

Ryan, Michael. "Building Castles in the Sky." *People*, December 7, 1987.

Schnayerson, Michael. "Power Blonde." *Vanity Fair*, January 1988.

Schwartz, John. "The Stars of Brick and Mortar." *Newsweek*, September 28, 1987.

Schwartz, Tony. "A Different Kind of Donald Trump Story." *New York*, February 11, 1985.

Sheffer, Ethel. "The Lessons of Lincoln West." *New York Affairs*, Vol. 8, No. 3, 1984.

Simonoff, Evan. "Deal of Misfortune." *Investment Dealers' Digest*, July 3, 1989.

Singer, Mark. "Trump Solo." *The New Yorker*, May 19, 1997.

Stem, Richard L., and John Connolly. "Manhattan's Favorite Guessing Game: How Rich Is Donald?" *Forbes*, May 14, 1990.

Stone, Michael, "Clash of the Titans: Business Tycoons Donald Trump and Jay Prizker." *Chicago*, October 1994.

Taylor, John. "Trump's Newest Toy." *New York*, July 11, 1988.

Tell, Lawrence J. "Holding All the Cards." *Barron's*, August 6, 1984.

Traub, James. "Trumpologies." *New York Times Magazine*, September 12, 2004.

Useem, Jerry, and Theodore Spencer. "What Does Donald Trump Really Want?" *Fortune*, April 3, 2000.

Van Meter, Jonathan. "Ivana! Ivana! Ivana!" *Spy*, May 1989.

Weiss, Philip. "The Fred." *New York Times Magazine*, January 2, 2000.

Wilkinson, Peter. "The New Fixers." *Manhattan, inc.*, January 1988.

DISSERTATIONS

Kroessler, Jeffrey A. "Building Queens: The Urbanization of New York's Largest Borough." Ph.D. dissertation, City University of New York, 1991.

GOVERNMENT DOCUMENTS

Corruption and Racketeering in the New York City Construction Industry. Interim Report by the New York State Organized Crime Task Force. Ithaca, N.Y.: ILR Press, 1988.

Details Supporting the Findings of Fact in the Special Investigation of the Federal Housing Administration. April 12, 1954–August 31, 1954.

German Federal Archives, Speyer. Friedrich Trump, papers and correspondence.

Housing and Development Administration Study Group. "New York City's Mitchell-Lama Housing Program: The Management of the Middle Income Housing Program." New York: Housing and Development Administration of New York, January 1973.

Kaiser, Frederick M. "Past Program Breakdowns in HUD-FHA: Section 608 Multifamily Rental Mortgage Insurance Program of the 1940s." Congressional Research Service, Library of Congress.

McKenna, William F. *Final Report on FHA Investigation*. August 31, 1954.

————. *Report to the Senate Committee on Banking and Currency*. June 29, 1954.

————. *Summaries of Federal Housing Section 608 Case Investigations Presented to the Senate Banking and Currency Committee*. n.d.

New York State. "Recommendations of the New York State Commission of Investigation Concerning the Limited-Profit Housing Program." April 1966.

New York State Housing Finance Agency Annual Report for Fiscal Year November 1, 1960, to October 31, 1961.

Ninth Annual Report of the Temporary Commission of Investigation of the

Senate of New York to the Governor and the Legislature of New York. February 1967.

U.S. District Court, Eastern District of New York. Archives relating to *In the Matter of Julius Lehrenkrauss* et al. 1934.

U.S. Senate. FHA Investigation, Hearings Before the Committee on Banking and Currency, Testimony of Fred Trump, July 12, 1954, pp. 395–420.

———. Testimony of Ian Woodner, August 4, 1954, pp. 1021–1123.

MISCELLANEOUS

American Institute of Architects, New York Chapter. "Report of the Sixtieth Street Yards Task Force." New York: June 1990.

Buckhurst Fish Hutton Katz & Jacquemart Inc. "Review of Riverside South Proposal." New York: July 1992.

Community Board Seven/Manhattan. "Draft Report of Community Board Seven/Manhattan on the Riverside South Proposal for the Uniform Land Use Review Procedure." July 22, 1992.

Cooke, Dr. C. M. *Tech Talk*. M.I.T. publication, February 1985.

Corporate Reorganization Reporter (Penn Central).

De Vita, Carol J. "The United States at Mid-Decade." *Population Bulletin*. Washington, D.C.: Population Reference Bureau Inc., March 1996.

Encyclopedia of New York City, edited by Kenneth T. Jackson. New Haven: Yale University Press, 1995.

Gould, Milton. "Fifth Avenue Coach Lines, Trump Tower and Roy M. Cohn." Chapter from an unpublished autobiography.

Henry Morrison Flagler Museum. "Whitehall: The Henry Morrison Flagler Museum." Brochure published by the museum in 1988.

Kelsey Story. Kelsey, New York History Committee, Kelsey Community Group, 1980.

Kroos, William. "A Peek at Richmond Hill through the Keyhole of Time." Richmond Hill Savings Bank, 1983.

Macri, Francisco. "Lincoln West or Who Trumped Whom." Unpublished autobiography written with Judith Murphy.

Moses, Robert. "West Side Fiasco: A Practical Proposal for the Restoration of the West Side Highway and Parkway to Public Use." November 25, 1974.

Penn & Schoen Associates Inc. "Report to Donald Trump on Public Opinion in America." October 1988.

Rose, Nelson. "Gambling and the Law: Recent Developments, 1998." Unpublished paper.

Scutt, Der. Unpublished professional diary, 1974–present.

Vital Statistics of the United States, 1950, Volume 1.

Acknowledgments

My earlier book, *The Trumps: Three Generations That Built an Empire*, published in 2000, looks at a century of American entrepreneurship as embodied in the careers of Friedrich, Fred, and Donald Trump. Since then, *The Apprentice* has made its debut on NBC, and Donald has added to his accomplishments one more: television star. Picking up the story where I left off, I have adapted and updated my earlier work to produce *Donald Trump: Master Apprentice*.

For the new book, I am indebted to a number of individuals, beginning with Donald Trump, Don Jr., and other members of the Trump family. They have been gracious and helpful, as have past and present Trump Organization staff, especially Norma Foerderer, Rhona Graff, and Charlie Reiss; NBC senior press manager Jim Dowd; and Michele Greppi, national correspondent for *TelevisionWeek*.

Editor Alice Mayhew and agent Gloria Loomis have been most understanding and supportive during this lengthy process; Roger Labrie, Emily Takoudes, and Miriam Wenger provided vital support. I remain indebted to Irving Alter, Wayne Barrett, George Blecher, Philip Blumberg, Cate Breslin, the Christleibs, Daniel Gutman, Alan Kleiman, Alan Lapidus, Richard H. Levy, Cam Mann, Caroline Mann, Ken Mollen, Eugene Morris, Mark Plummer, Sugar Rautbord, Marvin Roffman, Ethel Scheffer, Harvey Schultz, Der Scutt, and Paul Willen for their generous help on the original volume, and to Jamie Diamond for her assistance on the new book.

Finally, I want to thank Peter Mezan for help getting where I needed to be to finish; to Ann Banks, Carol Brightman, Jane Ciabattari, Grace Lichtenstein, Kathryn Kilgore, and Marilyn Webb for encouragement; and to Matt Stolper for his support and love along our ongoing journey.

In addition, I owe deep thanks to many others who spoke with me for the original volume and for the new book. The following list is only partial, for many asked that I not use their names. Thanks to Mike Abeloff, Heather Hillman Adams, Mark Advent, Frank Alleva, Joe Amoroso, Dennis Anderson, Dick Anderson, Engler Anderson, Wally Antoniewicz, Peter Arnell, Jonathan Ameson, Arthur Arsham, Valerie Asciutto, Ken Auletta, Pat Auletta, Ken Austin, Mark Bachmann, Mike Bailkin, Jerry Ballan, Jonathan Barnett, Ben Barowski, Neil Barsky, Kent Barwick, Richard Bass, Foster Beach, Abraham Beame, Laurie Beckelman, Phyllis Becker, Paul Bekman, Paul Belica, John Belmonte, Henry Benach, Arthur Bender, Alicia Berg, Milton Berger, Ted Bergman, Stanley Berman, Bob Berne, Dick Bernstein, Lee Bey, Daniel Biederman, Bronson Binger, Philip Birnbaum, Harry Blair, James Blair, Newell Blair, Bob Blanchette, Ron Bleecker, Bernie Blum, Stanley Blumberg, Charles Boch, Joe Boling, Steve Bollenbach, Patricia Bosworth, Leonard Boxer, Lily Brant, Peter Brant, Jeff Breslow, Fred Briller, Bonnie Brower, Michael Brown, Bobby Brownstein, John Brugman, Frank Bryant, Victor Btesh, Horace Bullard, Karen Burstein, Clayton Burwell, Javier Bustamente, Brendan Byrne, Conrad Cafritz, Arthur Caliandro, David Cameron, John Cantrill, Frank Cardile, Hugh Carey, Larry Carlet, Scott Carlin, Rafael Carmona, Catherine Cary, Haywood Cash, Anthony Castellano, Joe Center, Herbert S. Chason, Andrew Chertoff, Joe Coccimiglio, Joseph Cohen, Joseph M. Cohen, Matthew Coleus, Michael Conway, Peter Coombs, Scott Coopchick, Michael Corbisiero, Philip Corbisiero, Jacques Cornet, Rochelle Corson, Mary Roche Cossman, Gaylen Crantz, Jennifer Crisafulli, Felix Cuervo, Ngaire Cuneo, Jim Czajka, John d'Alessio, Linda Davidoff, Howard Davidowitz, Allison Davis, Gordon Davis, Pamela Day, Mary D'Elia, Michelle DeMilly, Herbert Denenberg, Kevin DeSanctis, Mario di Genova, Ken di Pasquale, Stanley Diamond, Richard Dicker, Cary Dickieson, John Digges, Bill Digiacomo, David Dilgard, Frank Diotte, David Dischy, Ted Dobias, Paul Doocey, Paul Dorpat, Louis Droesch, Linda Dufault, Paul Duke, Seymour Durst, Andre D'Usseau, Paul Dworin, Harriet Economou, Julius Edelstein, Michael Edelstein, Rick Edmonds, Owen Edwards, Bill Ehlers, Ned Eichler, Al Eisenpreiss, Stan Ekstut, Arthur Emil, Paul Erlham, Spencer Ervin, Mitchell Etess, Stu Faber, Hilbert Fefferman, Murray Feiden, Marcy Feigenbaum, Murray Felton, Chris Ferro, Jane Field, Joe Fisch, Rob Flanagan, Al Formicola, Cathleen Fostini, Molly Foti, Tim Frank, Fran Freedman, Bill Frentz, Christian Freund, Dale Frey, Fred Fried, Bernard Frieden, Louis Friedman, Steve Friedman, Hugo Friend, Sidney Frigand, Charles Frowenfeld, Bart Frye, Roy Gainsburg, Tom Gallegher, Martin Gallent, Alex Garvin, Bernie Gavser, Fina Farhi Geiger, Peter Gelb, Jeff Gerson, Victor Gerstein, Marvin Gersten, Mae and Moe Gherman, Jack Gibson, Andy Giffuni, D. L. Gilbert, Frank Giordano, Bob Giraldi, Stephen Girard, Norman Glickman, Ginny Gliedman, Homer Godwin, Richard Goeglein, Hadley Gold, Marty Goldensohn, Julius Goldberg, Paul Goldberger, Charles Goldie, Brian Goldin, Lowell Goldman, Jerry Goldsmith, Pat Goldstein, Sally Goodgold, Warren Goodwin, Edward S. Gordon, Dick Gottfried, Martin Gottlieb, George Grace, Gertrude Grady, Phyllis Grady, Ross Graham, Roberta Brandes Gratz, Ace Greenberg, Donald Greenberg, Shirley Greene, Libby Greenwald, Michele Greppi, Jordan Gruzen, Eleanor Guggenheimer, Michael Guider, Fred Halla, Mai Hallingby, John Halpern, Albert Hanna, Franklyn Harkavy, Chester Hartman, Nikki Haskell, Ashton Hawkins, Bob Hawthorne, Don Hayes, Heather MacIntosh Hayes, Judge John Hayes, Doug Healey, Dan Heneghan, Lee Hereth, Bob Herman, Philip Hess, Jud Higgins, Steve Hilbert, Raymond Hillman, Richard Hillman, Stanley Hillman, Dieter Hoch, Alan L. Hoffman, Archie Holeman, Ben Holloway, Myron Holtz, Stan Holuba, Bob Horowitz, Tom Hoving, Dave Howard, Philip Howard, Bill Hubbard, Gertrude Rice Hughes, John W. Hyman, Glen Ingalls, Steve Jacobson, Jerry Jagendorf, Herman Jessor, Philip Johnson, Richard Johnson, W. Taylor Johnson Jr., Anthony Jordan, Mike Kabealo, Richard Kagle, Richard Kahan, Blair Kamin, Henry Kanegsberg, Joe Kanter, Teddy Katsoris, Sandor Katz, Richard Katzive, Ben Kazan, Leon Kazan, Scott Keller, Tom Keller, Charles Kimble, Jeanne King, Eric Kingson, Jeff Kone, Arthur Kopit, Oliver Koppell, Joe Kordsmeier, Ann Rudovsky Kornfeld, John Koskinen, Victor Kovner, Howard Kramer, Richard Krauser, William Kroos, Ted Krukel, Irwin Kuhn, Donald Kummerfeld, Dorotha Kuritzkes, Benjamin Lambert, Morris Lapidus, David Lefever, Samuel LeFrak, Ken Lehrer, Franz Leichter, Henry A. Leist, Florence Lemle, Henry Lemle, Steve Lesko, Darrell Leury, Joel Levin, Ted Levine, Alfred Levingson, Bill Levitt, Dick Levy, Harold Liebman, Matthew L. Lifflander, John V. Lindsay, Ralph Lippmann, Clem Long, Paul Longo, Mike Lunsford, Patricia Lynden, Tom Macari, Bernice Able MacIntosh, Maggie Mahar, Bill Maloney, John Manbeck, Norman Marcus, Peter Marcuse, Ron Marino, Billy Markovitz, Rich Marrin, Donald Martin, Dr. Alexander Martone, Peter Martosella, Arlene Marx, Robert Masello, Christopher Mason, Jesse Masyr, Al Maurer, John McAnally, Tex McCrary, Patrick McGahn, John McGarrahan, Sean McGowan, Bill McKenna, Bob McKinley, Frances McNulty, Carol Melton, Bill Merusi, Olive Messenger, Ruth Messinger, John Meyers, Ted Meylor, Charlie Miesmer, Betty Miles, Ben Miller, David Miller, Ron Millican, John Minikes, Ken Moelis, Milton Mollen, Scott Mollen, Sandy Moorhouse, Alex Mooring, Tom Morgan, I. M. Moriyama, Mark Morris, Claude Morton, Eric Moskowitz, Ed Murphy, Gerard Murphy, Peter Murphy, Michael Musaraca, Mary Musca, Jarle Nakken, Burton Natarus, Hal Negbaur, Donald Neier, Martha Nelson, Jay Neveloff, Barbara Nevins, Jesse Newman, John Nichols, Jerry Nisman, Bruce Nobles, Jim Nolen, Don Noonan, Enid

Nordland, Craig Norville, Jay Noyes, V. L. Nussbaum, Timothy L. O'Brien, Martin O'Connell, Jack O'Donnell, Paul O'Dwyer, Jeffrey Oechsner, Michael Onorato, Allen Ostroff, Harold Ostroff, Senator Frank Padavan, Thomas Palmer, Victor Palmieri, Maurice Paprin, Roland Paul, Charles Payton, George Peacock, Ruth Peale, Henry Pearce, Charles Perkins, Steven Perskie, John Phillips, Frank Pino, Ken Platt, Sandra Kazan Pomerantz, Eric Posner, Lou Powsner, Bill Price, George Puskar, Alex Quint, Richie Rada, Morris Raker, Raquel Ramati, Julian Rashkind, Arthur Ratner, Ceil Raufer, Sugar Rautbord, Richard Ravitch, Walter Reade, Charlie Reiss, Barbara Res, James Revson, Jack Reynolds, Everett Rhinebeck, Richard Rice, Marty Riche, Bernard Richland, Peter Ricker, George Rinaldi, Don Robinson, Jerry Robinson, Steve Robinson, David Roeder, Marvin Roffman, Philip Rogers, Michael Romano, Lewis Roper, Richard Rosan, James Rosati, Irwin Rose, Nelson Rose, Steve Rosen, Bart Rosenberg, Bob Rosenberg, Wilbur Ross, Randall Rothenberg, Fred Rovet, William Ruben, Howard Rubenstein, Dave Rudovsky, George Ruebel, David Saltzman, Peter Samton, Tim Samuelson, Phil Satre, Mike Scadron, John Scanlon, Michael Scerbo, Roger Schafer, Larry Schafran, Robert Schearer, Alison Rhoades Schechter, Stuart Scheftel, Dan Schiffman, Bernd Schmitt, Doug Schoen, Gerald Schrager, Henning Schroder, Gary Schuller, Harvey Schultz, David Schuster, Edward Schuster, Conrad Schwartz, Gail Schwartz, Harry Schwartz, Joel Schwartz, Lynn Sharon Schwartz, David Sciarra, Mark Scott, Robert Selsun, Paul Selver, Lloyd Semple, Lou Sepersky, Vivian Serota, Jack Shaffer, Graham Shane, Peter Shapiro, Richard Shapiro, Sam Shapiro, Mary Frances Shaughnessy, Sol Shaviro, Sin-ming Shaw, Ivan Shomer, Paula Shore, Claude Shostal, Lorenz Shrenk, Fred Siegel, Mark Alan Siegel, Steve Siegel, Harvey Sieglbaum, Lisa Sihanouk, Sam Silber, Jim Silver, Leo Silverman, Larry Silverstein, Mike Simmons, William Simon, Marla Simpson, Marilyn Singer, Dusty Sklar, Wendy Sloan, Adrian Smith, Carl Smith, David Smith, Nathan R. Sobel, Donald Soffer, Peter Solomon, Florence Stelz Spelshouse, Jerry Speyer, David Spiker, Edith Spivack, Blanche Sprague, David Stadtmauer, Roger Starr, Martin Steadman, Andrew Stein, Ralph Steinglass, Robert Steingut, Conrad Stephenson, Henry Stern, Jeff Stern, Paul Stern, William Stern, Harvey Stinson, Charles Stocker, Roger Stone, Artie Storrs, Larry Straus, Brian Strum, Robert Sturges, Phil Suarez, Joe Sukaskas, Frank Sulloway, Betty Swetz, Stephen Swid, George Syrovatka, Myles Tannenbaum, Gary Tarbox, Breina Taubman, Larry Tell, Niles Thompson, Nancy Boyd Tickel, Elizabeth Tilyou, Jack Toby, Ernest Todham, Richard Tomlinson, Patrick Too, John Torrell, Henry Trefousse, Jane Trichter, Matthew Troy, John Trump Jr., Ginny Droesch Trumpbour, Stan Turetsky, William Bruce Turner, Margaret Uhl, Charles Urstadt, Jan Van Heinigen, Jonathan Van Meter, Carmine Ventiera, John Vinci, Jessie Voeller Conrad, Arnold Vollmer, Nicholas von Hoffman, Charles Walker, Jeffrey Walker, Abe Wallach, Al Walsh, Joe Walsh, John Walter, Karl Walther, Stanley Waranch, Robert V. Ward, Marvin L. Warner, Nick Warnock, Howard Weingrow, Andy

Weiss, Allen Weisselberg, Rick Welch, Tim Welch, Margo Wellington, William Wenk, Celeste Wesson, Howard West, George White, Dave Wiederecht, Mike Wiener, Bob Wildermuth, Murray Weinstein, Louis Winnick, Sally Wiseman, Ivan Wohlworth, Phil Wolf, Philip Woodhouse, Donald Woodward, Sidney Young, Brad Zackson, Robert Zajonc, Aja Zanova-Steindler, Lillian Zeh, Carl Zeitz, Beverly Ziegler, Howard Zipser, John Zuccotti, and Howard Zuckerman.

Index

ABOUT THE AUTHOR

Gwenda Blair is the author of the best-selling *Almost Golden: Jessica Savitch and the Selling of Television News*. Her work has appeared in the *New York Times*, *Newsweek*, *New York*, *Esquire*, *Smart Money*, and other newspapers and magazines. She lives in New York City and teaches at Columbia University's Graduate School of Journalism.